ROY MILLWARD
and
ADRIAN ROBINSON

The
Welsh
Borders

EYRE METHUEN · LONDON

First published 1978
© *1978 Roy Millward and Adrian Robinson*
Printed in Great Britain for
Eyre Methuen Ltd
11 New Fetter Lane, London EC4P 4EE
by Cox & Wyman Ltd
Fakenham, Norfolk

ISBN 0 413 28210 4 (hardback)
ISBN 0 413 39080 2 (paperback)

Contents

To our children
Glenys, Margaret, David, Stephen and Matthew

Illustrations

MAPS

Acknowledgements and thanks for permission to reproduce photographs are due to Dr J. K. St Joseph and the University of Cambridge for plates 4, 16, 34 and 39; to Aerofilms Ltd for plate 12; and to H. Tempest (Cardiff) Ltd for plates 5, 35 and 38.

Preface

Unlike many parts of Britain, the Welsh Borderland is not immediately recognisable as a geographical region. By definition it is a strip of country on either side of the boundary dividing England and Wales and in this political sense it can rightly claim distinctiveness over the past thousand years. To think of it solely in these historical terms would be misleading, however, for the area also possesses a unity based on its transitional character, lying as it does between the English lowlands to the east and the Welsh uplands to the west. Throughout the hundred-mile strip between the Dee estuary in the north and the Severn shores in the south there is an intermingling of lowland and upland, the miniature counterparts of larger-scale features which reach their full expression in neighbouring territories. In south Shropshire, for example, the scarp and vale countryside of Wenlock Edge recalls the chalk landscapes of south-east England, while the Ludlow Dome is simply a smaller-scale replica of the Weald. On the other hand, the high plateaus of the Black Mountains and Brecon Beacons have their parallel in the uplands of central Wales. Everywhere the impact of a varied succession of rock types is apparent and is largely responsible for the diversity of the landscape, perhaps the most notable characteristic of the region. Some of the oldest rocks in Britain are found in the borderland and go back in time for hundreds of millions of years, perhaps when life was beginning a hesitant start in its most primitive form. At the other end of this long time-scale the events of the Ice Age, a mere yesterday on the geological calendar, have also played a major role in fashioning the scenery of what has become increasingly recognised in recent years as one of the few remaining unspoiled parts of southern Britain. It was during this glacial period that the borderland became a battleground between competing ice masses, each seeking to occupy the lower ground, with Welsh ice from the uplands to the west coming into conflict with another ice sheet over the Cheshire Plain.

With the final melting away of this ice blanket, vegetation was quick to colonise the bare ground and it was not long before man was on the scene. At first his impact on the landscape was slight but over the past five thousand years it has gradually gained momentum so that today we see a countryside which is almost entirely man-made. To appreciate it to the full it is necessary to climb some of the isolated hill tops which are scattered throughout the borderland. Often the summit is crowned by an Iron Age hill-fort and from its ramparts there are distant horizons to be scanned, while the wider canvas affords a closer insight into the interwoven themes of landscape history.

Each part of the borderland has made its own distinctive contribution to the events of the past five thousand years. In the Middle March, for example, the great earthwork of Offa's Dyke reaches its fullest expression, taking us back in time to the end of the eighth century when an attempt was made to establish an agreed political frontier. Elsewhere the succession of Norman castle towns, each the centre of a Marcher lordship and associated with families like the Lacys and Mortimers, claim attention. In the country beyond the Wye there are castle settlements like Skenfrith and Grosmont which recall the period when an attempt was made to push the boundary farther to the west, almost into the heart of the Celtic lands. Perhaps the greatest visual impact made by man occurs in the northern March, where nature endowed valuable metals and coal that became the basis of an industrial society. Fortunately, and in comparison with other parts of the country, the borderland has few scars of past mineral working and even these have begun to heal.

A book by itself cannot make the landscape come alive, and it is necessary to explore the region both by car and on foot. For this purpose we have given National Grid References (sometimes with letter prefixes for general location) as an aid to identification throughout the various chapters. The new 1:50,000 Ordnance Survey maps provide an admirable cover to be used alongside the text and also in the field. In some cases we have used the old county names where these are more meaningful, with their present equivalent alongside.

As in our previous books we have had considerable help and encouragement from our wives. Gwyneth Robinson prepared the maps while Helen Millward was once again responsible for the index.

I

A view from the tops

Throughout the long corridor which straddles the border of England and Wales for 120 miles from the Dee to the Severn, the landscape is one of telling contrasts. Deeply set basins, nestling within enclosing hills, or long corridors of river flood plains penetrating deep into the heartland of the Welsh mountains give rise to an intermixture of lowland and upland seldom matched elsewhere in Britain. It is not always easy to appreciate these contrasts of relief, especially when travelling by car through the hedged countryside of Herefordshire or Shropshire. To fully understand the essential elements of the borderland scene, especially the richness stemming from its diversity, it is necessary to leave the lanes and climb the nearest accessible hill top. Although the view revealed is unlikely to be panoramic to the same degree as, say, from the top of Great Gable in the Lake District or Elidir Fawr in Snowdonia, the hill tops of the border country offer the only satisfactory means of assimilating the broader setting of the region without losing sight of its rich diversity.

Halkyn Mountain in the north may be something of a misnomer, for it just fails to reach the thousand-foot contour at its highest point of Moel Gaer (SJ 2169), but nevertheless it gives outstanding all-round views from its summit ridge. On a day when a cool north-westerly air stream is bringing in clear polar air from the Irish Sea, the all-embracing view summarises the essential ingredients of the borderland scene which is repeated, with minor variations, throughout the hundred-mile zone to the south until the Severn shore is reached near Chepstow. From the worn ramparts of the Iron Age fort which crowns the summit of Moel Gaer, the view extends eastwards across the flat terrain of the Cheshire Plain. In the middle distance the broken line of the Peckforton Hills (SJ 5256) stands out where the harder sandstone beds

13

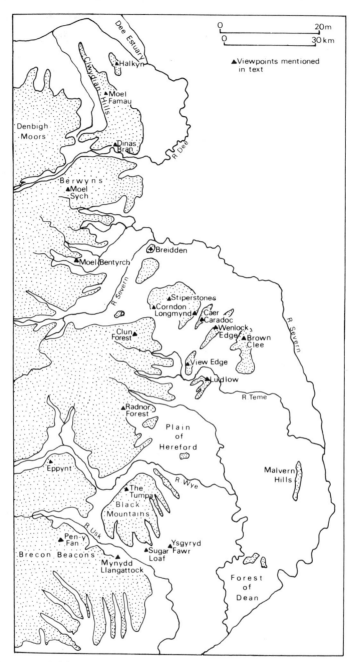

1. *The main relief features of the borderland countryside with prominent vantage points marked.*

project through the softer marls and boulder clay. The pastoral setting, with its multiplicity of green-hedged fields and the occasional isolated clump of planted woodland, is characteristic of many parts of lowland Britain, and seen here in close juxtaposition to the Welsh hills, serves to define the borderland landscape in a physical sense.

Along its north-eastern edge, Halkyn Mountain looks out over the sand-choked estuary of the Dee backed by the low, long line of the Wirral peninsula masking the urban agglomeration of Merseyside. In the medieval period, when Chester was unrivalled as the principal town of this region, the navigable approach through the mobile sands of the Dee estuary was of vital importance to the well-being of the port and city. Silting and haphazard changes in the main navigable channel, together with the rise of Liverpool, led to a continuous decline in the usefulness of the Dee artery, although from time to time the city fathers and private entrepreneurs attempted to combat the natural changes by straightening and embanking the main channel. As early as 1677 the River Dee Company was founded, but its early efforts came to nothing and it was not until 1733 that training works were begun along the important inner section from Connah's Quay to the outskirts of Chester. With the limited resources of the period over $1\frac{1}{2}$ million tons of material had to be removed by spade and transported by cart, a stupendous operation which took over twenty years to complete. Large areas on either side of the main embanked channel were now fit for reclamation from the natural saltings and over 3,000 acres were taken in during the latter half of the eighteenth century. As a result, the whole landscape was transformed from one of sand flats and marshland to the neat chequerboard pattern we see today. Some of this reclaimed land was later used when the expansive site of Shotton steelworks was laid out in 1908, now sending forth columns of smoke or bursts of steam though its future is problematical and by no means assured.

The view westwards from Moel Gaer is one of complete contrast. Beyond the low foothill zone in the immediate foreground the land rises to the ridge line of the Clwydian Hills, the first major hill range of the Welsh uplands and the outer rampart of the higher and more majestic mountain systems hidden from view to the west. Throughout its length the crest of the Clwydian Hills consists of a series of low swells or moels separated by high-level cols or the occasional major breach such as that achieved by the River Wheeler (SJ 1071). (Many of the moels themselves provide excellent all-round viewpoints and for this reason were sought after by Iron Age man when he established his line of forts crowning isolated summits like Foel Fenlli (SJ 1661), with its fine prospect overlooking the Vale of Clwyd and the more distant uplands to the west. A traverse of the countryside from Halkyn Mountain to the Clwydian Hills is a journey back in geological time. Halkyn itself is formed of Carboniferous Limestone, here in its massive, uncompromising form. Being resistant to erosion, partly due to its inherent hardness but also a result of its capacity to 'swallow' surface drainage and thus nullify the effects of river erosion, it stands out above the general level of the surrounding countryside. Where the limestone beds are less pure, surface drainage is possible, though even here there is always the possibility that the stream or river will disappear underground. This is the fate of the River Alyn, which often vanishes completely from its gorge-like valley between Loggerheads and Cilcain (SJ 1865). Progressing farther west, the beds of limestone gradually give way to the shales, sandstones and mudstones of the older Silurian formation. Some of these beds have been compacted by past earth movements and now offer considerable resistance to the denuding forces of water, wind and frost. It is this fact that has led to the creation of the almost continuous summit ridge of the Clwydian range, with Moel Fammau the highest point at over 1,817 feet (SJ 1562).

Though the gradual approach to the Clwydian Hills from the east has much to commend it, especially in the limestone scenery around Logger-heads, the most impressive view of the hill mass is from the floor of the Vale of Clwyd. A sharp wall rises steeply out of the flat floor of the Vale, broken only by a succession of combe-like valleys scoured out of the scarp face. The whole character of the region owes much to past earth movements which let down and preserved the softer and younger Triassic sandstone formations between a set of parallel faults. The older and harder Silurian beds were left as upstanding blocks, one of which forms the Clwydian range. The major fault runs close to the scarp foot and separates two different groups of strata, perhaps differing in age by as much as fifty million years. Its main impact is a topographic one, for it is responsible for the creation and maintenance of the great unbroken scarp wall which overlooks the towns of the Vale from Ruthin (SJ 1258) in the south to Rhuddlan (SJ 0278) in the north.

Past earth movements, leading to the disruption of rock strata, have played a major role in fashioning many of the individual elements which make up the border landscape. The Vale of Llangollen, for example, owes its alignment and straight form to a series of parallel faults. The rock strata were weakened and shattered to the extent that both river and ice erosion found little difficulty in etching out the broad vale. One fault, the Aqueduct (named after Telford's famous canal crossing of this section of the Dee valley) has had the effect of displacing the rocks both vertically and laterally. As a result, the Carboniferous Limestone which on the south side of the valley extends only as far west as Froncysyllte (SJ 2741), has been carried five miles along the northern side where it forms the magnificent scalloped and gently curving escarpment of the Eglwyseg Rocks, undoubtedly one of the finest topographic elements in the whole borderland (SJ 2244).

Throughout the complex sequence of change which has led to the present form of the Vale, the isolated knoll of Dinas Bran (SJ 2243) has survived. It is formed of tough, uncompromising Silurian shale, even though it is within a very short distance of the main Eglwyseg limestone outcrop. This can only be explained by the presence of the Aqueduct fault which runs through the col separating the knoll from the limestone escarpment. The summit of Castell Dinas Bran makes both an excellent viewpoint and defensive site. From prehistoric times right down to the early thirteenth century, defensive works have crowned its top. Remains of the last castle, built out of the local Silurian shale dug out from a deep trench on its southern flank, still survive in a ruinous state. From the valley floor, some 500 feet below, the ruins present the necessary picturesque outline which many builders of castle follies in later centuries sought to emulate. It is, however, from the castle ramparts on top that the view over this section of the borderland countryside is so rewarding. The deep incision which the Dee makes into the surrounding plateau, albeit fault-guided, is immediately obvious. Gently sloping platforms and benches strung out along the opposing valley side are given prominence by the pattern of their hedged fields with belts of darker woodland masking the steeper slopes. Each bench or flattening of a spur represents a remnant of an earlier valley floor when the ancestor of the present River Dee flowed at a much higher level. Later downcutting by the river, aided by changes which took place during the Ice Age (see pages 43–59), has gradually brought about the present form of the Vale, the end product of an evolutionary process which has occupied many millions of years.

A circuit of the top of Castell Dinas Bran leads, on the other side, to a close view of the Eglwyseg Rocks which run away in a gentle curve to the north-west. Hard bands of limestone, the teeth of the escarpment, stand out defiantly in the face of the weathering agents which are constantly seeking to destroy. That they have achieved some measure of success is shown by the apron of limestone boulders which litter the lower part of the scarp. Mass movement is still taking place and the single track road which skirts the escarpment foot is frequently covered with debris from rock slides and boulder falls. Much of the impressive character of the Eglwyseg Rocks is derived not so much from its massive bare rock crags but rather from the way in which the edge has been scalloped into a series of rounded buttresses set between short combe-like valleys which now contain only the occasional

1. *Eglwyseg escarpment, with the harder beds within the limestone standing out as bare rock scars.*

seasonal stream. During the Ice Age, however, these scarp-face valleys must have contained rushing torrents of water from the melting snowfields of the plateau top above. Considerable quantities of debris were brought down by these meltwater streams and today they form great boulder fans. They also provide areas of deeper soils and sheltered sites where the ash and sycamore can grow. All the farms which nestle under the scarp face are sited on or near these boulder fans to take advantage of shelter, an adequate depth of soil and an assured water supply.

The limestone country which dominates the northern marchland in such areas as Halkyn Mountain or the Eglwyseg Crags assumes less prominence farther south due to faulting and a thinning out of the massive beds. Before the limestone outcrop finally peters out near Llanymynech (SJ 2620) it is responsible for a succession of low hills which have been intensively quarried for stone. Away to the west the country has been carved out of the older Silurian and Ordovician beds and forms a foothill zone leading in steps to the higher ridges of the Berwyn range. The grain of the rock outcrops is from south-west to north-east and this has been faithfully reflected in the landscape as both streams and major rivers alike have cut their valleys in this direction. The regional dip, however, is to the south-east, and this is reflected in the courses taken in the upper reaches of rivers such as the Tanat, Cain and Banwy. When ice was sweeping across the area from the much higher ground to the west, it also took this south-easterly course and it seems probable that many of the gorge sections of the river valleys came into being at this time as the ice forced its way through towards the English Plain. Thus two main lineaments, one to the north-east and the other to the south-east, came into being and this has resulted in the countryside being split up into a series of rectangular blocks. Occasionally, where softer rocks outcrop, the valley sections have been widened to become basins, some large enough to be given regional names like Mochnant. Many of the basins acquired richer soils as downwash carried debris from the surrounding slopes, and were thus favoured as centres of early settlement, as at Llansilin (SJ 2028).

The plateau tops at heights of 1,000 to 1,200 feet are bleak in contrast to the sheltered basins. Although the rocks of shale, sandstone and mudstone have been tightly folded, erosion has shaved off the top surface to give a bevelled plateau with few eminences rising above the general accordant level. Viewpoints are correspondingly rare and it is only occasionally and somewhat fortuitously, as at the hill-top village of Llanfihangel-yn-Ngwynfa (SJ 0816), that it is possible to survey this low dissected plateau country of the Middle March. In the middle Banwy valley the isolated hill mass of Moel Bentyrch (SJ 0509) provides a good all-round viewpoint from its 1,100 foot summit. From its rounded top – a typical moel – the prospect eastwards is that of a typical 'tyddyn' landscape of small, long and low farmhouses each set within its own fields which have been laboriously reclaimed from the waste in past centuries. Occasionally a former 'hafod' or summer dwelling-house remains, though all have now ceased to play their former role as a temporary shelter when the lowland cattle were grazed on the upland pastures during the summer months. Many original hafods became permanent farms over the course of time and it is only in the place-name that we are allowed a glimpse into the past. A former hafod stands by the roadside in the hilly country leading up to Lake Vyrnwy (SJ 0214), while lower down in the valley the 'hendre' or home farm has also survived.

Pleasant rather than dramatic summarises the landscape of this relatively quiet backwater of the borderland, for although bare rock outcrops do occasionally appear on the steeper hillsides, much of the land is draped in a thick cover of head, a stony soil dating from the more extreme climatic conditions of the end of the Ice Age. It is only near the combe-like heads of valleys like the Tanat and its tributaries which drain the slopes of the Berwyns that we obtain the first glimpse and foretaste of the ice-fashioned scenery which reaches its full expression in the highest mountain areas like Snowdonia. Occasionally, as at the head of the Afon Rhaeadr, a hard rock band outcrops to add another facet to the scenery. A three-mile journey by narrow road up the valley from the small market town of Llanrhaeadr-ym-Mochnant (SJ 1226) leads to the impressive falls of Pystyll Rhaeadr which, because of its height, has given it the title of 'one of the seven wonders of Wales'. A hard bed of the igneous rock called felsite is responsible as it crosses the upper part of the combe forming the valley head. A small stream, the Disgynfa, tumbles over the edge and then drops over a hundred feet passing through a circular arch before finally spilling out of a pool to drop yet again to the stream bed below. Even today, when the senses tend to be blunted by the media, the first sight of Pystyll Rhaeadr makes an exciting prospect. How the early Victorian tourists who had walked many miles from the nearest railhead must have marvelled at the scale of the fall. Their appetites doubtless had been whetted by the writer of a guide book whose description of a fall conjured up visions of Niagara rather than a single jet of water. In spite of its shortcomings the fact remains that with a drop approaching two hundred feet it is one of the highest waterfalls in the Principality.

The narrow band of felsite which makes such an impact at Pystyll Rhaeadr is a foretaste of the scenery which has developed in the neighbouring county of Shropshire from similar hard igneous rocks, including basalts, andesite and dolerite. Breidden and its associated hill of Moel-y-Golfa (SJ 2914), rising abruptly out of the Severn Plain which it overlooks to the north, is perhaps the most impressive scenic feature of this sector of the March. At its highest point, where it tops 1,200 feet and is marked by Rodney's Pillar, the view is principally to the north and west. The northern face of Breidden is particularly steep and quarries have bitten deeply into its flanks in search of valuable road metal. At one time the dolerite of the hill justified the building of a railway around its northern edge but this has long been closed, although its former course can still be clearly made out on the ground around the village of Criggion (SJ 2914). The view, both from Rodney's Pillar and from the crest of the complementary Moel-y-Golfa to the south, justifies the climb through the woodland and bracken scrub. Around this barren rocky island the Shropshire Plain is one of agricultural plenty with its chequerboard landscape of neat fields set within closely trimmed thorn hedges. Here is lowland Britain at its best and it is only the large, rather formless Long Mountain to the south or the purple line of the Berwyns away to the west that serve as a reminder that this is border country. It is at Breidden that the River

Severn finally breaks out of the constricting influence of the Welsh uplands and as it enters the Shropshire lowlands it signifies its freedom in a series of expansive meander loops which glisten in the sun when seen from the summit of Breidden.

A comparable viewpoint farther south is the conical-shaped Corndon Hill (SO 3096), lying somewhat apart from the other south Shropshire hills. Like Breidden it, too, is composed of the tough, uncompromising igneous rock dolerite. The rock forms a lens-shaped mass occupying the top half of the hill and to some the intrusion is seen as a good example of a laccolith. Rising to over 1,600 feet, Corndon towers well above the surrounding countryside, especially that to the south and west where the small River Camlad is occupying a spacious valley altogether out of proportion to its size. The apparent anomaly is explained by the fact that this lowland was once the site of a glacial lake which, as it found an escape-route in the west, cut the impressive gorge of Marrington Dingle (SO 2794). The igneous rock of the Corndon complex has another claim to fame, for on the flanks of the hill above the village of Hyssington (3194), early man, perhaps fortuitously,

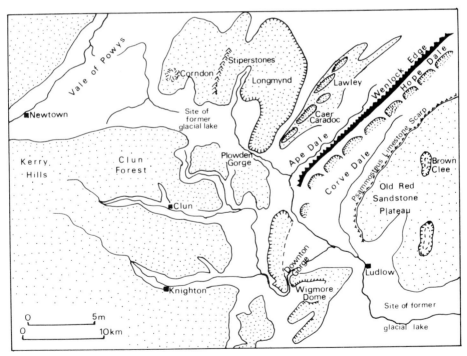

2. *The hills of south Shropshire and their associated morphological units.*

2. Stiperstones ridge of quartzite with projecting tors and debris slopes around.

found a variety of the rock which could be shaped for his flint tools. Over the centuries of prehistoric time this 'factory' produced considerable numbers of worked stones which were distributed far and wide across the country.

From Corndon summit the view to the east takes in a succession of plateaus, ridges, scarps and valleys. Throughout this varied south Shropshire landscape there is a close relationship between the type of rock and the resulting scenery. The Stiperstones ridge, for example, with its jagged outline reminiscent of the spine of some prehistoric monster, owes its origin to a narrow outcrop of white quartzite. The tilted rock strata has been eroded into a series of upstanding rock crowns which recall the hill-top tors of Dartmoor. The heather and bilberry slopes around are littered with quartzite boulders which during the arctic conditions of the closing stages of the Ice Age must have been prised away from the main rock outcrop and then rafted downslope on a slowly moving cushion of ice. The surviving rock outcrops of the ridge were also subject to attack by weathering, principally frost shattering, and the result has been that they have been carved into unusual shapes which merit descriptive names like Devil's Chair (3699).

Beyond the Stiperstones ridge which, at over 1,700 feet, provides an admirable viewpoint comparable with Corndon Hill, the land falls away to the lower, dissected country drained by the headwater streams of the River East Onny. In turn this gives way to the abrupt western edge of the Longmynd plateau where a major fault has brought to the surface some of the oldest rocks in Britain, pre-Cambrian grits, shales, conglomerates, flagstones and occasional ribs of volcanic rock. Although of varied lithology, the rocks share a common hardness which makes the Longmynd stand out as a rather featureless plateau of convex slopes falling away steeply on every side. It is only along the eastern edge, where it overlooks the Church Stretton valley, that the Longmynd has been successfully attacked by the forces of erosion. Deeply cut valleys, locally termed batches, serrate the edge and although the present streams are quite inadequate to the task, they are the undoubted successors to much more voluminous ancestors which, as the snowfield melted away on the plateau top at the end of the Ice Age, were assured of copious supplies of water to assist their downcutting. Some of the batches provide sheltered, picturesque hollows and one in particular, the Car-dingmill valley, close to Church Stretton (4494), is a well-known local beauty spot. It is now possible to cross this southern section of the Longmynd by car, for in recent years the narrow road over the top has been metalled and made passable for cars. The climb up the eastern face of the Longmynd is particularly steep but if the car is left near the summit and the short walk made to the end of one of the spurs the reward is a magnificent view over the sharply defined Stretton valley, a minor rift where the rocks have been let down between two sets of faults. On the far side igneous rocks outcrop once again to form a succession of whale-backed hills like Ragleth, Caer Caradoc and The Lawley. In the case of Caer Caradoc the natural contours of the hill-top have been modified by Iron Age man when he turned the summit ridge into a defensive strongpoint. This is one of many strategically placed forts running throughout the borderland region (4795). The climb to the summit of Caer Caradoc is not difficult and is best made along recognised paths from the Church Stretton to Hope Bowdler road (B4371).

With so many hills standing in splendid isolation, this part of the bor-derland is not lacking in outstanding viewpoints. To stand on top of Caer Caradoc with its panoramic views on all sides is to be taken back two thousand years when Iron Age man scanned the surrounding countryside from his vantage point. Today's scene of well-ordered fields and stone cottages would be missing, but the basic elements of the landscape, in particular the succession of scarps and vales which lie to the east of Caradoc, would have been apparent, perhaps more wooded than at present. For almost seventeen miles the straight line of Wenlock Edge remains unbroken. A thick and almost pure band of limestone is responsible for the escarpment which, although seldom more than 300 feet high, forms a continuous wall. Now much of the scarp slope and crest is covered with woodland, so many of the views that A. E. Housman knew and wrote about are no longer available. The succession of Silurian beds, of which the Wenlock Limestone is one of

23

the lower formations, continues to outcrop in a series of narrow bands straddling the countryside to the east. Overlying the limestone is a bed of shale which has been etched out to form Hope Dale just below the Wenlock ridge on its eastern side. Another limestone band, the Aymestrey, slightly more creamy in colour than the grey Wenlock formation, now intervenes and immediately the land rises to form a series of wooded knolls of which Callow Hill (SJ 4685) is the highest. Unlike Wenlock Edge, the Aymestrey Limestone does not give rise to a continuous scarp, for small streams in Hope Dale have successfully breached it at a number of places, forming batches similar to those of the Longmynd. Ultimately these small streams, following the south-easterly dip of the limestone beds, break out into the much more open Corvedale. Here, too, it is a bed of shale which gives rise to the wide vale. Running through its centre there is an outcrop of sandstone which forms a raised ridge so favoured for the siting of villages like Holdgate (5689) above the damp pastures of the valley bottom. During the Ice Age much of Corvedale must have lain beneath the waters of a shallow lake impounded both by ice and the surrounding higher ground. When the glacial lake finally drained away it left a rather immature pattern of drainage so that even today there is a curious parallelism in the courses of the River Corve and its near neighbour, the Pye Brook.

Once again in this wooded scarp and vale countryside it is the straight edge formed of a limestone bed which defines the south-eastern margin of Corvedale. In this eastward traverse the successive beds are becoming younger so that here, in the vicinity of the Clee Hills and the marked bench surrounding them, it is the Old Red Sandstone formation which outcrops. The twin knolls of Brown Clee (SO 5986), known as Abdon Burf and Clee Burf, both rise to over 1,700 feet and form the last outposts of the borderland hills before the true lowlands of the Midland Plain are reached. It is the fortuitous survival of a hard, resistant band of dolerite near the summit of Brown Clee that is responsible for the existence of the hill as a dominating element in the present landscape. What nature has failed to do, man has succeeded, for the hard, dark rock (dhu stone) has been extensively quarried as a roadstone. In spite of the untidyness which mineral working brings in its wake it is worth climbing to the summit of Abdon Burf for the platform it provides for viewing a large sector of the border country.

The scarp and vale country of the Wenlock area continues west of Ludlow, for the same geological formations are present. There is one marked difference, however, for now the various limestone and shale beds have been folded by past earth movements into a major dome-like structure – the Bringewood anticline. Thus although the same rock types are present, the linear grain of the Wenlock area now gives place to a horseshoe pattern with infacing escarpments overlooking the lowland centre of the Wigmore Basin. The steep scarps are nearly everywhere covered with woodland so that they stand out clearly in contrast to the pastoral benches and the rather marshy centre in the area known as The Willows (SO 4271). Before drainage works were carried out here in the last decade, the River Teme often broke its banks and for a time each winter there was a temporary lake after a period of heavy rain. As well as the upfold structure there has been considerable faulting of the various rock formations. Around Leinthall Earls (4467) there is a repetition of the limestone and shale outcrops and with it a corresponding duplication of the scarp and vale scenery. Occasionally the faulted rocks have been shattered as a result of earth movements so that even small streams find their task of erosion so much easier. The gorge-like section of the Mary Knowl valley (4972) owes its origin to this factor, the present stream having little difficulty in eroding deeply into the narrow band of broken rock. The presence of the two main limestones, in addition to their considerable impact on the scenery, has led to their use as a valued building material. Throughout the area where either the Wenlock or Aymestrey Limestone is close at hand, it has been quarried extensively in the past for local churches, cottages, imposing manor houses and even the more substantial marcher castle of Wigmore (4069). Its only rival in the past has been the Holdgate Sandstone from Corvedale, although increasingly in the present century the ubiquitous red brick and Welsh slate have made deep inroads into the area.

The small-scale diversity which occurs within the overall pattern of unity, so much a part of the border country, is given further expression in the area known as the Plain of Hereford. Plain is something of a misnomer, for although there are tracts of lowland in the valleys of the Rivers Wye and Lugg, there is also a liberal scattering of isolated flat-topped hills with a marked relief. Once again it is the geology which exerts a controlling influence over the landscape form. The Old Red Sandstone, the ever-present rock type throughout much of Herefordshire, is made up of beds of red and grey marl which erode very easily. But at intervals in the succession there are more compact sandstones and cemented nodular limestones. The latter have long been known from their local name of 'cornstones', for it was believed that the soil derived from them was ideal for growing cereals. Together with the hard sandstone bands, they resist erosion so that where they survive they give rise to tabular hills like those of Wormsley (SO 4148) and Dinmore (4851) which rise in spectacular fashion from the surrounding lowlands.

Seen from within or from the higher ground of the Black Mountains in the south-west, each of the cornstone knolls presents a similar picture of a flat-topped plateau ending in a sharp cornice before the rapid drop of the scarp edge begins. The latter can be as steep as 1:3 in places and is therefore often left in woodland. At one time the isolated hills must have formed part of a continuous plateau surface but erosion has breached the hard cap beds and then bitten deeply into the softer marls beneath. We can glimpse at the process of reduction in the present-day Wormsley Hill lying to the north-west of the city of Hereford. Streams working back by headward erosion have been successful in etching out deep, bowl-shaped combes into the

3. *Cornstone hill country of central Herefordshire with the flat-topped plateaus rising abruptly from the marl lowland.*

flat-topped plateau so that today Wormsley really consists of a number of distinct hill elements like Merryhill, Credenhill and the larger but more irregular Nupton Hills. The present streams in the combes seem incapable of accomplishing erosion on the necessary scale and therefore once again we must envisage more powerful ancestors, perhaps fed with meltwater from snow- and icefields, as the creative force. We can also see in the present landscape some evidence of river adjustment which has occurred in the past. The small stream which occupies the gap between Merryhill and Credenhill has succeeded in cutting back northwards and capturing the headwaters of a

26

former eastward-flowing stream which runs south from Tillington Common (4545), the point of diversion being close to Brinsop Court.

Wormsley Hill, rising to 881 feet on its northern edge, forms an ideal vantage point from which to survey the greater part of the cornstone country. To the north-east lie the isolated knolls of Butthouse Knapp and Pyon Hill, which have the appearance of being left behind in the half-completed reduction of the landscape. Beyond lies the sharp edge of the Dinmore Hills, a diamond-shaped mass with well-defined scarps on its west and south sides and breached by a glacial channel now followed by the River Lugg in the east. Dinmore, like the other cornstone residuals, is very flat on top but has been deeply scored by a central combe valley running from Broomwell Farm (4751). Just below the farm an especially prominent cornstone bed outcrops on the valley side and can be traced with the eye as it gives rise to a marked break in the slope. Elsewhere the nodular bed of limestone has been quarried for use as a building stone and for making flag fences around some of the farms.

This is but one instance of the use made of accessible local materials, especially in the past when the area formed something of a backwater, isolated from the mainstream of human activity. A much more durable stone than the cornstone for building purposes was a hard grit, variously coloured grey, green or red, which was extensively used for church and cottage alike. The Norman church at Wormsley and the nearby farmhouse are both built of this variegated sandstone. Before improving communications from the middle of the last century onwards allowed Welsh slates to be imported, many of the roofs were covered using a local fissile sandstone which, though not ideal because of its weight, did keep out the weather. On Garnons Hill (3944) there is a sandstone layer which cleaves readily into slabs about an inch in thickness and in the past it has been extensively quarried for roofing purposes, including the nearby Mansell Grange Church. Another quarry close by on the south side of the hill was opened up when the Hereford Turnpike Trust decided in 1853 to surface the road (the present A438) under their charge. Perhaps the best-known use of the local sandstone is in the church of Kilpeck (SO 4430). Here the richly carved doorway, with its representation of the Tree of Life, shows how local craftsmen were able to work the sandstone to perfection in a simple village church.

The River Wye, which perhaps plays the same role in the southern borderlands as the River Severn does in the north, meanders across the Herefordshire Plain in a series of great sweeping loops. It draws its water from the uplands of Wales well to the west and its valley serves to unite both

27

the English and Welsh sections of this part of the borderland. From Builth Wells (SO 0451) the river runs in a south-easterly direction in a narrow valley section but at Llyswen (1338) it turns at right-angles to enter a broader valley through Hay ultimately to reach the Hereford lowland after rounding the corner of the Black Mountains. In this dog-legged course the river effectively splits the Welsh plateau into three distinct blocks, Radnor Forest and its environs to the north, the Black Mountains to the south and the mass of Mynydd Eppynt in the west. Each consists of a high tableland, deeply dissected in places but, due to variable rock types and the different effects of erosion, each with a distinctive form.

Radnor Forest has the character of an upland island ringed by sharply defined slopes. Much of the plateau top lies at a height of 1,600–1,700 feet though it rises to over 2,000 feet in the centre of the dome. In places, isolated tumps like the Whimble (SO 2062) rise well above the general level and give good vantage points over the Forest and surrounding countryside. The Silurian mudstones and shales weather to give mainly rounded slopes but occasionally, as in the Great Creigau (crags) and Whinyard Rocks, more tenacious beds break through to the surface. Extensive deposits of head drape the lower slopes and are well exposed in many of the forestry tracks. Gully erosion is common in these soft, unconsolidated deposits and from the top of the Whimble the prominent gashes, known as the Three Riggles, stand out on the side of Harley Dale (1862). A marked pattern of radial drainage has been established running outwards from the domal centre of the Forest. If the present streams seem inadequate in relation to their deeply carved valleys, their predecessors, fed by snowmelt, could have accomplished much erosion in the relatively soft mudstones. Radnor Forest seems to have preserved a wealth of local descriptive names for many of its topographic features, names like 'Water-break-its-neck' for a waterfall as it tumbles out of a hanging valley.

The name Forest is a medieval designation and refers to a hunting area, although in the present century the Forestry Commission, through active planting especially along its eastern margin, have given parts of the area a wooded appearance. It nevertheless retains its island character for there are no roads and few tracks crossing the plateau top. Much of the area is still unenclosed and carries great flocks of sheep which are brought down to New Radnor for shearing. With the thick blanket of stony clay known as head covering much of the plateau top and draping even its steepest slopes, the soils are capable of maintaining improved pastures. Forestry has also benefited, for the trees grow quite quickly, especially if sheltered when young. Plantations now extend almost up to the 2,000 foot contour on the eastern flanks, and if agreement could be reached many other parts could be afforested. The only unfavourable area lies in the south-west close to the spa town of Llandrindod Wells where an upfold brings to the surface the older and more rugged Ordovician rocks. Some are igneous in character and give rise to broken ridges like that of Llandegley Rocks (1361) and the Carneddau range close to Builth Wells (0655). In the past this rugged terrain has provided good defensive sites like that of Cefnllys, set on a windy, rocky spur above the wooded gorge of the River Ithon (0862). The first use of the site was made by Iron Age man, who carved out a single rampart around the spur crest. In later centuries the Mortimers, one of the great Marcher landowners, built a castle and this was followed by the laying-out of a new town early in the fourteenth century. Although mainly a military settlement designed to maintain a hold of this part of the border country, Cefnllys had a weekly market and a supporting borough charter. Today there is little to suggest the former glory of the place, save perhaps for the lonely church which lies down in the valley well away from the exposed spur where the town was laid out.

The succession of igneous rocks which outcrop in various parts of this tiny enclave have had another effect on the landscape, for they give rise to mineral springs. In the last century many were exploited in order to develop the string of spa towns, each with the suffix 'Wells', including Llandrindod, Builth, Llangammarch (SN 9347) and Llanwrtyd (8846). Little now remains to indicate their former importance although they still retain the air of an inland resort. Those in the south-west of the area are overshadowed by the towering escarpment of Mynydd Eppynt. Much of the plateau top is a military area with restricted access but the few roads which cross it serve to emphasise its expansive character. Before it became a military exercise area its steep western face and barren top always presented something of a barrier between the even higher uplands to the west and the richer lowlands of the Wye valley and the Plain of Hereford. The cattle drovers were undeterred and in order to avoid the turnpike tolls they used the tracks across Mynydd Eppynt en route for the fattening pastures of England. There is a stark reminder of the past in the shell of the former Drovers Arms inn (9845), now abandoned to the elements and the gunners using the nearby artillery ranges. The best view of the Eppynt landscape is a mile farther along the road (B4519) just before it begins to descend the imposing north-west-facing scarp. On the plateau top the Old Red Sandstone formations have weathered to give gentle slopes which grade almost imperceptibly into the shallow valley bottoms. It is only on the scarp face itself that any harder sandstone beds are exposed as crags but even here it is the underlying Silurian flagstones which make the greatest impression, particularly in the side walls of Cwm Graig

4. *Scarp edge and dip slope valleys of the Black Mountains. The view takes in the sharp cornice of Pen-y-Beacon and the sub-scarp shelf known as The Allt.*

Dhu (9647). This is one of a number of short valleys which head back into the scarp face and during the Ice Age must have nourished their own snowfields and perhaps tiny glaciers which helped to extend their steep backwall.

Compared with Mynydd Eppynt, the tableland of the Black Mountains is a much more impressive topographic feature and serves to illustrate how a slight change of rock type can have such a profound effect on the resulting scenery. While it is true that the summits of the Black Mountains rise to over 2,600 feet at Pen y Gader-Fawr (SO 2328), which is almost a thousand feet higher than the top of Eppynt, mere height alone is not a sufficient explanation of the striking difference between the two adjacent tablelands. Both have been fashioned out of a great slab of the Old Red Sandstone formation and in each area the lowest beds belong to the Downton and Ditton Series, and are mainly mudstones which can be as much as 3,500-feet thick. Some beds of siltstone and sandstone occur within the soft marls and locally these

30

serve to strengthen the formation. Really tough and tenacious beds are missing so that both in Eppynt and the lower dip slopes of the Black Mountains a gentle flat-topped plateau results. On the higher, north-westerly summit ridges of the Black Mountains a completely different situation exists, for the red beds of marl are overlain with a cap rock formed of a succession of sandstone, grit and conglomerate beds. It is these harder beds, belonging to the Brecon Series, which form the impressive scarp crest towering above the middle part of the Wye around Hay (2342), an excellent centre for exploring this part of the borderland. Seen from below, the sharp cornice formed by Pen-y-Beacon (2436) and The Tumpa (2235) stands out in spectacular fashion, especially when seen against a southerly light. Both are now accessible, for a metalled road runs from Hay-on-Wye up over the scarp crest at a height of 1,778 feet and then makes a more gradual descent along the side of one of the many dip-slope valleys to the monastic ruins of Llanthony (2827). From the high col – part of an ancient crossing of the Black Mountains known as the Gospel Pass – it is only a climb of another 500 feet to reach either Pen-y-Beacon to the north or The Tumpa to the west. Both give excellent all-round views, especially westwards across the Wye valley into the plateau country of mid-Wales. This is true Marchland which the Normans in the twelfth century attempted to control by building strategic castle towns like Painscastle. Just below the scarp crest there is a marked bench, locally known as the Allt, which has been fashioned out of a sequence of relatively resistant sandstone beds. The shelf is remarkably flat at about the 1,200-foot contour but its edge has been deeply cut into by youthful valleys which run down to the Wye. Much of the area is open common land and still provides rough grazing for the valley parishes below.

In contrast to this abrupt north-west face of the Black Mountains the complementary dip slope is one of gradual descent with long spur ridges separating the wide-open valleys. Bare rock outcrops are common, especially on the north-east-facing slopes where the harder conglomerate beds outcrop. Much of the valley side is, however, covered with a thick deposit of head and in a number of places has been subject to rilling and gullying as a result of heavy rains on the plateau top. Each of the dip-slope valleys has its distinctive setting. The most interesting are the Grwyne Fechan and Grwyne Fawr, which are narrow and twisting with extensive forestry plantations on their sides. The Vale of Ewyas is more open with a through-route linking a succession of older settlements. Ewyas is the regional name of a former princedom which goes back to the sixth century. Before the Norman Conquest a castle was built at Ewyas Harold (3828) by Ralph, Earl of Hereford and when he died in 1057 it passed to his son Harold who ultimately gave his name to the settlement and surrounding district. Another prominent Marcher family were the Lacys and after the Conquest they acquired an adjacent manor which ultimately became Ewyas Lacy, taking in the former centres of Rowlstone (3727), Watterstone (3425), Clodoch (3227) and Longtown (3229). At each of these a motte and bailey castle was thrown up using the soft red marls for the earthworks and the harder sandstone for the main castle buildings. It is here in this tiny corner of Herefordshire that the true character of the border region emerges in that both the physical and human threads are drawn close together. Throughout its turbulent history Ewyas has maintained a distinctive, almost independent existence, with its pattern of life often dictated by circumstance but nevertheless reflecting its natural setting and available resources.

In the Vale of Ewyas itself, as opposed to the larger region around it, there are many distinct facets which reflect both the natural and man-made history of the area. The lower part of the valley is much narrower than farther upstream, the restriction being due to harder beds within the Brownstone formation. At Cwmyoy (2923) they form bare crags, below which there are extensive areas of rumpled ground associated with past landslips. Some are quite recent and have caused the medieval church of St Martin on the side of Hatteral Hill to subside. Although some restoration was carried out last century, both its tower and chancel walls lean noticeably. Beyond Cwmyoy, the valley once again opens out as the priory remains of Llanthony are approached. In this quiet remoteness of a Black Mountain valley it is easy to appreciate those qualities of the landscape which first drew William de Lacy in the early twelfth century to found a priory church endowed with the lands of the manors at Cwmyoy and Oldcastle. The other prominent Marcher family of this area was also involved in religious foundation, for in 1147 Robert, son of Harold of Ewyas, founded the Cistercian Abbey of Dore (3830). Although no parts of the original building remain, there is some later twelfth-century fabric incorporated in the present building which, after restoration, still functions as a church.

Abbey Dore lies at the entrance to the Golden Valley, the most open of the succession of river valleys which dissect the dip slope of the Black Mountains. The name has often attracted attention and various suggestions have been made as to its origin. The usual explanation is that it is a misnomer for the river name Dore from the French for gold. It is likely, however, that the river name itself is of great antiquity and is an adaptation of the Celtic word 'dwr', simply meaning water. Whatever the origin of its present name, the Golden Valley can claim to be the richest jewel in this dip-slope landscape. Being wider and more open than its neighbours, its floor carries rich crops of grain from its deep, alluvial and glacial soils. Downwash from the adjacent slopes, particularly from the cornstone beds which outcrop high up on the valley sides, make it extremely fertile and rich farming country. Its agricultural prosperity once prompted local farmers to promote a narrow gauge railway running the whole length of the vale from the main-line junction at Pontrilas (3927) through Abbey Dore, Vowchurch, Peterchurch and Dorstone before climbing to the col at the upper end and linking with the Wye valley railway near Hay-on-Wye (see pages 195–6).

On statistical grounds the Brecon Beacons can claim to be the most spectacular of the high tablelands of the southern Marches. It is some 500 feet higher than its nearest rival, the Black Mountains, and with its thicker capping of the resistant Old Red Sandstone conglomerate it presents an even more impressive escarpment face to the north. Its greater height and aspect have also led to it being subject to prolonged glacial attack during the Ice Age so that huge amphitheatres have been cut into its edge, each with bare rocky crags encircling the steep backwall. In the details of this glacial sculpture we are constantly reminded of the great ranges of North Wales, Snowdonia, the Arennigs, Aran Mountains and Harlech Dome. Nothing quite as dramatic occurs elsewhere in south Wales so that on uniqueness alone it fully justifies the setting apart of the area as a National Park.

The rounded contours of the Brecon Beacons plateau-top and southerly slopes towards the coalfield give little hint of the abrupt, angular edge on its northern side. Precipitous slopes, carved out of alternating layers of shale, sandstone and conglomerate, form the backwalls of cwms which nurture the many streams running northwards to join the Usk. The intervening spurs are formed mainly of sandstone which weathers to give smooth outlines. At times the spurs are flattened sufficiently to form an underscarp bench which recalls the similar feature of the Allt below the Black Mountains crest. The easiest approach to the Beacons top is by the track which leads up from the main Merthyr Tydfil to Brecon road (A470) at Storey Arms (SN 9820). An alternative though longer approach to the scarp crest is by the old route running south from Brecon up the side of the Cwm Cynwyn to a high-level col at a height of 1,961 feet (SO 0320). From this point there is a scarp crest walk westward to Pen-y-Fan at 2,909 feet and Corn Du at 2,863 feet. From these high points on the Beacons rim the view on a fine day is especially rewarding, taking in not only the great expansive sweep of the plateau lands to the south but, more impressively, the intimate details within the scarp face and the foothill country running down to the Usk valley. Beyond there is the gradual rise of the back of Mynydd Eppynt and, under conditions of

33

exceptional visibility, the rising mass of Pumlumon can be faintly seen in the far distance.

The scalloped edge to the Beacons only occupies a few miles to the east of the Merthyr to Brecon road. Continuing farther eastward the Old Red Sandstone formations are replaced by the Carboniferous Limestone and with it there is a corresponding change of scenery. The same basic elements of flat-topped plateau and northward-facing scarp remain but there is a change

5. *Alternating sandstone and shale formations making up the almost precipitous north face of the Brecon Beacons.*

in the detail as the distinctive qualities of limestone as a rock assert themselves. Mynydd Llangattock has a scarp edge which recalls the Eglwyseg Rocks overlooking the Dee valley in the north. Past quarrying has accentuated the steep profile for the bare rock crags provided a reasonably acces-

34

sible source of limestone, needed by the ironworks of the coalfield area to the south. A tramway was built around the northern edge by following the contours just below the scarp. This has now been made into a road over part of its length so that the area is accessible both from Clydach (2213) in the east and Llangattock in the Usk valley (2117). Although the limestone top is bleak and windswept, the shelter given by the scarp face has led to a distinctive woodland growing up on the steep north-facing slopes. A nature reserve has been established here at Craig-y-Cilan (SO 1915) to preserve vegetation which includes the rather rare whitebeam (Sorbus minima), a close relation of the mountain ash. The area can be entered using old quarry tracks. Close by are narrow clefts in the limestone which lead into one of the largest cave systems so far discovered in Britain with no less than nine miles of tunnels and passages. The entrance to the cave Agen Allwedd (SO 188158) – now closed by an iron door – lies high up on the cliff face near the end of the path. Another cleft is Eglwys Faen (stone church) and from its name it has been suggested that it once functioned as a retreat during the formative years of the Celtic Church. Its secluded site recalls the sea cave of St Ninian on the shores of the Isle of Whithorn in Galloway.

The cave of Eglwys Faen lies near to one of the few scarp-face valleys which allow access to the plateau above. On top one is confronted with a treeless waste of short, tussocky grass with many boggy hollows, quite unlike the limestone areas of the Pennines. A covering of impermeable clay allows water to collect on the surface and the lack of an adequate natural drainage pattern adds to the problem. Numerous conical hollows – swallow holes – pit the surface in places and their presence indicates subterranean collapse of the underlying limestone beds. Everywhere there is a feeling that this is the last outpost of 'natural' scenery before the industrialised landscape of the coalfield is reached only a few miles to the south at Brynmawr and Beaufort.

For an appreciation of the more distinctive features of limestone terrain it is necessary to travel a dozen miles to the west to the headwater reaches of the Mellte and Hepste rivers around Ystradfellte (SN 9313) as they drain the dip slopes of Forest Fawr. In the deeply set Mellte valley below the village the stream runs underground for part of its course and can be heard and occasionally seen down a crevice in the rock. Great boulders choke the stream bed but lower down it re-emerges as a normal river once the Millstone Grit formation is reached. Hard bands of sandstone then take over and create a number of impressive waterfalls around Clyn-gwyn (9210). An even more impressive fall, Sgwd-yr-Eira (fall of snow), occurs on the nearby Hepste river where it is possible to walk behind the curtain of water on a natural ledge cut into the underlying soft shale. The few square miles of country

35

around Ystradfellte are worth exploring in detail for the area abounds in surprises and natural curiosities.

East of the Brecon Beacons and Black Mountains the country assumes a much less dramatic appearance as the harder beds are replaced more and more by thick red marls. For the most part it is a maze of minor valleys which lead to the Monnow trench as it crosses the area in a north-west to south-east direction. Rising above the general level is the monadnock of Graig Syfyrddin (SO 4021), with its top reaching to over 1,400 feet at its southern end. The other major topographic break in this ridge-and-valley countryside is provided by the distinctive shape of Skirrid Fawr (3318), lying about three miles north-east of Abergavenny. Although this isolated hill takes on different appearances when seen from various directions, its most distinctive view is from the main Abergavenny road (A465). Along its western side there is a great cleft caused by the slipping of the hard capstone beds in the distant past. From the ramparts of the Iron Age fort which crowns its elongated summit there are good views both of the surrounding foothill country as well as more distant vistas of the Malverns and Cotswolds on a clear day. Perhaps because of its great rent on its side, Skirrid Fawr has always had a mystical and religious association connected with the Crucifixion. In medieval times a chapel, dedicated to St Michael, was built on its summit. Only the footings now remain but the climb to its 1,600-foot summit is worthwhile because of its isolated setting. In the past the ascent was looked upon with a great sense of achievement and an early traveller, the Reverend William Coxe, recalls in his *Historical Tour of Monmouthshire*, published in 1801, how he was 'filled with animation and lassitude, horror and delight' on reaching the top.

This foothill country of north Gwent, with its scattering of isolated castles at Skenfrith, White Castle and Grosmont, forms an admirable introduction to the Forest of Dean for the harder, upper beds of the Old Red Sandstone which are absent here now make a reappearance once the Wye valley is approached. They include the quartz conglomerates which, although only about 100 feet thick, form an impressive rim to the plateau of the Forest of Dean. The rocks have been gently downfolded into an elongated basin shape with the youngest beds (belonging to the Coal Measures) outcropping in the central part. Between the hard rocks of the rim and the rolling landscape of the interior there is a discontinuous outcrop of the Carboniferous Limestone. It is most pronounced along the western margin between Coleford and St Briavels (SO 5504) and is significant in that the limestone contains small pockets of haematite which have been worked intermittently since Roman times. In the area known as the Scowles (6004), mining has created a jumbled landscape of pits and chasms as the shallow pockets of iron ore have been extracted. Ample supplies of charcoal and the availability of water from the swiftly flowing streams descending the plateau edge to both the Severn and Wye, led to numerous furnaces and forges growing up in the marginal valleys of the Forest. Today the industrial scene has changed with no ironworks or working collieries. Former waste-tips are now covered with woodland and

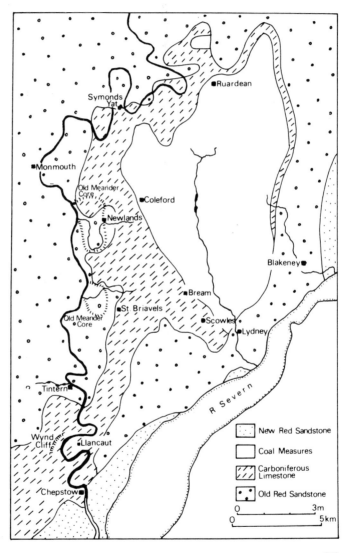

3. *The geology of the Forest of Dean plateau and Wye valley.*

37

one south of Cannop (6011) has been adapted to provide one of the few good vantage points in the Forest.

The woodland which today covers much of the area is largely coniferous and has been planted by the Forestry Commission who, in 1938, created the first National Forest Park here. On the drier, less-fertile sandstone soils trees like the Norwegian Spruce, Douglas Fir and Corsican Pine have grown well. Around Blackpool Bridge (6508) the stands of Norwegian Spruce were planted as long ago as 1901 and are now mature. In keeping with the Forest Park image, a 'Forest Garden' has been planted in the Abbots Wood near Soudley Pool (6511) and here the visitor is able to see stands of the various trees labelled and their date of planting shown. With so much of the area now under woodland the regional name of Forest of Dean is once more applicable. This was not the case in the last century when, after a long period of almost continuous exploitation, the plateau presented a very bare appearance. The voracious appetite of the local iron industry, with its great demand for charcoal, and the oak timbers needed for the hulls of the Navy's ships had virtually removed all the original natural vegetation.

The history of the Forest as a royal hunting chase where the king could pursue the wild boar and deer goes back to the time of Edward the Confessor in the eleventh century. Although the hunting laws were vigorously enforced at the outset, later centuries saw the development of small clearings in the forest and sporadic settlements began to spring up. Gradually the whole appearance of the area began to change. None of the trees which we see today has survived from the original forest cover of Edward the Confessor's day and even the great oak at Newlands (5509), now standing broken and dismembered in the centre of a field, is unlikely to be more than 700 years old. The largest stands of 'natural' woodland are today found around Speech House (6212) with the holly trees perhaps dating back to the early seventeenth century and the scattered oaks all that remain of the great scheme of planting begun in 1689. Other plantings took place in the eighteenth and early nineteenth centuries with conifers used to protect the young oak saplings. Once the conifers were seen to flourish on the poor soils they gradually took over so that deciduous trees are now only grown in special situations.

The most impressive scenery of the Forest lies around its margins, particularly where it overlooks the Wye valley. A well-known and much visited spot is Symonds Yat (5616), where the River Wye makes a great sweep to the north after a preliminary incursion into the limestone edge around Welsh Bicknor. The viewpoint lies at the northern end of a long spur of limestone which lies within the meander loop of the river and, although now somewhat

6. *The tidal Wye with one of its large meander loops at Llancaut.*

commercialised, is well worth a visit. A platform hewn out of the knobbly and worn limestone provides a view to the north with the wooded Huntsham's Hill in the foreground and the sweeping curve of the river disappearing temporarily around it. To the west lie the steep slopes where the Wye enters its gorge section, a much-favoured part of the valley for the Victorians who built their cottages in tiers amongst the deciduous woods. Much of the present splendour of the area is the result of a sequence of events over a relatively long period of geological time. Initially the river must have been flowing across a broad plain at a much higher level than at present and it was during this phase that it developed its great meander loops. A subsequent uplift of the Forest of Dean plateau forced the river to cut down and it was at this stage that the gorge and its incised meander loops came into being. On the outside of each meander loop the river has tended to undercut the steep slopes and created rocky precipices which are very much a part of the Wye scene. Within the inside of many loops there are areas of flat ground which form excellent farmland as at Liveoaks Farm (5397) and Llancaut (5396). Both benches lie about 250 feet above the present valley bottom and must represent a stage in the history of development of the river. There are other indications in the present valley of its earlier evolution for at both Redbrook (5310) and Bigsweir (5304) there are former meander loops now lying high and dry above the valley floor. At one point the Redbrook meander core lies almost 400 feet above the present river and this is an indication of how much downcutting has taken place since the loop was severed and then abandoned.

Although the rejuvenated river flows through a deep trench for much of its length between Ross and the sea beyond Chepstow, there are variations in valley form depending on the different types of rock encountered on its twisting course. At Lower Lydbrook (5917), for example, where the river makes its first real bite into the Forest of Dean plateau, the valley side slopes are not excessively steep as the rock type involved is the relatively soft shale. Only a mile downstream, however, at Coldwell Rocks (5615), harder limestone beds are encountered and the river cliffs are almost vertical. From this point the river makes a long detour to the north alongside the edge of Coppet Hill. This is formed of quartz conglomerate which is tough and resistant to erosion. After rounding Huntsham's Hill, the river flows southwards again and enters its limestone gorge at Symonds Yat. Immediately both sides of the valley crowd in with bare scars like the Seven Sisters Rocks (5515) breaking through the woodland cover. Before Monmouth is reached, the river has once again escaped its containing wall of limestone and for some miles towards Tintern it runs through Old Red Sandstone Rocks. Although the valley width is still restricted with room only for river, road and former railway, the side slopes are less steep and a more open appearance results. Once the river enters the limestone again below Tintern there is an immediate return to steep river cliffs. With so much mature woodland on its banks, good viewpoints are limited, though the climb to the top of Wynd Cliff (5297), by over 300 steps, can be rewarding. Another vantage point, this time on the other bank, is at Wintour's Leap (5496) by the side of the B4228 road. The view here is of hedged fields within the Llancaut meander loop and the steep limestone bluff of Wynd Cliff rising beyond, the whole setting enhanced by the sweeping curve of the river itself.

The best way to appreciate the river scenery of the Wye Valley would be to follow in the footsteps of the early tourists who made the journey by boat. From the mid-eighteenth century onwards they came in ever-increasing numbers to see for themselves the picturesque beauty which the guide books praised in most fulsome language. This lower section of the Wye had long been used for commercial purposes but it was not until 1745, when John Egerton, Vicar of Ross, had a pleasure boat built to carry his friends and visitors down through the Wye gorge, that the possibilities of tourist traffic became apparent. Another fillip came from the visit of the Reverend William Gilpin in 1770. He was soon aware that it conformed to his ideas of what the idealised landscape should contain. Much of his voyage down the river was marred by heavy rain but this did not deter him from substituting his own veiled impressions of the gloomy grandeur. By the first decade of the nineteenth century, tourists were flocking to the area, their appetites whetted by the writings of Gilpin, Archdeacon Coxe, Clark Heath, a local man from Monmouth and others. They usually embarked at Ross and took two days to make the journey down-river to Chepstow. At various points they left the boat to visit the local iron forges, wireworks and paper mills as well as the great centrepiece of the voyage, Tintern Abbey. Industry was not looked upon with disfavour, for 'the agitation and uproar of the great forge hammers served to add to the wildness and terror of the rocky gorge'. The stretch below Tintern provided the greatest excitement, and as one traveller put it, 'the beauties are so uncommonly excellent that the most exact of critics of landscape would scarcely wish to alter a position in the assemblage of woods, cliffs, ruins and water'. One can only wonder whether this view still prevails in a car-conscious age.

The border country of Wales ends in the south with a landscape similar to that with which it began in the marshland shores of the Dee estuary. The scale is different, for the levels which border the Severn shores are considerably more extensive. There is also a different history of settlement and reclamation. The region is typified by the Caldicot Levels which extend in a narrow strip from the mouth of the Wye to the estuary of the Usk. Inland the marshland is well defined by the rising ground from Llanwern (3688) through Magor to Caldicott and Portskewett (5088) – the former coastline. A land surface existed here towards the end of the Ice Age but as the sea level rose it was subsequently drowned from about 10,000 B.C. onwards. Various deposits were laid down similar to those accumulating on the Severn shores today, at first gravels and then thick beds of silt. As the surface rose, it became out of reach of all but the highest spring tides and vegetation was able to establish itself. As layer upon layer accumulated and decayed, they formed thick beds of peat which underlie much of the present marshland surface. Samples taken from the peat and subjected to pollen analysis suggest that this occurred from about 750 B.C. i.e. towards the end of the Bronze Age. Here we have the first hint of a land surface but it was far too marshy and liable to flood to allow any human settlement. It is not surprising, therefore, that no prehistoric remains exist in the Caldicot Levels. The situation changed in Roman times and pottery dating from the first to third centuries suggests that some settlement was taking place at this time, possibly as the result of a slight drop in sea level. The occupation surface at this time was well below the present level but this is due, in part, to more recent compaction of sediments. The peat beds have certainly shrunk and one result has been the leaning tower of Whitson Church (3883), recalling many similar occurrences in the Fenland.

Sea level seems to have been relatively low throughout Saxon and Norman times and this undoubtedly encouraged settlement in the marshes. There was an ever-continuing threat of inundation in later medieval times which led to the building of higher sea banks. These proved only partly effective and there are many records of flooding from the sixteenth century onwards. One particularly severe flood happened in January 1606 when waves overtopped the sea defences and surged inland. A contemporary manuscript account, with woodcut drawings, shows that extensive damage was done to property. A plaque on the side of Nash Church marks the level reached by the floodwaters at that time. Other storms have followed in succeeding centuries, often with gale-force winds rapidly veering from south-west to north-west. These storm surges, which are similar in character to that which caused the east-coast floods in 1953, represent a real threat to the marshland today even though the sea walls have been strengthened and raised in height. At Goldcliff (ST 3281), where the sea wall is tied to a solid rock outcrop, the rising ground allows extensive views over the marshland with its straight ditches and hedge boundaries. The name Goldcliff – an inlier of Keuper and Rhaetic rocks – comes from the mica in the beds which glistens in the sun. It is the only solid rock outcrop in the whole of the Caldicot Levels and it was here that the Roman Goldcliff Stone was discovered in 1882. Although its exact significance is unknown, one suggestion is that it was a boundary mark, implying land ownership and land division in Roman times. Caerwent (4790), a Roman town, lies only a few miles to the north on the edge of the levels, so the suggestion is not without support. Much of the marshland scene of today must date from much later centuries. One tangible record dates from 1245 when the Cistercian monks of Moor Grange Farm were given permission to dig ditches and 'make them as they saw fit' in order to drain the damp pastures. This was but one episode in the sequence of events, both natural and man-made, of the past 8,000 years which has transformed the area. The last and biggest change to the landscape has been the laying out of the great Llanwern steelworks on the marsh to the east of Newport. Like the Shotton works on Deeside, the cheap marshland gave an expansive site needed by the industry, as well as good rail links and an importing port for raw materials.

2

The Glacial Invasion

The borderland concept is given further expression if the events of the Ice Age are considered in relation to the evolution of the present landscape. Although the whole of the glacial period lasted well over a million years, it is the closing stages, extending back about 50,000 years, that have had the greatest effect. Even in this period conditions were not equally cold so that any ice sheet affecting the area tended to both advance and retreat. At times also, particularly in the northern borderlands, there were two competing ice masses. From the west came the ice sheet nurtured in the high mountains of central and north Wales. When it reached out eastwards into the hills and basins of the borderland country it found itself in conflict with ice that had moved in from the Irish Sea and through the Cheshire Gate to occupy large parts of the Midlands. The boundary line between the two ice masses was never static but ebbed and flowed like the man-made frontiers of historic time.

Ice both erodes and deposits and it is from the debris which it leaves behind on melting that we get the clearest indication of its former extent and pattern of movement. The Welsh ice brought with it clays which are typically blue-grey in colour and fragments of rock which had been plucked from the slates, shales and igneous rocks of Snowdonia, the Arans, Arennig Ranges and Berwyn Mountains which lay across its track as it moved eastward. In contrast, the boulder clay dumped by the Irish Sea ice is predominantly chocolate-brown or red-brown in colour and commonly incorporates both fairly local material from the Wirral Peninsula and the Cheshire Plain and far-travelled erratics which can be matched with parent rocks from Criffel in Galloway and the mountains of the Lake District. The deposits of the Irish

43

Sea ice also tend to contain thick beds of sand or gravel as well as chalk flints which must have come from the bed of the Irish Sea.

The whole glacial story is complex and is only now being unravelled after 150 years of painstaking research by geologists and geomorphologists working on the deposits. Fortunately the landforms associated with the ice are relatively easy to identify so that it is possible to piece together the main processes and events which have been responsible for the evolution of the present landscape. With such a large area involved, extending over 120 miles in a north–south direction, the effects vary considerably in different parts. For example, in the Middle March where the influence of the ice from the Welsh uplands was dominant, great glaciers moved down the valleys of the Teme and Wye causing temporary lakes to develop in some of the lowland basins and ultimately changing much of the former drainage pattern of the area. In the southern Marches the highest parts of the Black Mountains and Brecon Beacons had their own snowfields which nurtured glaciers capable of considerable erosion. Even in the past ten thousand years, ice has once more accumulated in many of the hollows before spilling out into the surrounding countryside and leaving behind morainic mounds of debris as they melted. This varying impact of ice on different parts of the borderland has undoubtedly contributed to the diversity of its landscape. Together with the

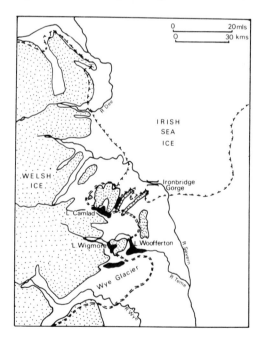

4. *Glacial competition between the Welsh and Irish Sea ice sheets and their associated impounded glacial lakes.*

44

marked variations in rock type, it has made the region one of infinite variety in its constituent parts.

The most important role which the glacial deposits play in the present landscape is nowhere better displayed than in the countryside around Mold (SJ 2464), though similar patterns occur on a smaller scale throughout the region. The town of Mold, with its regular pattern of streets, lies on the south side of the Alyn valley which extends westward without any real watershed across into the Wheeler valley and thence into the Vale of Clwyd. During the Ice Age, water was trapped in the Vale and then forced its way through the Wheeler–Alyn gap, carrying with it considerable quantities of debris in an easterly direction. These deposits form the low terraces of sand and gravel (kames) which now line the present valley sides. At the eastern end near Padeswood (2762) the hummocky surface of drift represents further accumulations left behind by the ice as it melted. Its 'basket of eggs' form, well seen on the golf course and forming some of the hazards, can be likened to the drumlin swarms which occur in many glaciated areas and which are believed to have arisen as a result of moulding of ground debris by the sole of the glacier. Some, however, believe the hummocks are simply kames of river-deposited debris which has been washed out of the glacier snout. Whatever the true origin of the deposit, it gives rise to a fresh-looking landscape which on the geological time-scale was formed only yesterday. This is characteristic of much of the area and emphasises that too little time has elapsed since the end of the Ice Age for other agents of erosion to have modified the glacial scenery. Even though the mounds are formed of soft, unconsolidated material, their sides are still remarkably steep. In some parts the natural shape of the mound has been used to advantage. On the valley side, one mile south of Flint (2371), the builders of the Norman castle used the landform for their castle motte.

The Welsh ice from the west seems to have begun to melt some time before that of the Irish Sea ice which occupied much of the Cheshire Plain. For a brief period lakes were formed between the ice front and the hills of Wales and as water flowed from one to another in a southward direction it carved out new valleys. Most of these became dry after the ice and the lakes disappeared. Only in a few cases did the overflow valley become part of the present-day drainage system. Another legacy of the period was the creation of entirely new lines of drainage. This is well shown by the River Alyn which, from its source in the Clwydian Hills to the Cheshire Plain, passes through a series of abrupt turns, largely as the result of the disruption caused by an ever-fluctuating ice margin. Originally the river flowed northwards along the

45

foot of the Carboniferous Limestone escarpment through Cilcain (1865) and thence to Nannerch (1669), where it uses the present valley of the Wheeler on its way into the Vale of Clwyd. At one stage in the Ice Age, however, the original valley route north of Cilcain was blocked by an ice lobe so that the River Alyn had to forsake this course and cut a new exit to the east. The result in the present-day landscape is the magnificent limestone gorge running down to Rhydymwyn (2066). Part of the former route, prior to ice diversion, is shown by the wide and open valley north of Cilcain which is now completely dry. A second diversion from its original course took place in the vicinity of Padeswood and again this has led to the creation of a gorge section around Caergwrle (3057) through tough sandstone beds. The final feature of the River Alyn to excite attention is the great loop at Bryn-Alyn (3353), just north of Wrexham, where the river turns back on itself from south to north. This situation is most likely to have arisen when the lake into which it was flowing in the Wrexham area suddenly changed its outlet from south to north. When the lake finally drained, the river followed the northern exit. Great quantities of debris were brought into the lake by the River Alyn and it is on these deposits that much of the present town of Wrexham is laid out.

Away from the Welsh foothills the borderland ice has left a very different imprint on the present landscape. It seems that at one stage the Welsh ice pushed well out into the plain of north Shropshire and met the Irish Sea ice along a curved line running from Perthy (SJ 3633) through Loppington (5437) and then north-east towards Whitchurch. Along this zone of contact both ice sheets contributed a plentiful supply of debris in the form of clays, rock fragments, sands and gravels. Today this morainic material forms a broad belt of country standing well above the general level of the surrounding area. Its highest point occurs near Perthy where it reaches 487 feet but throughout the area there are many hillocks which top the 400-foot contour. Groups of whale-backed hillocks or drumlins occur widely and are believed to have formed as the almost stagnant ice exerted a moulding action over the ground moraine. Many of the farms of the area are sited on their crests to take advantage of the drier site amidst the succession of rather boggy hollows.

Around Ellesmere (3934) many of the deeper hollows are still filled with water to give rise to a distinctive landscape of small lakes or meres. Some, like Whitemere (4133), are deeply set within wooded hillocks, while others simply occupy the lowest parts of shallow valleys and have irregular outlines. In nearly every case the shape of the mere is a reflection of conditions left behind after the ice had melted, although occasionally there has been some modification due to silting up around their shallow margins, now often a reed or alder swamp. It is generally accepted that the meres are natural bodies of water and not man-made like the Broads of East Anglia. As yet there is no proper integrated drainage system covering the area and in some cases artificial dykes have been dug to get rid of the water. Some of the original meres must have disappeared quite quickly after the end of the Ice Age and in their place damp peaty hollows formed, known locally as mosslands. The peat developed as the result of reed and sedge colonising the wetter places. As layer upon layer of vegetation decayed, so the surface was gradually raised and sphagnum moss was able to colonise the upper parts. In mosslands like Whixall and Fenn's Moss (4836) the peat shows a distinct stratification due to the decay of the two different types of vegetation.

It is to these mosslands that we must turn for an insight as to the way in which the landscape has evolved over the past ten thousand years. The technique of pollen analysis, in which the distinctive shapes of different pollen types are assessed quantitatively and related to known vegetation, has provided a means of working out the post-glacial vegetation history of the region. At Whixall Moss, after about 8,000 B.C. when the climate became much warmer, the open water of a former mere gradually gave place to marshland colonised by damp-loving vegetation. Birch saplings began to establish themselves in the surrounding area, for it is the pollen of this tree which is found in the lowest peat layers of the present mossland. Thereafter the pollen of pine, willow, hazel and oak are found in ever-increasing quantities indicating that conditions were becoming favourable for a more mixed vegetation in the lands around. This situation continued into historic time although the area was never suitable for settlement until artificial drainage works were undertaken in the last century. Even then it was squatters who took up residence and their humble cottages are still found around the edge of the moss. Some peat-digging for fuel took place but in recent years the workings have been largely concerned with the horticultural market and the peat used as packing for early potatoes and tomatoes.

Although no less important in the fashioning of the present landscape, the impact of ice invasion in the Middle March was very different from that farther north. There are two main reasons for this. Firstly, only Welsh ice was involved, at least during the final and most effective period, as the extent of the Irish Sea ice was limited to the area north of the latitude of Wolverhampton. This gave greater freedom to the glacier tongues coming down from the ice fields of central Wales and enabled them to push well out into the English lowlands. The other main difference arose from the fact that the Middle March countryside, whose main outlines had been determined long before the Ice Age, consisted of a mosaic of small basins and enclosing hills.

The advancing ice tended to seal off the drainage from these basins, causing temporary lakes to form which would ultimately find a new outlet over the lowest ice-free col. The great outrush of water from the impounded lake would quickly cut a deep gorge so that when the ice ultimately melted it might become part of a newly established drainage system. The Middle March landscape abounds with examples of entirely new river patterns replacing the original drainage lines.

The maximum extent of the Welsh ice in south Shropshire and the adjacent Hereford Basin can be determined from the distribution of rock fragments (erratics) left behind in the glacial drifts after the ice has melted. Stones and even large boulders, which are sufficiently distinctive for their source to be easily recognised, include the Hanter Hill gabbro and the Dolyhir Limestone. Over fifty years ago it was realised that the Welsh ice must have formed a great piedmont glacier which spread out into the Herefordshire lowland and came to rest in the rolling country of the Kyre uplands at Grendon Green (SO 5956), seven miles east of Leominster. Its

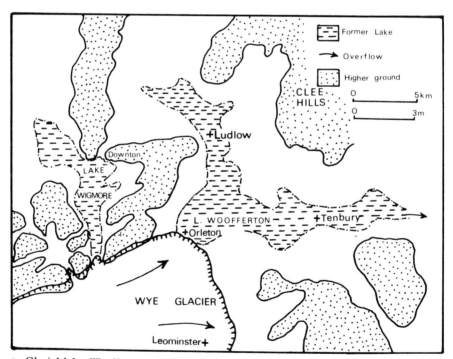

5. *Glacial lakes Woofferton and Wigmore in relation to the Wye Glacier at its maximum extent.*

48

7. *The site of the pro-glacial Lake Woofferton with the rising ground of the Ludlow anticline in the background.*

northern boundary is marked by a prominent moraine on which the village of Orleton is situated (4967). The morainic ridge rises some fifty feet above the flat country and presents a fairly steep face to the south, presumably where it was once in contact with the ice. The whole feature is well seen from the old railway bridge a mile to the south-west. Ice must have stood at Orleton for a considerable time and allowed meltwater streams to lay down a thick succession of sands, gravels and laminated clays, the latter possibly associated with a temporary lake which developed to the north and which was later to have a profound effect on the drainage pattern of the area.

Detailed studies of this corner of Herefordshire have been made in recent years by Cross and Hodgson, using a whole range of techniques in order to unravel the complexities of the glacial history. Their work has shown that an extensive lake once existed between the Wye valley ice front at Orleton and a similar containing ice wall near Ludlow, four miles to the north. This site of Lake Woofferton, as it has been termed, is today marked by low, rather featureless country as one might expect from a former lake floor. The lake changed its size and shape from time to time but at its maximum extent it ran back northwards through the present Whitecliffe gorge at Ludlow as far as Stanton Lacy (4978). Here it was in contact with another ice lobe which had pushed southwards through the Church Stretton valley. Eastwards, a long arm for the lake ran up what is now the Teme valley to beyond Tenbury Wells (5968). The lake shore was at a height of approximately 300 feet and its

49

main overflow was over a low col some distance to the east of Newnham (6469). Huge volumes of water poured out from the outlet and quickly eroded and lowered the soft marls of the gap. In time this would cause the level of the lake to drop and gradually reduce its size with possibly only the eastern Teme valley arm existing at the end. When the ice finally disappeared and the lake completely drained, the new post-glacial drainage of the Teme would have no difficulty in following the easterly course already marked for it.

The new River Teme, now flowing eastwards to join the Severn, has completely reversed its direction compared with its pre-glacial ancestor. The latter once had its source region near Newnham, gathering water from the upland country to the north and south and then flowing westwards ultimately to become part of the Wye drainage system. Evidence for this lies in the narrowing form of the present Teme valley to the east when it should be widening downstream. In addition, many of the Teme's tributaries join the main river in an upstream direction which again suggests some anomaly. The high-level terraces of the middle part of the Teme valley as well as those of its tributaries, the Rea and Ledwyche Brook, also provide evidence of a former westward-flowing drainage system. The glacial history of this section of the Teme provides an outstanding example, perhaps unique on this scale, of a major river undergoing a complete reversal in direction over the past 20,000 years.

8. *The former floor of Wigmore Lake set between two enclosing limestone scarps.*

The events of the Ice Age were also felt along another stretch of the Teme valley, namely in the Vale of Wigmore to the west of Ludlow. In pre-glacial times the river, coming from the Welsh uplands, turned south at Leintwardine (4073) and then continued in this direction through the Vale of Wigmore and past Aymestrey (4265) into the Lugg valley and thence to the Wye. For a brief period the valley near Aymestrey was blocked by ice and this caused a lake (Lake Wigmore) to form in the flat country east of Wigmore. Water poured into this lake, bringing with it a huge amount of debris. Some of this can be seen in the gravel pit at Yatton (4266) where the workings have exposed a thick deposit of fluvio-glacial material. On top there is a plastic stoneless clay – a true lake sediment – while below there are beds of flat stones together with a wide band of sand showing marked current bedding. All this is part of a huge delta which streams from the ice front lying to the south built out into the lake. As more water was added, so the level of Lake Wigmore rose until it was able to overtop the lowest col in the encircling wall of hills. This was at a point close to the present Downton-on-the-Rock village (4277). The overflow quickly cut a deep gorge which is still very much part of the present landscape. After the ice melted and the glacial lake drained away, the River Teme used this outlet and it became part of the circuitous course of the present river.

This part of the borderland has innumerable examples of drainage diversions similar to those of the Teme, as rivers were forced to adopt new routes in the face of the disruptive effects of ice invasion. In most cases they are

9. *Drumlin topography near Shobdon with rounded swells enclosing small meres.*

51

marked by the river taking an unlikely route through a narrow gorge when an easier and more direct passage appears open to it. The gorge of the River Lugg between Sned Wood and Mere Hill (SO 4065) is a good example. Here we can also see an earlier and now abandoned route marked by the dry valley running to the south-east towards Mortimer's Cross (4263). Many of these valley sections only functioned for a relatively short period but so powerful was the erosive power of the river swollen with meltwater from the ice sheet that the gorges so created are important elements in the present landscape, dissecting the foothill country into distinct blocks. The valley sides are too steep to be farmed and have now been planted with conifers, a now familiar scene in the borderland.

The main cause of all this disruption and drainage modification in the hill country to the west of Aymestrey was the blocking effect of the Wye glacier. This occupied the big lowland basin extending eastwards from Presteigne (3164) and now drained by the Lugg and Arrow rivers and their tributaries. As it moved slowly eastwards, the great tongue of ice moulded the debris along its sole and the result has been a succession of low swells which collectively are termed kettle moraine. Many of the deeper hollows are still occupied by lakes as around Shobdon (4062) and Titley. With its gentle relief and rich diversity it was ideal country for landscaping when the great country estates were established from medieval times onwards. The morainic landscape is well seen alongside the B4362 road from Mortimer's Cross to Presteigne, especially around the village of Shobdon. The largest lake is just west of the village and is now part of a caravan site. Most of the country is well drained and makes high-quality farmland but there are negative areas like Coombe Moor with its bogs and rushes. Here perhaps we catch a glimpse of the sort of landscape which was common to many parts of the borderland immediately after the ice had melted and new drainage lines had yet to be established.

When the Wye glacier was at its most powerful stage much of the Herefordshire lowland, including the cornstone hills, must have been covered by ice. Later, as melting took place, the surface level of the ice fell and first the cornstone hills and then the middle ground would reappear. One persistent glacier lobe which seems to have continued as the ice melted elsewhere was in the middle part of the Wye valley upstream from Hereford. The ice was hemmed in on its south-western side by the edge of the Black Mountains while to the north lay the Wormsley Hills. For a time the snout must have halted along an arc a few miles west of Hereford where a belt of morainic debris gives rise to distinctive ground. Its hummocky terrain between Stretton Sugwas (4642) and Kingstone (4235) rises to almost 400 feet in places and suggests that the ice front must have persisted here for a considerable time. Small pits have been opened up in the moraine from time to time and these invariably show a complex sequence of deposits, often with gravels overlying a thick red, sandy bed of boulder clay. The River Wye has bitten deeply into the moraine at Weir Cliff (445417) and exposed some fifty feet of deposits. While this stillstand of the ice front was taking place along the Stretton–Kingstone line, the ground moraine of the glacier was being moulded into a succession of low swells and hollows. Some are now filled with water like Blakemere (3641) and it has been suggested that these arose as masses of dead ice were trapped in the boulder clay and subsequently melted, leading to a collapse of the deposits above. Many of these surface dimples, some with lakes and others without, have no natural outlets and show how little the landscape has changed since the ice finally left the area.

The retreating Wye glacier also halted for a time along the line between Norton Canon (3847), Staunton-on-Wye (3744) and Bredwardine (3344), and in doing so left behind the most impressive morainic feature of the Hereford lowland. The ridge, which reached a height of 384 feet just south of Norton Canon, rises over a hundred feet above the surrounding countryside. It is seldom more than a thousand feet in width but it is distinctly hummocky with low swells along its crest line. Few sections are available for study but there is no doubt that it is composed of glacial debris from the stony character of the soils in the fields around. The steepness of its sides suggests that the moraine marks a temporary re-advance of the ice front, a common enough event, for in the closing stages of glaciation the margins would fluctuate considerably depending on the vagaries of the climate. When the Wye glacier did finally retreat it left behind a ridge which was high enough to impound a temporary lake near Letton (3346), which today forms an area of flat, badly drained ground that sometimes becomes flooded in winter.

Much of the impetus given to the Wye glacier as it spread its ice lobe into the English Plains must have come from the accumulating snowfields of the Welsh plateau to the west. The height of the ice in the main trunk stream is not known exactly but it must have approached the 1,000-foot contour. It was certainly high enough to pass through the low col at Scotland Bank (2943) at the north-west end of the Black Mountains and into the Golden Valley. Evidence for this is provided by the erratics of Silurian rocks in the upper part of the vale which could only have come from a distant source to the west. The large size of the Golden Valley, especially its broad, flat floor crossed by the River Dore, a clear misfit, implies that ice had some part to play in its shaping. The ice probably did not extend down the valley beyond Vowchurch (3636). On its retreat a small lake existed for a short time in the

53

vicinity of Dorstone and this would account for the rather flat and marshy character of this part of the valley today.

During the final stages of the Ice Age the summit plateaus of the Black Mountains projected well above the ice level, rather like the nunataks of Antarctica today. Small snowfields undoubtedly developed in the combe-like heads of the valleys but true glaciers originating from within seem unlikely. The extreme cold at heights of over 2,000 feet along the crest ridge must have led to intense frost action and the gradual accumulation of shattered rock fragments. There would also be mass movement of debris downslope when thaw conditions prevailed in the warmer summer months – the process known as solifluction – so the landscape cannot have escaped modification. The effects of these periglacial processes, though not dramatic, are nevertheless unmistakable. Much of the valley slopes are covered with a thick deposit of red clay with rock fragments embedded in it. This 'head' material is usually taken to indicate extreme cold conditions with a prising away of bare rock surfaces by frost action and their subsequent removal downslope as a thin veneer of slow-moving sludge. In some parts the head has given rise to a succession of minor terraces lining the valley sides. Good sections are to be seen in the hedge banks and in the roadside cuttings above Capel-y-Ffin (2531) on the old Gospel Pass route. The presence of head usually leads to good soils, for the deposit is not lacking in minerals and is usually well drained because of its many rock fragments. The slopes of the Black Mountains were formerly much more farmed than at present. Unfortunately, in the past fifty years the relative isolation of the area and the attraction of better wage rates in the towns has led to a steady depopulation. Many farms have been abandoned and their buildings remain as ruins amidst steadily deteriorating pastures and fields. The inherent fertility of the glacially derived soils still remains and in such a situation forestry seems the only way of realising the full potential. In this there is a direct conflict with the sheep farmer and also the visitor seeking wide panoramic views from the tops.

Although it is now taken for granted that ice has played a major role in putting the final touches to the landscape canvas through etching, smoothing and draping the surface, this was not always the commonly held view. Biblical accounts of the flood undoubtedly led many early geologists to believe that 'foreign' rocks must have been carried to their present situation by a much higher sea level. Andrew Ramsey, an eminent geologist who unravelled many of the complexities of rock succession by his extensive mapping in both north and south Wales, once thought that the major northern edge of the Brecon Beacons, with its impressive corrie basins, was a former sea cliff. He also noted in 1846 that the drift deposits around the border town of Kington were nothing more than 'the dregs of matter removed from the land' by the action of some primeval sea. Ramsay was writing at a time when geological ideas were in the melting pot. Only a decade before, the Swiss Agassiz and the Reverend Buckland had put forward the 'revolutionary' view that glacial processes, like those occurring in the Alps, were once actively shaping our own landscape. Marine shells found in deposits at heights of over a thousand feet were not carried by a gigantic flood but rather the result of the great transporting power of mobile ice sheets. Once these views began to command respect, a completely different approach to landscape evolution was available. Landforms whose origin had previously defied explanation were now subject to the new theory. As Charles Darwin put it after re-visiting Snowdonia where he had earlier failed to recognise the significance of what he had seen, 'a house burnt down by fire could not tell a clearer story'.

It was not until 1883 that the real truth emerged as to the origin of the features of the Brecon Beacon scarps which Ramsey had earlier thought of as an ancient sea cliff. In that year Professor Edgeworth David described the landscape in terms of the erosional and depositional effects of a major glaciation. On at least two occasions the Beacons accumulated snow and ice to such an extent that great tongues moved both northwards into the Usk valley and southwards to reach the Vale of Glamorgan. In the case of the Usk glacier it probably filled the valley to a height of about 1,000 feet when at its most powerful. At this time there was a further supply from Mynydd Eppynt in the west, so that it could divide near Crickhowell (2118) with a tributary glacial tongue moving east into the Crwyne Fawr valley while the main Usk glacier turned south-east towards Abergavenny. The former was sufficiently powerful for it to force its way as far as Llanfihangel Crucorney (SO 3220) where it came to an abrupt halt. It was here that it left behind a long curving moraine extending right across the valley. The main border railway (Shrewsbury to Newport) passes through the western end in a long cutting. On its northern side the morainic edge is particularly steep as it was once cut into by the River Honddu. South of the morainic ridge, which rises about 150 feet above the valley floor, there is an ill-drained area which marks the former site of a glacial lake – Lake Triley. This had only a short life for it quickly disappeared once the ice bank to the south melted. As a result of ice interference, the River Honddu, which had formerly flowed south to join the Usk at Abergavenny, was now forced to make a sharp turn to the north along an old glacial channel to join the River Monnow near Pandy (3322). This is one of the many modifications to the earlier drainage pattern which occur throughout the border region. It has lasting significance in that the gap it vacated has been used as a major through-route for both road and rail.

While the tributary glacier of Gwyrne Fawr was bringing about changes in the Llanfihangel Crucorney area, the main Usk glacier had come to a halt only a short distance down the valley in the vicinity of Penpergwm where it left its mark as a terminal moraine stretching towards Gilwern (2414). In retreat, the Usk glacier had periods when the ice front came to a temporary halt and it is at these stages that further morainic belts were laid down across the valley floor, like those near Llangattock (2117) and Llandethy (1220). In the grounds of the nearby Buckland House, the landscaping of the parkland has taken advantage of the broken contours of the ground moraine and converted its natural hollows into ornamental ponds. The same natural landscape also makes a fine basis for laying out a golf course and here, as near Mold in north Wales, the events of thousands of years ago have been turned to advantage in this leisure-conscious age.

One major feature of the present landscape of the southern borderlands which owes its origin to the events of the Ice Age is Llangorse Lake (SO 1326). It occupies a broad enclosed lowland to the north of the Usk valley in front of the sharp edge of the southern end of the Black Mountains. The lake must have been larger in the past for its margins are surrounded by land which is only just above its present level. This is especially so on the northern side where there are large expanses of fen near the church. Llangorse, like so

10. *Llangorse Lake, one of the few remaining water areas which have survived since the end of the Ice Age. The island 'crannog' is marked by the clump of trees.*

56

many Welsh names, is purely descriptive and means the church of the fen. The lake came into being as ice from the Wye valley in the north pressed southwards towards the Usk. This was only a brief interlude, however, and soon the Wye ice retreated again towards its main centre. It did so in a series of stages punctuated by halts or stillstands of the ice front. Each is marked by belts of morainic debris which sometimes make a vivid impact on the present landscape. As the low ground in front of the retreating ice front became exposed, so it was flooded with meltwater to a height of about 630 feet above Ordnance Datum. At this early stage the lake probably had two overflow outlets, one at Pennorth (1026) in the south-west and the other at Bwlch in the south-east. Further retreat of the Wye valley ice to the north ultimately allowed a lower drainage outlet for the lake to emerge and the present route via the Afon Llynfi was established. Although there has been some lowering of the outlet it has not, as yet, proved sufficient to allow the lake to drain away completely, though this will be its ultimate fate. Close to the present shore, set on a morainic islet within the lake, there is a crannog, an early lake dwelling built on wooden piles, recalling similar features found in the Somerset Levels. It is probable that it was in use when the lake was much larger and therefore given greater natural protection.

It is on the high plateau of the Brecon Beacons that glaciation has had its greatest visual impact. While the valley glaciers of the lowland were slowly pushing forward, scraping and scratching rock surfaces in their path and incorporating myriads of rock fragments in their ground moraine, a very different glacial process was taking place on the surrounding heights. The crest line of the Brecon Beacons reaches almost 3,000 feet and would therefore have been high enough to nurture and maintain considerable snowfields. These in turn would serve to supply the ice streams of the many valleys running down from the scarp face. The open form of these valleys and their abrupt combe-like heads betray the effects of past ice erosion. The small streams which occupy the valleys today are quite incapable of bringing about the present form, so we must look to the past and to the moulding forces of ice for an explanation. The past, in this instance, is not too distant, for in a deteriorating climatic situation from about 8500 B.C. onwards, corrie glaciers once more developed in these deep hollows under the Beacons scarp. For a brief period of perhaps no more than 500 years, the ice steadily and effectively gouged out the hollows while frost-shattering on the bare rock slopes above contributed a steady supply of debris with which to arm the glacier and help it in its task of grinding out the hollow. When the corrie glacier finally melted, this debris was left as an arcuate rim around the entrance.

In nearly all the Brecon Beacons corries there are two separate morainic ridges fronting the amphitheatre. The earliest formed ridge is usually well down the valley and is often no more than a series of gentle swells lying across the floor. In contrast, the upper and most recent moraine forms a more distinct ridge, often rising fifty feet above the general level. At one time small circular lakes were ponded behind the moraine but in most cases they have drained away. In Cwm Llwch (SO 0022) a small lake has survived, possibly because the ice gouged out a rock basin as well as leaving behind a morainic barrier. Where a former lake has drained away and left behind a succession of deposits it is often possible to determine approximately when the corrie hollow was last occupied by ice by using the method of pollen analysis. Although this method does not give an absolute dating (radio carbon assaying is necessary for this) the pattern of the post-glacial vegetation changes in Britain is now so well established that it is possible to fit an individual site into the general record. For the Brecon Beacons corries we believe that the glaciers which laid down the outer set of moraines were active about 15,000 B.C. when the country as a whole was undergoing its last major glaciation. These corrie glaciers subsequently melted completely and for a period of several thousand years much warmer conditions prevailed. Shortly after 9000 B.C. cold conditions set in once again and for a period of only 500 years a mini-glaciation occurred. It was at this time that snowfields once more developed in the earlier formed corrie hollows and under steady accumulation and pressure gradually created small glaciers. These did not extend down the valleys as far as on the earlier occasion and when they finally melted they left behind another ring of morainic material much closer to the corrie head. The great amphitheatre of Craig Cerrig-gleisiad, now a nature reserve (9622), shows the arrangement well for although the former lake is now nothing more than a boggy hollow, the rim of morainic mounds is almost as fresh looking as when it came into being just over 10,000 years ago.

The intensity of glaciation in the Brecon Beacons, compared with that on the nearby Black Mountains, might appear puzzling at first sight. It is clearly not simply a question of height, for the Beacons tops are only about 200 feet higher than their Black Mountain counterparts. The basic geology of the two areas is broadly similar with a succession of Old Red Sandstone beds outcropping in both areas. Perhaps the most acceptable explanation takes into account the relative situation of the two regions and the differences in orientation of the plateau edge. There is reason to believe that during the Ice Age the prevailing winds were similar to those of today, that is from the south-west. The Beacons would have received a greater precipitation in the form of snow than the Black Mountains and therefore developed more extensive and deeper snowfields. With the long dip slopes south of the

Beacons crest completely open to the south-west, considerable accumulations of snow and ice would take place on and in the lee of the scarp crest. It is in this situation that the greatest amount of glacial erosion would take place and the result has been a succession of corrie hollows facing northwards towards the Usk valley. This northward aspect would also favour erosion in that snow and ice would tend to persist longer here, especially during the closing stages of the Ice Age. In contrast to the Beacons, the Black Mountains would have received a lower precipitation in the glacial period, just as it does at the present time. It also lacked the great south-west-facing plateau gathering ground which was to nurture the active corrie glaciers just below the Beacons scarp. Its own scarp, facing north-west rather than north, would not experience minimal insolation figures so that once again it would be less likely to sustain active corrie glaciers for so long a period. The result has been that the Black Mountain scarp has not been scalloped to anything like the same extent and has a form which emphasises the controlling influence of rock type rather than the erosional effects of ice.

These contrasts of detail and degree in the landforms of areas like the Black Mountains and Brecon Beacons occur throughout the Welsh borderland and contribute to the great diversity which is so marked a characteristic of its landscape. The events of the Ice Age, often initiated and controlled from outside the area, have played a major role in this. While in some cases it led to the creation of entirely new landforms, like the overflow valleys of the Middle March countryside west of Ludlow and substituted a completely different drainage pattern from that which had existed previously, the effect of glaciation was often far more subtle. The smoothing effects of ice deposition, the creation of vast deposits of head under periglacial conditions and the blanket effect which they have had on valley-side slopes as well as creating fertile soils, are just as much the result of the glacial invasion as its more dramatic effects. Both have made their distinctive contribution to creating a landscape which was to influence man when, through the events of history, the area was destined to become a human as well as a physical borderland.

3

The Prehistoric
Foundations of the
Border Landscape

The longest period in the story of man's shaping of the landscapes of the
Welsh borderland is that occupied by the thousands of years of prehistory, a
period of which there is no written record of human activities. The movements of peoples, the social organisation and the economy of the inhabitants
of the hills and plains that extend between the estuaries of Dee and Severn
can be inferred only from such indirect evidence as the designs of pottery, of
stone and metal tools and ornaments, and objects in the landscape such as
burial mounds, high ramparted earthworks and sinuous cross-country dykes
that are the obvious handiwork of men. The record of prehistoric communities, as every fresh discovery in archaeology reveals, is woefully incomplete. Nevertheless, more than enough is known to show that some tracts of
the Marchland, such as the Severn plain about the Wrekin or the limestone
hills of the Vale of Clwyd, have long acted as centres of settlement. It is
evident also that many features of the present landscape of the border
country are of prehistoric origin. The summit ridge of the Clwydian Hills is
followed by an ancient trackway that was used by traders with Ireland in the
closing centuries of the Bronze Age. Scores of borderland hill tops, sites that
are now so often inaccessible because of densely planted fir trees, bear the
weathered earthworks of Iron Age camps.

The earliest evidence of man in the Welsh Marches dates back to the Ice
Age when Palaeolithic hunters left proof of their occupation of caves high in
the limestone hills that flank the Vale of Clwyd. Between this remote time

and the raising of Offa's Dyke about A.D. 780, the relics of many centuries of prehistory and the Dark Ages lie scattered about the landscape. In themselves alone these handfuls of broken pottery, a long-lost stone axe or bronze weapon, a burial-place plundered by unknown treasure-seekers, can tell us little of the evolving environment of those prehistoric centuries. Only when the finds of two hundred years of archaeological investigation are studied in their relations to each other and against the background of the topography of the marchland is it possible to perceive, however dimly, the elements of a prehistoric Human Geography. For instance, the hill country around Clun has been scoured for more than half a century by enthusiastic local archaeologists in search of prehistoric stone tools. Thousands have been collected ranging over a span of time that probably stretches from the Neolithic to the late Bronze Age, from before 3000 B.C. to 1000 B.C. The abundance of such prehistoric finds from the long ridge that separates the Clun and Teme valleys led Dr L. F. Chitty, the most eminent of Shropshire archaeologists, to the belief that here ran the line of a prehistoric trackway leading out of central Wales towards the Severn at a crossing near Bewdley. This ancient track was followed by the cattle drovers of the medieval centuries. Today it can be pieced together from quiet lanes that run close by some of the finest Iron Age forts of the Marches.

Many other features of the prehistoric development of the March country lie invisible in the present landscape even to the eye of the most discerning traveller. They have been brought to light only through the use of the more refined exploratory techniques of the professional archaeologist. In the Severn Plain around Shrewsbury, aerial photography has revealed the sites of farms that were worked in Roman times. Likewise the airborne archaeologist has gathered new evidence that has led to a radical reinterpretation of the history of the Roman town of Viroconium. Even more subtle methods than those of the aerial photographers, whose pictures pick out the faintest traces of former landscape features in crop marks, are encountered when the botanist recovers prehistoric pollen from peat-bogs and lake muds. A statistical analysis of the different kinds of preserved pollen leads towards a knowledge of the changing vegetation of prehistory. The highly original work in this field that has been carried out in the English Lake District and parts of Ireland has not been matched in the Welsh borderland, largely because the region lacks the remote mountain tarns that elsewhere have accumulated the pollen-preserving muds of scores of centuries. Even so, it is possible to sketch the main features of the vegetation of the marcher zone from the Neolithic to the close of the Iron Age over a time-gap of some four thousand years. Up to a thousand feet and more above sea level, forests with

61

the oak as a dominant species must have been extensive, if not continuous. At higher levels, towards the precipitous crest of the Brecon Beacons or on the long spurs of the Black Mountains, open stunted forest merged into heathlands and rough grassy pastures. The two zones of natural vegetation in the Marches probably served communities with differing economic structures in those prehistoric centuries. The dwellers along the valleys seem to have been arable farmers; a shred of undoubted evidence for this belief may be found in the pollen grains of cultivated crops discovered at a Neolithic site near Builth.* The uplands above the thousand-foot contour probably favoured pastoral communities. The grazing of sheep and goats by prehistoric farmers helped to press back the forest frontier, beginning a process of woodland clearance that was not to end until the great medieval attack upon the lowland forests had spent its force.

Much research is still wanting before the full story of the evolution of vegetation in the Welsh borderland becomes clear. Sir Cyril Fox's classic work on Offa's Dyke, a result of several summers' detailed investigation of this Mercian earthwork in the field, hinted at the extent of forest along its track at the time of its construction towards the end of the eighth century. Fox believed that the straight sections of the dyke were built across open country where long sighting lines were available to its engineers. In other places the earthwork follows a gently sinuous course, a pattern that may have been imposed by the problems of demarcation through woodland. For a short distance in the Severn valley about Welshpool and for many miles of the middle Wye between the Radnorshire Hills and the country below Ross, Offa's Dyke disappears from the landscape. Sir Cyril Fox explained the absence of the dyke from these riverine plains with the proposition that the extensive tracts of dense oakwood rendered a defensive earthwork unnecessary. Forests, it seems, formed the dominant feature of the landscape of the lowlands and great river valleys of the Marches throughout the prehistoric period. In the uplands, research is slowly bringing to light a more complex picture of the changing natural environment of prehistory under the influence of climate and man. In Neolithic times, large tracts of grassy heathland probably occupied the Brecon Beacons, the Black Mountains, Radnor Forest, Longmynd and the other upland masses of the marchland. Evidence is now accumulating that the succeeding Bronze Age witnessed an extensive spread of open oak forest into the high country. Proof of this important change in the landscape comes from the Mynydd Troed tomb, a Bronze Age site, where the soil from beneath the burial has shown that the

*H. N. Savory, 'Prehistoric Brecknock', *Brycheiniog*, 15 (1971).

mound was raised in a clearing in an oak forest.* By the beginning of the Iron Age a change of climate to wetter and cooler conditions in Atlantic Europe brought about another modification of the upland vegetation of the Marches. The forests of the high ridges and exposed plateaus were replaced by a deep blanket of peat.

Not until the later centuries of the first millennium B.C. is it possible to discern a coherent pattern in the human geography of the Welsh Marches. In the final major division of prehistory, the Iron Age, the construction of a vast number of ramparted, embanked and ditched enclosures on exposed mountain tops and commanding spurs as well as on raised knolls in river plains has left abundant evidence in the present landscape of a distinctive organised society. Today the Iron Age camps are the last relics in the border country of a Celtic civilisation that evolved, flourished and was slowly extinguished over a period of time that extends for almost two thousand years. But the Iron Age cultures of the borderland which at the time of their fullness received an overlay of Roman civilisation for a little more than three centuries were established in a countryside that had already experienced several thousand years of human occupation.

It is hard to assess the influence of man on the border landscape in the pre-Iron Age cultures – the Mesolithic, Neolithic and Bronze Ages, to use the long-established conventional divisions of archaeology. Some of the earliest evidence of man's forerunners, the hunters and food-gatherers of Ice Age times, comes from caves in the narrow tracts of limestone country at the northern and southern limits of the Marches, from the Vale of Clwyd and the Wye valley. The Bont Newydd cave (SJ 0171), high in a wooded limestone escarpment above the Elwy, has yielded the bones of Ice Age animals – bear, bison, reindeer and *Elephas antiquus* – as well as the evidence of occupation by Palaeolithic hunters. From the limestone hills on the eastern flank of the Vale of Clwyd the caves of Ffynnon Beuno and Cae-gwyn provide key sites for the understanding of the long Palaeolithic period in the British Isles. There tools of early Aurignacian type have been discovered beneath a layer of boulder clay that was deposited in the final advance of the ice sheet from the Irish Sea. Apart from a handful of stray flints from different parts of the Marches, the caves of the limestone hills provide the only evidence of the many thousand years, perhaps as much as half a million, in which Palaeolithic hunters may have made their spasmodic intrusions into the region.

The Mesolithic period, whose hunting cultures occupy the time between

*D. P. Webley, 'Aspects of Neolithic and Bronze Age Agriculture in South Wales', *Bulletin of the Board of Celtic Studies*, 23 (1970).

the final waning of the Quaternary ice sheets and the appearance of the first farming communities, is known through the scattered, fragmentary evidence of flint tools. Most of the cave sites have yielded the tiny worked stone implements, microliths, that are characteristic of the sparse groups of Mesolithic hunters. At King Arthur's Cave (SO 5415), a natural refuge beneath a limestone crag above the gorge of the Wye, the Mesolithic occupation seems to date between 10,000 and 8000 B.C. The earliest known Mesolithic sites have been associated only with caves, but lately fresh discoveries have come to light that suggest a more widespread distribution of these hunting groups over the region. Microliths have been found buried beneath the peat on the spurs that slope gently southwards to the industrial valleys of south Wales from the crest of the Brecon Beacons. But the most exciting Mesolithic find in the Marches happened during an excavation at Rhuddlan in 1970 on a bluff above the River Clwyd, where once stood the Norman borough that preceded the founding of Edward I's new town at the end of the thirteenth century. The archaeological investigation aimed to unravel the topography of the twelfth-century town and to locate the site of the lost Norman borough-church. In the course of this work, evidence of a Romano-British settlement was turned up, a pit containing pottery of middle Bronze Age date was found and, most surprising of all, a number of pits with more than 10,000 flints of Maglemosian type showed that a Mesolithic settlement had existed at Rhuddlan.* The application of radio-carbon dating to the shells of hazel nuts from the Mesolithic layer suggested a date of 6789 B.C. with a marginal error of eighty-six years in either direction of time. The proof of the occupation of this site at the mouth of the Clwyd, perhaps for a substantial period of time about 9,000 years ago, seems to be evident from these finds.

In several parts of Britain archaeological finds from Neolithic times rank among the most important. For instance, along the coastlands of the Irish Sea numerous megalithic burial chambers suggest stable and well-organised settlements of farmers. The borderland of hills and valleys between Dee and Severn has little to show of this kind. Shropshire has no long barrows or chambered tombs and Herefordshire's record would be little better but for Arthur's Stone, a burial chamber with its huge capstone still intact that stands on the long ridge between the Golden Valley and the Wye. Farther south, along the Vale of Usk, firmer evidence of the presence of Neolithic farmers has been gathered by local antiquarians working in the now lost county of Brecknock, one of the oldest distinctive social units in the British

*H. Miles, 'Excavations at Rhuddlan, 1969–71', interim report, *Flintshire Historical Society Publications*, 25 (1971–2).

Isles that was destroyed by a clumsy and ill-considered replanning of local government in the 1970s. The primary settlement of the best land along the Usk had probably been achieved by the middle of the third millenium B.C. in a wave of Neolithic colonisation that came, it is believed, from the east, from earlier farming communities in the Cotswolds and by the Severn estuary. A particularly favoured part of Brecknockshire was the wide belt of lowland

11. *Arthur's Stone, a Neolithic chambered tomb on the long ridge that separates the Golden Valley from the Wye in a tract rich with the evidence of prehistory.*

between Mynydd Eppynt and the Black Mountains. Small fields, where the ground was worked by hoes, were cleared from a cover of mixed light woodland of oaks and ash and hazel. Such clusters of Neolithic farmers in widely scattered clearings among the mountains of the southern marchland were not out of touch with other regions of Neolithic Britain. For instance, a polished stone axe-head, recently found near Three Cocks, has been shown to be a product of the now famous axe-factory at the head of Great Langdale in the Lake District.

Much fundamental research is still wanting on the Neolithic period of prehistory in the Welsh Marches. From time to time finds are made that

65

change the sketchy generalisations that have so far been made about this remote epoch when farming first came to the British Isles. For instance, three previously unsuspected chambered cairns have been recognised in Brecknockshire over the past ten years – at Llanigon (SO 2337) under the scarp of the Black Mountains, at Rhos-fach (SO 1833) near Talgarth on the wide 1,000-foot bench that separates the smiling valley of the Afon Llynfi from the steep Black Mountain front, and among the broken wooded hills about Llaneglwys (SO 0739) where the Sclihwen Brook flows down to the Wye. The discovery too of Neolithic material from the high moorlands of Brecon has changed the view that the uplands were neglected until the Bronze Age.

But the most thought-provoking discoveries of Neolithic date have come from sites long known as belonging to man's occupation of the marchlands in later centuries. The inner hill-fort of Early Iron Age date at Ffridd Faldwyn (SO 2197), close to Montgomery, has beneath it pottery of Neolithic date, suggesting the presence of a settlement there long before the raising of the Iron Age earthwork. A similar relationship between an earthwork of the Celtic millenium in the Marches and an earlier Neolithic settlement became evident with the excavation of Gaer Aberllynfi (SO 1737) in 1951. This Iron Age fort, one of the few detailed explorations of such a prehistoric landscape feature that has yet been made in Brecknockshire, stands close to the confluence of the Wye and Llynfi. Pottery and flints of Neolithic Age were discovered under the inner rampart of the fort, lying on the original surface on which the earthwork had been raised. Here we have evidence of a Neolithic settlement, evidence that has been saved for us by the building of an Iron Age rampart over the same site some two thousand years later. The most puzzling feature of this seeming chance coincidence of the Neolithic and the Iron Age at one site is that the superposition of the Celtic Iron Age over settlements that have been occupied at a much earlier period in prehistory is not uncommon in Wales and the Marchland. At present the slender evidence of archaeology will not support the idea that there has been a continuity of land-use and settlement at such places over many hundred, even thousands, of years. When Sir John Conway Lloyd and H. N. Savory reported on their excavation of the hill-fort at Aberllynfi, they wrote that the Neolithic settlement 'was destroyed long before the building of the early Iron Age rampart'.* Again, pondering over the problem of the coincidence of material from widely separated periods of time, they wrote: 'such repeated superimpositions may be indicative of a certain community of needs and

* J. Conway Lloyd and H. N. Savory, 'Excavations of an Early Iron Age hill fort and a Romano-British iron-smelting place at Gwernyfed Park, Aberllynfi, 1951', *Brycheiniog*, 4 (1958).

habits between the Neolithic and Early Iron Age agriculturalists of Britain, just as the repeated absence of evidence for Bronze Age occupation may be indicative of different conditions and practices during most of that period.

The sketchiness of our knowledge about the prehistoric geography of the Marchland and the hint of revolutionary new ideas in the future is perhaps best illustrated from some recent work in the valley of the Rea Brook, a tributary of the Severn at Shrewsbury. It runs through a countryside that has none of the usual visual evidence of the Neolithic period. Crop marks on air photographs revealed the sites of three prehistoric farms, Iron Age estates, at Weeping Cross (SJ 5110), Sharpstone Hill (SJ 4909) and Lyth Hill (SJ 4706), all related to light sandy soils on the south bank of the Rea Brook. Weeping Cross, because of threatened housing development, was subject to a 'rescue dig' that revealed sufficient material to suggest 'continuous occupation' from the Neolithic through the Bronze Age until the final establishment of the Iron Age agricultural settlement, with its circular and sub-rectangular huts enclosed by ditches.

The evidence of the Bronze Age in the landscape of the Welsh Marches is as incomplete as that of its forerunner, the Neolithic period. Here and there we find the scattered hints of a culture period that lasted for much more than a thousand years. Gop Cairn (SJ 0880) in the north, on the hills that rise above the wide sands of the Dee estuary, must rank among the most impressive landmarks of the Bronze Age in the British Isles. It has a diameter of some three hundred feet and rises to a height of twenty-five feet. But that is about all that is known about the huge man-made mound on Gop Hill. Even its true date and origin need to be firmly established. Speculation has gone so far as to connect it with the burial of some wealthy person who might have been engaged in the metal trade with Ireland, a traffic that probably used the ancient trackway along the height of the Clwydian Hills. Bronze Age burial mounds of a humbler kind, rough overgrown hummocks that are hard to recognise in the countryside, are widespread in the uplands. More than two hundred cairns have been noted in Brecknockshire alone, mainly on the ridges of the Black Mountains, the Eppynt Moors and the long gentle spurs that stretch from the escarpment of the Beacons towards the south Welsh industrial valleys. Scarcely a dozen of these sites has been excavated. Flintshire too has clusters of burial cairns on the hills between the Vale of Clwyd and the Dee's coastal plain. None had been excavated before the 1950s with the aims and the techniques of the scientific archaeologist. Then in 1952 a cluster of six cairns and two hut circles (SJ 1662) on the Clwydian Hills close to Moel Fammau was investigated because it was threatened with destruction

67

as a result of afforestation. The publication of the findings in the journal of the Flintshire Historical Society shows only too clearly the value of exact local research in modifying the textbook generalisations of prehistory.* The first cairn building and burials at this site on Cefn Goleu took place between 1700 and 1400 B.C. The primary burial site 'shows certain morphological affinities with megalithic monuments'. Here it has been suggested that the chamber tomb tradition of the Neolithic peoples has been fused with 'the solitary beaker cist tradition' brought by the first Bronze Age settlers, the Beaker people. Research at this one place on the Clwydian Hills shows that the seemingly sharply drawn frontiers of prehistory, between the Neolithic and the Bronze Age, are blurred in the evidence left behind by a pastoral community from more than three thousand years ago in the marchland.

Archaeology's fragmentary evidence from the Bronze Age in the Welsh Marches presents some tantalising problems in creating a picture of the economy and society of those times. In the moorlands where the Irfon and its tributaries find their headsprings about Abergwesyn lines of stakes have been uncovered from beneath the peat in a hollow near Trallwm Farm (SN 8754). It is believed that they formed fences used in stock-raising and that they may date back to the middle Bronze Age. Another Brecknockshire site, the artificial island in Llangorse Lake (SO 1326) known as the Crannog, may also find its origins in the Bronze Age. Much has been lost and much probably still remains concealed that would reveal a variety and complexity in the communities of the Bronze Age that is not evident from the known remains of countless burial mounds and the occasional ring of standing stones half buried by heather.

The culmination of Britain's prehistory was the Iron Age, ten centuries and more when a Celtic society flourished in these islands. The marchland landscape displays to perfection and in abundance so many features of this epoch. Even today its place-names and the vocabulary and tones of dialects that are fast becoming extinct reveal the region's debt to a Celtic past. The most outstanding objects in the present landscape that date from the Celtic Iron Age are, without doubt, the enclosures marked off by grass-grown ramparts and ditches, the hill-forts. Just as a journey along Offa's Dyke unravels the topography of eighth-century Mercia's western frontier, so the network of Iron Age earthworks suggests, however darkly, something of the long-lost social and political organisation of this territory before the Roman, Saxon and Norman occupations gave it a marchland character.

*M. Bevan-Evans and P. Hayes, 'Excavation of a cairn on Cefn-Goleu', *Flintshire Hist. Soc. Pub.*, 13 (1952–3).

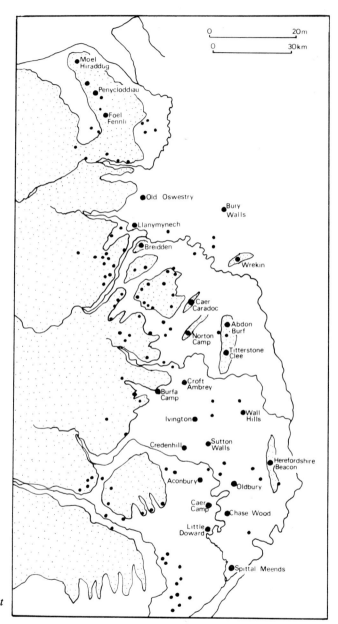

Moel
Hiraddug

Penycloddiau

Foel
Fennli

Old Oswestry

Bury
Walls

Llanymynech

Breidden

Wrekin

Caer
Caradoc

Abdon
Burf

Norton
Camp

Titterstone
Clee

Croft
Ambrey

Burfa
Camp

Wall
Hills

Ivington

Credenhill

Sutton
Walls

Herefordshire
Beacon

Aconbury

Oldbury

Caer
Camp

Chase Wood

Little
Doward

Spittal Meends

0   20m

0   30km

6. *Distribution of Iron
Age hill-forts with the
largest and most important
named.*

69

The Clwydian Hills illustrate the role of the Iron Age fort as an element of the modern landscape as clearly as any part of the Marchland. Five earthworks in magnificently commanding sites may be found in an eight-mile stretch of that upland. Three of the Clwydian forts – Foel Fenlli (SJ 1660), Moel Hiraddug and Pen-y-Cloddiau (SJ 1267) – must rank among the most extensive of these earthworks in the whole of the Marches, for they successively take up twenty-nine acres, thirty-six acres and sixty-five acres. The last and biggest of all, Pen-y-Cloddiau, encloses a hilltop at more than 1,400 feet above the sea. The defences alone cover twelve acres and consist of four ramparts and three ditches. The date of its building and the intentions of those who raised an earthwork of such grandeur that it was to make a permanent impression on the landscape still remain a complete mystery. Pen-y-Cloddiau has not been excavated and there is no superficial evidence of hut circles or platforms to suggest that it was occupied for any length of time. In fact, only Moel Hiraddug among the five forts of the Clwydian Hills has been subject to a rigorous modern archaeological investigation, and that was a rescue dig in 1954–5 provoked by the advancing face of a limestone quarry. On the gentler eastern slope of this long narrow hill that forms the northern end of the Clwydian range, Moel Hiraddug flaunted a complex of earthworks consisting of three ramparts and a counterscarp bank. Inside the fort were some two dozen hut circles. The evidence that came from Dr Bevan-Evans's excavation generally confirmed the speculations about the neighbouring hill-forts that had been made largely from the relationship of their shape and design to other long-known hill-forts in the Welsh Marches and southern England. The excavation suggested that the first earthworks had been raised about 350 B.C. and that this high-lying place with its magnificent prospect of the lower plain of the Clwyd had been finally abandoned about 150 B.C., more than two centuries earlier than the usually accepted date for the last occupation of so many of the Iron Age sites in Wales and the Marches.

The long line of hill-forts on the Clwydian range, among the finest in the British Isles, opens up an even wider country of the mind as archaeologists begin to speculate about their origins and their meaning. There seems little doubt that they represent important elements in the society of the British tribe, the Deceangli, that occupied this part of north-east Wales at the time of the Roman Conquest. J. Forde Johnson, in his description of the hill-forts of this region, came to the conclusion that they were built for strategic purposes. In his article in the valuable local historical journal, *Flintshire Historical Publications*, he says 'the impressive scale of their ramparts leaves no doubt that they are true hill-forts in the military sense, and not mere cattle enclosures'.* Apart from the size and complexity of the ramparts, the location of several of the forts suggests a strong strategic motive in their construction. Three of them command from precipitous slopes the chief gaps that lead through the range of hills into the Vale of Clwyd. Moel-y-Gaer (SJ 0970), at Bodfari, occupies an isolated, precipitous summit above the Wheeler Gap. Moel Arthur (SJ 1466), from a height of almost 1,500 feet, commands a narrow passage through the hills into Dyffryn Clwyd, while from an even greater height the rough ramparted enclosure of Foel Fenlli with its two dozen hut circles glowers down on another corridor through the hills, the Pen Barras Pass. Even so, it is far from clear what part these lonely hill-top sites played in the unrecorded inter-tribal conflicts of the Celtic Iron Age. It is equally arguable from the shapes, layout and sites of the Iron Age earthworks that they were raised to serve the day-to-day peaceful purposes of the economy of the Deceangli. The 'forts' themselves might have been used to shelter cattle, sheep and goats that were grazing the summer pastures of the Clwydian range. Professor Leslie Alcock in his wide-ranging investigation of Iron Age sites in Britain has suggested that the spaces between the ramparts of multivallate forts might have served for the penning of livestock. Were they perhaps used as corrals in the sorting of animals, or was their chief function to provide the greatest safety from the raids of wolves and other predatory wild animals?

That the series of Clwydian forts acted as focal points in the management of the upland pastures seems a highly probable explanation of their origins. Transhumance, the movement of cattle and sheep to mountain pastures during the summer months, was part of the Welsh economy in the Middle Ages. A cluster of primitive huts or an isolated steading – the hafotai – would serve this high grazing ground. The houses of the summer settlement were inhabited from May until September by shepherds and their women-folk who were engaged in milking and the making of cheese and butter. The origins of transhumance as a way of life are lost in prehistory, in all probability dating back to the wide use of our mountain pastures in the later Bronze Age. If this argument has any meaning for the prehistory of the Clwydian Hills, one would look for the permanent settlements of these hill pastoralists in the lowland plain along the Vale of Clwyd. Here the almost continuous use of the land at certain favourable sites along the vale has practically obliterated all traces of prehistory from the landscape. One can only guess at the places where the Iron Age dwellers of the lowlands based themselves, but the recently excavated site of the Norman borough field at

*J. Forde-Johnston, 'Fieldwork on the hill-forts of North Wales', *Flintshire Hist. Soc. Pub.*, 21 (1964).

Rhuddlan points to the presence of prehistoric communities at favourable places along the River Clwyd. One minor piece of evidence from the 'forts' on the hill tops suggests that they may have been connected with the rich valley plain at the foot of the western scarp of the Clwydians. The ramparts of Pen-y-Cloddiau stretch unbroken along its northern and eastern outlooks for three-quarters of a mile. The entrance on the lower south-eastern flank seems to be linked to an easy way from the Vale of Clwyd that climbed the gentler, open slopes of the spur above Llangwyfan (SJ 1166). As the mind's eye ranges backwards in time, a vision forms of the early summer procession of livestock and shepherds making their way by winding trails to occupy the camps along the height of the Clwydian Hills.

The mystery that surrounds the problem of the hill-forts and their role in Iron Age society is scarcely dispersed by the few fragments of archaeological evidence that have so far been recovered from the sites in Clwyd. For instance, some Roman coins were discovered within the ramparts of Foel Fenlli (SJ 1660). They would seem to point to trade between the native Deceangli, the dwellers of the hill-forts, and the invading Romans after the middle of the first century. It may be that this ramparted and ditch-encircled hill top, close to the line of the Bronze Age ridgeway, served as a place for summer markets and fairs. In many other parts of Britain there are traditions of markets held within the enclosing ramparts of Iron Age camps. Defence, the management of summer pastures and gatherings for trade and commerce, all may have played a part in the economic and social functions of the cluster of hill-forts on the Clwydian range. The scanty evidence that until now has been forthcoming from these sites does not suggest the presence of permanent communities, communities that have sometimes been described as 'towns', at these bleak, exposed sites on the highest hill tops of north-east Wales. The identification of the cores of Iron Age settlement in the Vale of Clwyd is all but lost to us, but it seems likely that Llanelwy (St Asaph) (SJ 0374), raised on a low, fertile ridge at the convergence of the Clwyd and Elwy rivers, formed a focus of Iron Age settlement at the seaward end of the vale. A clue to its prehistoric importance may perhaps be read in the choice of this place as a Roman station on the line of the road from Deva (Chester) to Segontium (Caernarfon). The directions of Roman roads and the location of their military settlements in the border country and Wales were deeply influenced by the existing pattern of Celtic settlement. It cannot be finally determined whether the main Roman road into north Wales crossed the Vale of Clwyd at Llanelwy because this was geographically the best passage across the plain westward into the hill country or whether this place between the two rivers was chosen because an important Iron Age settlement already existed there. An even more intriguing site in the exploration of this problem of the recognition of the foci of Iron Age settlement in the lowland beneath the Clwydian Hills survives in Dyffryn Clwyd, the upper, mountain enclosed part of the vale, remote from the sea. Here, on the western edge of the vale, are the earthworks of an Iron Age fort at little more than five hundred feet above sea-level. Craig Adwy Wynt (SJ 1254) is a complicated site made up of two enclosures whose western boundary is formed by a forty-foot-high limestone cliff above the deepening valley of the upper Clwyd. Nothing is known about its detailed archaeological history, but Craig Adwy Wynt's association with the Iron Age and its central location in Dyffryn Clwyd, an ancient unit of settlement that was to coincide centuries later with a medieval Welsh cantref and, later still, the Marcher Lordship of Ruthin, offers a high probability that this formed the permanent quarters of that part of the Deceangli tribe living in the inner vale.

The Clwydian Hills and their related lowland to the west provide a pattern of Iron Age settlement that can be followed through with many variations into the central and southern Marchland. To the east and south of the tribal lands of the Deceangli lay the territories of the Cornovii. The core of this Celtic Iron Age polity lay in the plain of the middle Severn, a fertile and favoured region amidst which the ancient mass of the Wrekin stands up like a dark island from the rich greens and golds of the cornfields and pastures of mid-Shropshire. Today the Wrekin is perhaps the most commanding element in the landscapes of the West Midlands. It stands as the badge and the identifying symbol of Shropshire and it must ever have been so. Perhaps this hill of mountainous proportions, now transmitting television programmes to the ancient territory of the Cornovii from a mast within the ramparts of its huge hill-fort, was the focal point for that people when the Romans came here to found a fort and then to build a town at Viroconium (SJ 5608) on the bank of the Severn.

The frontiers of this kingdom, centred on the Severn Plain about the Wrekin, are hard to determine. In the north the Cornovii must have controlled much of the area of the later county of Cheshire, if one is to accept Ptolemy's reference to the legionary fortress of Deva, Chester, as within their territory. Only in the south is it possible to define a clear frontier with another neighbouring Celtic tribe, the Dobunni. Here, amid the lovely hill country of south Shropshire, where almost every spur and summit seems to carry traces of an Iron Age fort, a frontier was drawn through the Aymestrey Gap, across the hill tops of the Clees where Brown Clee alone carries the relics of three embanked earthworks on its upper slopes, thence eastward across the Severn to the Clent Hills.

The large number of Iron Age forts within the territory of the Cornovii hints at a vanished social organisation and a mobilisation of labour and engineering skills of which these lonely places in the contemporary landscape are the final relic. As in the Clwydian Hills, the patterns of these Iron Age structures in the landscape may point to the distribution of population and the focal tracts of the economy of the Cornovii. Shropshire possesses ramparted earthworks of a scale and grandeur to match those of the territories of the Deceangli. Most of the major hill tops – Wrekin, Breidden, Pontesford and Caer Caradoc – were landmarks which the Cornovii signalled by the construction of elaborate earthworks. Here too, as in the Vale of Clwyd, there is a hint that the embanked enclosures of the Celtic Iron Age were a feature of the lowland landscape as well as occupying the summits of outstanding hills. Old Oswestry (S J 2931) crowns the summit of a low clay hill, a drumlin, on the western edge of the plain. With its multiple ramparts it ranks among the biggest of the Cornovian 'forts' and rivals the Wrekin in its claim to be the focus of power in that Iron Age state. Old Oswestry was first excavated in the late 1930s by W. J. Varley, but the very extent of the site

12. *Old Oswestry, with its multiple ramparts, forms one of the most impressive relics of the Iron Age in the territory of the Cornovii.*

74

means that this earthwork has given up only a fraction of its secrets. The large quantities of pottery that Varley unearthed showed that this was an inhabited site, in all likelihood a permanent settlement. The character of the finds, especially the crude nature of the pottery, led Varley to believe that this was still an active settlement in the post-Roman decades, but a more recent view of the material claims that the potsherds are fragments of small ovens dating from almost a thousand years earlier in the early Iron Age.*

Farther south, in the southern borderland of the Cornovii, where the topographical pattern changes from the broad horizons of north Shropshire to a mosaic of hills, billowy plateaus cut through by valleys six hundred feet and more below the upland surface and tiny plains that once contained the transitory lakes of the Ice Age, we find a great abundance of hill-forts. Ffridd Faldwyn, close neighbour to Henry III's castle at Montgomery, has yielded evidence of the early occupation of its hill-top site that reaches back into the Bronze Age. Farther east, on a sharp strategic hill top above the Camlad near Bishops Castle, we find The Roveries (SO 3292) and southwards in the wooded hills about the River Clun there are the vast and almost inaccessible earthworks of Bury Ditches (SO 3283), inaccessible on account of the closely planted woodland that is a recent concomitant of so many Iron Age forts in different parts of England. These ancient objects in the landscape of the south Shropshire hills turn the mind back to the Clwydian range. Was this a frontier, a border zone, in the long-forgotten political geography of Iron Age Britain? Are the high, enclosed spaces, often with multiple ramparts, part of elaborate defence systems in strategically dangerous districts? It seems just as likely that the abundance of 'forts' among the south Shropshire hills may mean no more than the adaptation of a pastoral economy to a dissected topography. But if this is the sole explanation of the present distribution pattern of the hill-forts, it is strange that the most extensive tract of upland grazing, the Longmynd, whose summit ridge is traversed by a Bronze Age trackway, possesses no major earthwork of the Iron Age.

From the hills of the Middle March in the border country of Shropshire and Herefordshire has come new and striking evidence on the meaning of hill-forts in the society of the Celtic Iron Age. A long series of excavations between 1960 and 1966 at Croft Ambrey (SO 4466) has shown that settlement persisted there through several centuries. The works of man on this hill top that dominates the southern entry to the Wigmore basin evolved through several stages over a period of six hundred years. The earliest rampart, enclosing six acres of the hill top, was built between 450 and 300 B.C.

*S. C. Stanford, 'The function and population of hill-forts in the Central Marches', in F. Lynch and C. Burgess, *Prehistoric Man in Wales and the West* (1972).

Post-holes behind the rampart show that it contained a number of timber huts. At a later date, in the first half of the third century B.C., the settlement was expanded with the raising of the huge bank that has survived for more than two thousand years in the north Herefordshire landscape to mark the site of Croft Ambrey. The recent archaeological investigation of the site has shown that over the centuries of occupation the wooden buildings within the enclosure were reconstructed over and over again and the great gateposts that held the wooden doors blocking the entrance had to be replaced many times as their foundations became rotten. S. C. Stanford in his fascinating report of the field-work at Croft Ambrey through the early 1960s* records the emplacement of twenty successive gateposts before they were finally dug out at the time of the Roman Conquest. Croft Ambrey, he suggests, was disarmed and abandoned in A.D. 50 when Ostorius Scapula pursued his campaign in the Marches against the Celtic tribal leader Caratacus whose memory, as Caradoc, has been perpetuated in the modern name of more than one Iron Age fort. Even when Croft Ambrey had been deserted as a permanent settlement, the evidence of potsherds, beads and a mound of proved Roman date has led Stanford to the view that the hill top was still used as a sanctuary. As he writes, 'the population survived somewhere in the area and returned to worship outside their ancient stronghold'.

The conclusions that have been drawn from the long and careful excavation of Croft Ambrey throw new light on the human geography of the Iron Age. The pattern of the settlement within the enclosure has been clearly revealed. It shows rectangular four-posted timber buildings, some small huts that may have acted as granaries and other larger buildings that must have been dwelling-houses. The houses were built in a back-to-back plan and fronted the narrow, unmetalled streets that followed the contours of the hill top. Croft Ambrey was a permanently occupied village over a long period of time in the Iron Age. The excavation of the fort revealed the foundations of some three hundred timbered buildings. The clear evidence of rebuilding shows that dwelling-houses and barns persisted on the same plots of land over a long period of time. Some light too has been shed on the economy and the day-to-day life of the inhabitants of Iron Age Croft Ambrey. From many different archaeological levels the remains of charred wheat prove that corn was grown, ground, and baked into bread. The numerous finds of animal bones suggest the preponderance of sheep as the main source of meat. The tools of spinning and weaving – spindle-whorls, loom-weights of baked clay and bone needles – show that wool was spun and woven into clothing.

---

*'Croft Ambrey hill-fort', *Trans. Woolhope Nat. Field Club*, 39 (1969).

The way of life and economy of the hill-fort dwellers that can be sketched from the archaeological evidence at Croft Ambrey must have remained unchanged over several centuries. Its pattern is the same wherever an extensive dig has been made within the precincts of a hill-fort, but such close investigations have been rare up to the present time. A few miles to the south of Croft Ambrey, Dr Kathleen Kenyon made an archaeological investigation of Sutton Walls (SO 5246), a thirty-acre ramparted enclosure on a low hill above the flood plain of the River Lugg. Within the rampart were found the footings of timbered buildings with clay walls; there were the hollows of numerous storage pits. Hearths, an abundance of Iron Age pottery and great quantities of animal bones – the food refuse of several generations of occupation – all pointed to the persistence and continuity of settlement at this place. Unlike Croft Ambrey, the Iron Age layers of artefacts are followed by pottery of the Roman period that suggests a sequence of occupation until the fourth century A.D. The discovery of sickles, knives, daggers and nails as well as the slag associated with iron-working suggests that Sutton Walls was engaged in industry beside the corn-growing and pastoralism of a rural community. The long, rich sequence of settlement on this hill above the Lugg could mean that Sutton Walls was a centre of government in one of the tribal units of the Dobunni whose extensive territories embraced the valley and adjacent hills of this important tributary of the Wye.

Wherever modern field research has turned to one of the Iron Age hill-forts, fresh and often puzzling evidence has been added to support or question the established theories on their origin and functions. The most revolutionary insights concern their beginnings and the increasing likelihood that some of the forts were inhabited long after the Roman conquest of the March country in the first century A.D. Until lately, the building of the hill-forts has been placed in the later centuries of the first millennium B.C., mainly after 300 B.C. Now proof is gathering from several sites that settlements and the construction of ramparts may date back in time for more than an additional five centuries. A certain type of rampart, using a box-like construction with a timber framework, may have been in use at the beginning of the ninth century B.C. At another Iron Age fort, Dinorben, on the western edge of the Vale of Clwyd, a series of excavations in the late 1960s by H. N. Savory has yielded proof of more than a thousand years of occupation. Through the application of radio-carbon dating techniques to material from the earliest rampart, Savory was able to show that this ancient piece of the earthwork had been thrown up in the ninth century B.C. over the site of an open, undefended late Bronze Age settlement. Again, the oldest earthworks at Ffridd Faldwyn, the 'fort' close to Montgomery, probably date to 800 B.C.

77

A similar early date, at the close of the Bronze Age before the first of the great Iron Age invasions reached the British Isles, has been suggested for the beginnings of hill-fort construction on the Breidden and at the important lowland earthwork near Ludlow, Caynham Camp. Recent archaeological work and discussion of these discoveries is adding a new dimension, a greatly lengthened time-scale, to our appreciation of the hill-fort and its society in the marchland landscape. As S. C. Stanford has commented, 'the Welsh border hill-fort societies show a great degree of permanence . . . societies whose stability for such long periods makes the Roman occupation appear but a short and untidy episode in the history of these islands'.

The Roman 'episode' lasted for a little more than three centuries, long by any reckoning of the changing fortunes of history, but the active time-span of the Iron Age camps and their Celtic societies would take us back from our own day in the twentieth century to the period of the Norman Conquest. Even so, it is possible amid the enthusiasm generated by the exciting new arguments developing about the Iron Age to lose sight of the immense contribution of the Romans to the evolution of Britain. The Celtic world was deeply influenced by its exposure to this complex, closely organised Mediterranean civilisation. Traces of the Roman influence in the Marches are numerous and they reflect a culture far richer than that of the pastoral tribes dwelling in the hill-top camps whose names, the Deceangli, Cornovii and Dobunni, were handed down to posterity through the historians of Imperial Rome.

Without doubt the most original contribution of the Romans to the Iron Age landscape lies in the foundation of towns and the implications that these settlements held for trade, industry and the establishment of bureaucratic forms of government. The Roman towns of the March had a strong military flavour. In the north lay the greatest of legionary fortresses, Deva, the base of the Twentieth Legion. Today, as Chester, we can trace the outlines of the Roman fort and settlement in the street plan at the city's centre and in the stones of the wall that has undergone several rebuildings on the line of its Roman foundations. Caerleon mirrored Chester's role in the Roman subjugations of south Wales and at Caerwent, scarcely a dozen miles from the military settlement on the Usk, a Roman town spread itself over almost fifty acres. Today Caerwent (ST 4690) is a village, a scattering of farms and cottages, where fragments of the buried urban structure of almost two thousand years ago peep through in the present landscape and still determine some of its features. For instance, lanes and hedgerows follow the lines of former Roman streets and in places the extensive foundations of buildings are exposed to the light of day. Caerwent is an exciting place to explore,

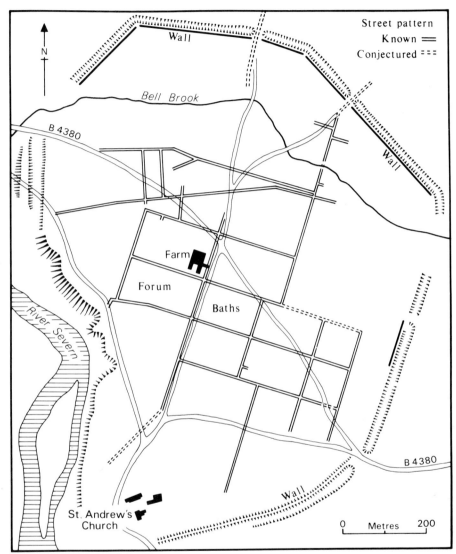

Street pattern
Known ==
Conjectured ===

Wall

Bell Brook

B 4380

Wall

Farm

Forum

Baths

River Severn

B 4380

Wall

St. Andrew's
Church

0   Metres   200

7. *Viroconium, one of the largest Roman towns of Britain and the most important of the Marchland settlements. The main outlines of the street plan are largely known from air photographs, for only part of the town has been systematically excavated.*

especially in the clear, low-angled sunlight of a spring evening, when one senses in a twentieth-century landscape the intersection of two planes of history and of two cultures, one urban and Mediterranean the other rural and belonging to the Atlantic world.

Wroxeter (SJ 5608), a Shropshire village on the bank of the Severn, contains the site of the grandest Roman town in the Marches, Viroconium. Recent research at Viroconium has shown a much more complex history in this urban settlement than was once suspected. Until lately, the history of Viroconium, fourth largest town of Roman Britain by area, was considered to begin with its foundation towards the end of the first century. Signs of burning and destruction were thought to mark the end of its urban life early in the fifth century when Anglo-Saxon, Pict and Irish raiders brought down the Roman order in an epoch of confusion. Today the archaeological research of the 1960s, on the ground and from the air, has revealed the beginning of Viroconium as a fortress settlement, a legionary fortress, about A.D. 50. Aerial photography by Dr A. K. J. St Joseph showed in the form of crop marks two parallel ditches to the north-west of the forum. It is evident that the ditches predate the laying-out of the town because at one place a large house was built over them. The insight into the first stage of Viroconium's evolution that is provided by an air photograph has been corroborated by recent archaeological findings beneath the grid-iron of streets at the centre of the town. There the remains of large and complicated timber buildings show the earliest stage in the development of Viroconium before the streets were laid down at the end of the first century. It seems most likely that these were the buildings of a legionary fort on the bank of the Severn, established perhaps about A.D. 50 as part of the Roman campaign in central Wales when the troops of Ostorius Scapula advanced against Caratacus. Further evidence for a primary military phase in the Roman occupation of the middle Severn basin has emerged with the recognition, from the air, of an auxiliary fort on the bank of the Severn some 450 yards to the south of Wroxeter. And in 1963 another aerial survey of the surroundings of Viroconium recognised a marching camp about $1\frac{1}{2}$ miles to the north at Duncot on Tern.

Wroxeter as a fortress lasted for little more than a generation. The military control of the Celtic marchland moved north-westward to the northern limits of the territory of the Cornovii, to Deva. By A.D. 90, on the site of the demolished fortress the Romans began building Viroconium, a new tribal capital for the Cornovii. Research has now revealed a most complex history of building with marked phases of active development and others when building languished, sometimes for decades. Renovation, rebuilding, changes of plan and in the purpose of buildings are all part of the complex story that has been published in numerous articles in learned journals and particularly in the transactions of the *Shropshire Archaeological Society*. It has been admirably set out in Graham Webster's book on *The Cornovii*, a work that puts together the incomplete and difficult evidence of the life and history of this tribe whose times and way of life lay outside the ambit of the written record.

The plan for the development of Viroconium that was started about A.D. 90 soon languished. The baths on the west side of the main street were never completed. When the building of Viroconium was taken up again about A.D. 125, a new forum was laid out on the site of the abandoned baths. The main features of the town plan must have been completed in this phase of building. For instance, the forum was finished about A.D. 130 according to the evidence of the inscription placed over its entrance by the Cornovii which told of its dedication to the Emperor Hadrian. Viroconium's prosperity was not continuous. Between A.D. 160 and 170 the forum and property to the south of it were seriously damaged by fire. In the subsequent rebuilding, the shops that had existed on the west side of the main street were replaced by a temple. Towards the end of the third century another and more catastrophic destruction hit Viroconium. The whole of the monumental front of the forum collapsed into the street where the stones bearing the incription of its dedication were to remain buried under the gathering soil of the centuries, to be turned up more than fifteen hundred years later by the spade of the archaeologist.

It has always been assumed that Viroconium, one of the largest towns of Roman Britain, had come to a violent end, sacked and destroyed by fire in the confusion of the Roman withdrawal from Britain. Research in the 1960s among the quiet fields of this buried city has uncovered an unsuspected late stage in its history that reaches into post-Roman times. It has been shown that the dramatic evidence of burning, presented in the earlier accounts of the end of Viroconium, could be explained as the rakings from the stoke-holes of the Roman baths. Now there is evidence that the occupation of the centre of Viroconium continued until the close of the fifth century. In a series of excavations on the site of the basilica between 1966 and 1973, Philip Barker was able to prove that buildings with timber frameworks and walls of wattle and daub had been raised over the floor of the Roman basilica. Barker rcognised the plan of a large building in which the capitals of the basilica had been used as foundations, 'pads', for timber posts. Against the upstanding wall of the basilica a number of 'lean-to' structures had been erected. The plan of this main building which covers much of the basilica site was of a Romano–British type, a winged corridor house with a central entrance. As Philip Barker has written, 'a powerful character built himself a kind of

13. *Viroconium — two facets of the present townscape of the Roman town by the Severn.*

country mansion in the middle of the city, surrounded with small buildings which are either stables or houses for his retainers'. Viroconium fell into a long decline; the modern archaeologist can find no evidence of a catastrophic holocaust. By the end of the sixth century the centre of the city was being used as a cemetery and the ground was at least two feet above the latest Roman street level. Viroconium had ceased to be a town, and the nucleus of a rural community, its successor, was now centred at Wroxeter.

14. *The stones of Viroconium are used again in the gateway to the parish church at Wroxeter.*

Just as modern research has uncovered fresh evidence for the history of Viroconium, so a reassessment of the impact of the Romans on the countryside of the western marchland has taken place. Perhaps the most striking of recent speculations is the view of S. C. Stanford, based on his excavations in and around Leintwardine, that for long after the conquest of Wales parts of the country between Severn and Wye retained a military character.* The Roman settlement at Leintwardine (SO 4074), Bravonium, on the bank of the Teme, had always been considered as a civil settlement – a small town and posting station midway between Kenchester and Viroconium

*S. C. Stanford, 'The Roman forts at Leintwardine and Buckton', *Trans. Woolhope Nat. Field Club*, 39 (1969).

on the line of Watling Street West where that road threads its way through the hills of south Shropshire and north Herefordshire. Stanford's excavations, first in 1958 and then in a continuing series until 1967, have shown that an important Roman fort was established at Leintwardine about A.D. 160 and that it was intermittently occupied until at least the middle of the fourth century. And this was not the only Roman strongpoint among the scarped and wooded hills of the Middle March. Aerial surveys have revealed two forts close to Leintwardine, one at Jay Lane on a hill to the north of the village and the other at Buckton (SO 391733) to the west of the Teme on a terrace slightly raised above the river's flood plain. Both were established and abandoned before the building of the large fort with its timber-laced rampart that covered a fourteen-acre site across Watling Street West. This reassessment of Leintwardine's role in the Roman occupation suggests that the uplands between the Wye and Severn called for military control long after the subjugation of Wales in A.D. 78. Watling Street West, connecting Kenchester and Viroconium between the Wye and the Severn, was probably established as a temporary frontier in the first century. Its frontier role is emphasised when we remember that there are seven Roman military sites, some described as temporary marching camps, within seven miles of Leintwardine. That this same tract of hills where Teme and Clun converge was important in the political geography of the Celtic marchland is shown by the relics of eleven Iron Age forts within ten miles of Leintwardine. Similar evidence, hinting at the unstable political character of the Marches for much of the Roman period, has been gathered from research in the 1960s at Walltown,* a small fort in the Forest of Wyre close to the long wooded corridor of the Severn below Bridgnorth. As Graham Webster has written, 'a sequence of Roman forts of permanent character has been proved on this site'. In his concluding remarks upon Walltown, Webster suggests that the study of the frontier zone in Wales has been over-simplified, 'problems and perplexities abound and much more evidence is needed from many more sites'.

The Roman interest in this western border zone of Britain was not only confined to the demands of strategy and military geography. Mineral working, a state monopoly of the Roman world, and other industries such as quarrying and tile-making have left their marks on the countryside. Among the Shropshire hills, in the area of longest military occupation, lay some of the richest mineral resources. Lead and small quantities of silver were extracted from ores mined in the hills around Shelve. Farther north, at

*C. I. Walker, 'Excavation at the Roman fort at Walltown Farm, Shropshire, 1960–61', *Trans. Shropshire Arch. Soc.*, 58 (1965).

Llanymynech (SJ 2622), the pits, galleries and caverns that riddle the slopes of the limestone hill that steeply overshadows this untidy quarrying settlement formed part of the workings for copper in the Roman centuries. Finds of pottery and coins, as well as the evidence of burials in the third and fourth centuries, amid the maze of ancient diggings at Llanymynech suggest that the miners for copper there lived underground in man-made caves.

The most exciting of the Roman industrial sites in the Marches must be at Linley Hall (SO 3492), where the West Onny emerges from the hill country between the Stiperstones and Corndon Hill, a land rich in lead. The Roman interest in this district is undoubted because five lead pigs have been recorded from hereabouts, all with a cast inscription mentioning the Emperor Hadrian. The site at Linley Hall covers twelve acres and its extensive and complicated earthworks can only be interpreted as containing an industrial plant. An aqueduct running parallel to the West Onny seems to have been built to draw water from the river, and it could have provided power for water-wheels in an ore-grinding and crushing mill within the enclosure where the hall now stands. The unravelling of the geography and technology of Roman lead-mining and ore-processing is indeed difficult in the Shropshire hills. Extensive mining in the eighteenth and nineteenth centuries about Shelve and Snailbeach has removed or obscured all evidence of Roman operations and the faint traces on the ground at Linley Hall, last described in the *Transactions of the Shropshire Archaeological Society* in 1856, only deepen the problems of interpretation.

Farther south, in the vicinity of the Forest of Dean, there arose one of the chief industrial regions of Roman Britain. The extraction of iron ore from shallow pits in the Forest of Dean probably goes back into the pre-Roman centuries of the Celtic Iron Age. The persistence of the dialect word 'scowles', a Celtic word, to describe the jumbled, overgrown holes and hillocks of ancient ore-workings, suggests the long history of the industry there. At Ariconium (SO 6423), a little to the east of Ross-on-Wye, an extensive Roman settlement. once described as a villa, is now known to be a complex industrial site where the iron ore from the country to the south was refined and forged. Not far away, at Whitchurch (SO 5417), another industrial site of Roman iron-processing was uncovered in the course of road-widening in the 1950s. Here, in Lower Vagas field, there had stood a furnace in the sixteenth century. Excavation revealed two earlier floors beneath the plant of Tudor times, one being medieval and the other Roman. The iron ore for this forge at Whitchurch must have been brought from the Dowards (SO 5416), a wooded hill embraced by the gorge of the Wye below Symonds Yat.

4

The Shaping of a Borderland

In the two centuries that followed the crumbling of Roman rule in Britain, the human geography of the Welsh Marches slowly took on a new shape. The exact date of the removal of Roman troops remains an enigma, but it could not have happened much later than the opening years of the fifth century. Claudian, the poet, says that Stilicho took troops away from Britain about the year 402. His lines, referring to this event, seem to contain a direct reference to the legion based at Chester, which he described as 'the legion that curbs the savage Irish and reads the marks tattooed upon the bodies of dying Picts'. The next great force to shape the evolution of the Marchland came only with the incursion of the Anglo-Saxons towards the close of the sixth century. The political intrusion of the Saxons into the Midlands began after a number of victorious battles in southern England. The first crucial event was the defeat of the British by Cuthwulf in a battle near Bedford in 571. The Battle of Dyrham, fought in the vicinity of Bath in 577, led the Saxons into the Severn valley and brought about the collapse of the political order that the descendants of the Romano British, the Dobunni, had maintained in that region around Gloucester. Almost two centuries separate the emergence of the West Midland state of Mercia from the extinction of the Roman political order, more than half of the time-span of the Roman occupation itself. The events of this period, transmitted to us imperfectly through half-forgotten legend and the heroic poetry of Wales, witnessed a reassertion of many of the traits of the pre-Roman Iron Age.

We have already seen that there is evidence for the reoccupation of some of the hill-fort sites in the centuries after the Roman abandonment of Britain.

There is even a tradition in the Marches that the hill-forts were used in the Middle Ages by the invading armies of Welsh princes. For instance, Owain Glyndwr is said to have encamped in the hill-fort at Wapley (SO 3462), high on the ridge overlooking the confluence of the Lugg and the Hindwell Brook, before he advanced on Pembridge and the plain of Hereford in 1401. But perhaps the most important feature of the geography of the Marchland in the post-Roman centuries was the emergence of a chain of tribal territories between the Dee and Severn, territories that were ruled by princes whose royal houses are recorded for us only in the wild, poetic legends of Dark Age Wales.

The successor state to the Roman order in the middle Severn valley and the northern march in the fifth century was the kingdom of Powys. The origins of Powys remain as obscure as all the attempts that have been made to define the extent of its territories. Equally it presents to us such baffling problems as the location of its reputed capital, Pengwern. One fact is certain, Powys came into existence in the fifth century soon after the extinction of Roman rule in Britain. Its very name, derived from the Latin, *Pagenses*, meaning the people of the countryside, hints at the early date of the creation of Powys. Again, there is the tradition that the political geography of Dark Age Wales found its roots in a reorganisation of government in the west in late Roman times, a reorganisation that was engineered by Maximus, an officer under Count Theodosius who was the ruler of Britain late in the fourth century. Maximus, his name transformed into Maxen Wledic, was to become part of the folk history of Wales and the Celtic peoples.

The core of this Dark Age kingdom is clear enough; it belongs to the basin of the middle Severn about Shrewsbury, the north Shropshire plain and the dissected hill country of the upper Severn and its tributaries. At its greatest extent, Powys perhaps reached from the estuary of the Dyfi to the sandstone hills of mid-Cheshire and south-eastwards across Shropshire to a frontier on the Severn in the tract of the Ironbridge Gorge. To the south, it stretched to the valley of the upper Wye to touch the northern bounds of the kingdom of Brycheiniog. The core of Powys was shaped out of the former tribal territory of the Cornovii in Shropshire and of the Ordovices among the hills of central Wales. The name of Powys lived until the reorganisation of Welsh administration by the Act of Union, in 1536, created the modern pattern of counties. Today, in the latter half of the twentieth century, Powys lives again as the name of one of the new areas of local government that have swept away a centuries-old pattern of counties in the interests of a fashionable doctrine that is summed up by the catch-phrase 'economy of size'. The new Powys is not a recreation of the political geography of the past because it includes, in its absorption of Brecon, territory that at no time belonged to the Dark Age and medieval princedom. The name Powys referred to a living political entity for more than a thousand years, but over the centuries the geographical shape of that body politic was to change immensely. The fifth-century kingdom that found an eastern frontier somewhere in the Midland Plain was to be reduced by the fifteenth century to the hill-lands of east-central Wales between the Berwyns and Plynlimmon. Its changing political shape under the pressure of countless years of border warfare can be ascribed to the advance of Anglo-Saxon Mercia from the east in the seventh and eighth centuries, the creation of an aggressive chain of Marcher lordships after the Norman Conquest, and harsh internal struggles among the princedoms of medieval Wales.

If it is difficult to determine the shape and extent of Powys in the centuries before the Norman Conquest, it is perhaps even harder to fix the internal details of its geography. We know of a long line of rulers, princes of the royal house of Powys, reaching back into the fifth century, but with no degree of

15. *Mathrafal, the mysterious castle-site in the Vale of Meifod that claims to have been the palace of the Dark Age princes of Powys.*

certainty can one locate the capital of their state or the site of a royal palace. The traditional capitals, suggesting an itinerant court, include Chester, Mathrafal and Pengwern. Mathrafal's claim to lie at the heart of Powys history in its earliest centuries is indeed strong. It lies close to the confluence of the rivers Vyrnwy and Banwy (sj 1310), deep among the wooded hills of Montgomeryshire and at the very centre of a territory that has always been part of Powys. Apart from the magic of its name, a word straight from the Arthurian dark age, Mathrafal arouses the imagination by the quietness and beauty of its site today. The earthworks of a medieval castle, weatherworn, green and crowned with ragged trees, overlook a sharply undercut river cliff of the Banwy. The rounded, wooded hills that encircle the site bear the relics of several Iron Age and Dark Age camps. Northward, the Vyrnwy opens into the smiling plain of Dyffryn Mefod. Mathrafal's claim to be one of the ancient centres of political power in Powys is reinforced by the history of Meifod (sj 1513), once a medieval market centre but now a modest village, its single street of houses strung along the wide arc of a vast churchyard. Meifod has been described as 'the old ecclesiastical capital of Powysland, the burial place of many of its princes'. Its huge circular churchyard, the shape of which can still be clearly traced, once enclosed a Celtic monastery. Even in the later Middle Ages its importance was still evident in the three churches that stood within the sacred circle of the Dark Age monastery.

The hardest problems in the interpretation of the geography of Dark Age Powys surround the identity of Pengwern. The puzzle of the location of this former seat of the court of her princes and capital of Powys becomes all the more exciting because of several references in medieval and Dark Age literature. The Legend of Monacella would seem to leave no doubts about the site of Pengwern when it records that Brochwel Ysgithrog, prince of Powys and earl of Chester, held his court 'in a city called Pengwern, now Shrewsbury'. Giraldus Cambrensis, writing in the twelfth century an account of a journey through Wales, recognised Shrewsbury as Pengwern. Supporters of the Pengwern–Shrewsbury hypothesis (and they include Eilert Ekwall, the great scholar of English place-name studies in the twentieth century), have claimed that the palace of the rulers of Powys stood on the hill top within the curving loop of the Severn where we now find St Chad's Church. Shrewsbury is certainly an ancient site, though the first documentary evidence of a settlement there occurs in a charter of Wenlock Abbey dating to 901. Then its English name is recorded. But there is a strong likelihood that the ancient heart of the town is built over an Iron Age camp. The 'bury' element of the modern place-name suggests some early earthwork that may precede in time the founding of the English settlement. The

Pengwern hypothesis is weakened by the fact that Shrewsbury also bears an old Welsh name, Amwythig, a name that was probably current at the time when Powys flourished. Archaeology has up to now been able to contribute little to the establishment of Shrewsbury as the capital of the Dark Age kingdom because it has produced scarcely any evidence from those times or the preceding Romano–British Iron Age.

The fullest description of Pengwern appears in a tale of the deeds of Cynddylan, a Dark Age hero of Powys, set down in a poem by Llywarch Hen. There we read that Cynddylan 'lived in his great hall at Pengwern in the white town by the woods'. The poem goes on to describe how this Welsh chieftain lost his life in a battle against the English in the seventh century and tells how his body was carried to be buried at *Eglwysau Basa*, the church of Basa. Here is the clearest topographical reference in this misty account of events in the remote history of Powys. Eglwysau Basa must refer to Baschurch (s J 4221), and it seems not unlikely that the site of Pengwern may be located among the sandstone ridges and the once extensive marshes and mosslands of the north Shropshire plain. A probable place is The Berth (s J 4223), one of the most mysterious and fascinating earthworks of the borderland. It lies scarcely a mile from Baschurch in a district where surviving pools and meres still testify to the marshy wilderness that must have existed here in centuries past. The Berth today consists of two circular enclosures with low grassy ramparts. They are joined to each other by a faintly raised causeway. Around the edge of the ring-like enclosures a tiny, lazy stream

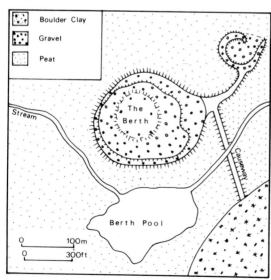

8. *The Berth in its geological setting to show the natural advantages of the gravel knoll set in the peaty mosslands.*

meanders, broadening out, to the south of the main earthwork, into the Berth Pool. Another and longer causeway provided a passage across this shallow valley in times gone by when its string of marshes and stagnant pools must have formed a natural moat for the two ring-works within. Was this indeed the long-forgotten Pengwern, palace of the princes of Powys?

The claim of The Berth to be the true location of Pengwern carries much strength, and H. P. R. Finberg in his important essay, 'Mercians and Welsh',* was confident that the answer lay in this forgotten object of the north Shropshire landscape. Only an archaeologist can settle this debate, and lately Graham Webster, in the closing pages of his study of the Cornovii, has suggested that 'the real Pengwern' may be revealed if a detailed excavation of the hill-fort at Bury Walls (SJ 5727), poised on the edge of a sandstone escarpment overlooking the plain of the middle Severn, should uncover the post-holes of the Great Hall of Cynddylan.

Powys dominated the territory of the Northern and Middle Marches from the Dee to the upper Wye in the post-Roman decades. Similarly, the southern March saw the evolution of Dark Age kingdoms out of the tribal territories of the Iron Age. The upper valley of the Usk formed the core of Brycheiniog, a kingdom that maintained its freedom from intrusion from the Anglo-Saxon east until late in the tenth century. The landscape and the place-names of Brecknockshire still bear witness to the remote decades of the fifth century when the kingdom of Brycheiniog came into being. Tradition has it that the founder of this little state contained within the fertile basin of the upper Usk was Brychan, whose father, Anlac, was an Irish chieftain. Even though Dark Age history expresses the evolution of states in the terms of the deeds of heroic individuals, there is no doubt that the waves of Irish colonists who made plantations along the western coast of Britain from the Clyde to Devon in the fifth century played an important part in the emergence of Brycheiniog. The region of densest Irish settlement was in south-west Wales. Here lay the kingdom of Dyfed, whose rulers of Irish origin were probably already established in late Roman times. Dyfed occupied the peninsula of Pembrokeshire and reached out to an eastern frontier in the Towy valley. It was from this direction that the Irish colonists, Goidelic Celts, must have reached the attractive lands of the Usk. Their most likely route of entry into the region was along the Roman road from the Towy plain at Llandovery across the Mynydd-bach Trecastell (SN 8330) into the headstreams of the Usk. The proof of this Dark Age Irish element in the development of Brecon has been handed down to us through the place-name

*In *Lucerna-studies in some problems of the early history of England* (London, 1964).

elements of the county that are of Goidelic origin. For instance, the suffix *ach*, a Goidelic term, is found repeated twenty times in Brecknockshire in the name Clydach. Again, the county has yielded seven inscribed stones from the Dark Age centuries, stones with a script of Irish origin that have been found in greater abundance farther west in the coastlands of Wales.

Recent research has added a new and striking piece of evidence for the presence of Irish settlers in Brecknockshire with C. B. Crampton's work* on settlement patterns in the uplands that encircle the plains of Usk and Llynfi. In the rough pastures above the 1,000-foot contour, Brecknock has a higher proportion of common land than any other county in Britain. On the Mynydd Illtyd (SN 9726), a long, open ridge to the south of the Usk crossed by a Roman road, Crampton has recognised, through air photographs and ground surveys, evidence of cultivation and field systems of three widely different ages. Most obvious are the farms with their shelter belts of trees that form ragged piecemeal enclosures from the common land in the nineteenth century. Earlier still we find the faint evidence of medieval ploughland, distributed in blocks across the gentle hill-slopes and displaying the characteristic patterns of ridge and furrow. The medieval cultivation of these uplands probably dates to the two centuries after A.D. 1000, a period of notably warmer climate when the frontier of farming expanded into the harsher lands in many parts of western Europe. Fainter still, and from an earlier epoch, the hills of Brecknock bear a different pattern of fields. Air photographs reveal networks of tiny rectilinear fields, each covering only a fraction of an acre. Mostly they are largely obscured by the medieval ploughland and the later efforts to reclaim the commons. The most striking feature of the oldest field patterns is the contention by C. B. Crampton that their boundaries may still be recognised on the ground in roughly defined lines of scrub gorse. He believes that the gorse was deliberately planted as a hedge, perhaps originally among other species, including hawthorn, that have since died out. Faint marks on highly enlarged air photographs and striking patterns among the blazing gold of gorse in spring guide the mind back to some remote period of cultivation on the Brecknockshire hills. The dating of such tenuous evidence is hard indeed, but an important clue may lie in a circular earthwork, composed of a single bank and ditch, on Mynydd Illtyd. This camp is entangled in the pattern of early, rectilinear fields. In fact, the interior of the camp was cultivated in the same way, suggesting that the earthwork was already there when the field system was sketched out. After an examination of fossil seed-content from the top-soil of the camp, C. B.

---

* 'Ancient settlement patterns in mid-Wales', *Archaeologia Cambrensis*, 116 (1967).

Crampton believes that it dates from the Iron Age. If the irregular patterns of tiny rectangular fields on the upland commons were created after the raising of a camp in the Iron Age, later to be largely obscured by the ridges of medieval ploughing, it seems most likely that they belong to a Dark Age context, perhaps to the Irish migrants who laid the dynastic foundations of Brycheiniog.

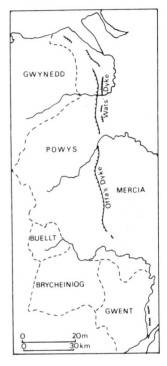

9. *Political map of the borderland in the eighth century (after Rees).*

If Brycheiniog looked to the Irish coastal settlements of western Wales for its origins, another Dark Age kingdom, Gwent, was turned towards the Severn estuary and the east. Its territories occupied most of the lower Usk valley and reached along the Wye from below Hereford to the Severn shore. Gwent, by reason of its eastward outlook, suffered from exposure to Anglo-Saxon settlement and aggression. Its political geography is chequered too by internal dynastic dissension. Despite the pressure of external influences from the east in the evolution of Gwent, one may still discern in the landscape of today elements from its Celtic Dark Age history. One of the districts of Gwent, the *cantref* known as Erging or Archenfield, remained deeply embedded in its Celtic past until the twelfth century. Archenfield belongs to

93

southern Herefordshire, bordered on the east by the Wye and to the west by the Monnow and the dark face of the Black Mountains. Both the Welsh and English names of the district, Erging and Archenfield, seem to be derived from the name of the Roman settlement, *Ariconium*, where the iron and metal-working industry of the Forest of Dean had been located. Erging, as we know it at the time of the Norman Conquest, may represent the remnant of a much larger political unit that reached to the Malvern Hills and the banks of the Severn.

Saxon colonisation after the seventh century and the later military organisation of the Norman marcher lordships failed to efface all memories of Erging from the south Herefordshire landscape. Place-names and, above all, the dedications of churches are a reminder of the Christianity that survived here from late Roman times. The place-name element *eccles*, of Celtic origin describing a church or chapel, probably refers to a site of early Christian worship. Eccleswall (SO 6523) in the parish of Linton-by-Ross lies close to one of the most important parts of the March in Roman times. It stands on the southern fringe of Ariconium, one of the major iron-working centres of Roman Britain whose name was the progenitor of the Dark Age Erging. Here, it seems likely, stood the chapel of a Christian community in the late Roman centuries.

Dark Age Erging is glimpsed more fully through its association with one of the most famous missionary saints of the Celtic world, Dubricius or Dyfrig. The references to Dyfrig in the *Liber Landavenis*, a collection of charters of the cathedral church of Llandaff gathered together in the twelfth century, show that he was born in the middle years of the fifth century. The account of his life in *The Book of Llandaff* records that Dyfrig was the son of one of the kings of Erging, one of a royal line that is recorded down to the year 570. Erging as viewed through the pages of the *Liber Landavensis* seems to be a post-Roman kingdom, a territory with its own line of princes, that fell into decline towards the close of the sixth century. Dyfrig devoted his life to strengthening the fabric of the church in the territory of Erging. He was born at Madley (SO 4138), a place in that most delectable tract of the Welsh Marches, the Wye valley above Hereford, whose name sums up the complex evolution of the territory of Erging. The first element of the name is derived from the Old Welsh, *marle*; it means *the good place*. The termination is the Old English element, *leah*, that is found widely in the areas of later Anglo-Saxon settlement and which describes a woodland clearing. Madley as a name expresses the slow transformation of Erging into Saxon Archenfield under the impetus of colonisation from the east after the beginning of the seventh century. The location of Madley, too, suggests the important part played by Roman roads in determining the pattern of settlement in the successor kingdoms to the Roman order. It stands scarcely half a mile from one of the main roads through the March country where Watling Street West, linking Caerleon and Viroconium, descends towards the crossing of the Wye and the site of Magnis, Kenchester (SO 4342), on the river's northern bank.

Dyfrig established two important religious foundations in the same district of Erging, first a monastic community at Hentland (SO 5426) in a secret place to the south of the Wye where the river makes its way in great sweeping meanders between Hereford and Ross. The parish church of Hentland, which may well occupy the holy ground of Dyfrig's fifth-century monastery, stands at the head springs of a tiny stream that drains swiftly to the Wye. This medieval church, much restored by the Victorians, bears little visible witness to its links with Britain's oldest form of Christianity except in a dedication to the founder of the monastery, St Dubricius, and in its lonely site in a parish of scattered farms. The layout of settlement in Hentland, a dispersed pattern without a village core, is suggestive of a ground-plan that has long been associated with the Celtic West. The hamlets and farms, too, of the surrounding countryside hark back to the centuries before the Saxons with such names as Pencoyd, Tretire, Treaddow, Hendre and Pengethley. Unconsciously, the present landscape of south Herefordshire remembers Erging.

St Dyfrig's school at Hentland trained scholars and missionaries whose names have been commemorated in scores of dedications through Wales and the borderlands, among them St Teilio and St Samson. Dyfrig's community at Hentland was later moved to a fresh monastic site beside the Wye at Moccas (SO 3542). Moccas lies only half-a-dozen miles from Madley and the important north–south line of communication through the Marches by Watling Street West. It stood upon one of the important entries into Brycheiniog and west Wales. Moccas seems to have fallen into obscurity as a monastic centre after the close of the sixth century.

With the impending expansion of Anglo-Saxon influences from the east and the eclipse of Erging as a kingdom, new border states were about to emerge in the pre-Conquest Marchland. They included kingdoms of the Magonsaetan in the Lugg valley, and of the Wreocensaetan, the territory, as the name says, of the dwellers around the Wrekin. All that is left to remind us of the land of Erging, lost in the scarce-recorded centuries between the withdrawal of the Roman armies and the coming of the Saxons, is a scattering of Celtic place-name elements among the familiar and homely Saxon designations of south Herefordshire and a cluster of church dedications to Dyfrig, St Dubricius, the only member of the obscure line of Erging's royal house to leave his mark on history. We find the majority of the dedications to St Dubricius in the country between the Wye and Monnow, reaching westward to the Golden Valley. Hentland, Whitchurch, Ballingham and St Devereux among others must mark the territory where Dyfrig preached and founded churches in the latter half of the fifth century. This was the essential core of Erging.

The seventh century was one of the critical epochs in the evolution of the territory that extends between the Dee and the Wye, a period as important in its political development as the decades around 1100 when the mosaic of Norman marcher lordships came into existence. By the middle of the seventh century the true marchland character of the zone was apparent. The westward expansion of Mercia from the core of this English kingdom in the Trent valley towards the hills of Wales meant that a borderland between two cultures, Welsh and Anglo-Saxon, had been created. Two peoples with different racial histories, languages, social customs, laws, forms of Christianity and political organisation interlocked among the hills and valleys of the March. In the opening years of the seventh century the Marches were still part of the Celtic World, a fact that is proved by a record of a conference of British bishops that was called together by St Augustine in A.D. 603 at which the River Severn was regarded as the boundary between the lands of the English and the British. Less than two centuries later another kind of boundary, an earthwork more than 120 miles long, had been raised by King Offa of Mercia through the hills of the borderland to define the territorial limits of Celt and Anglo-Saxon. The whole of the Severn basin eastward of Welshpool lay within the control of Mercia. In the region of the Middle March, the zone of deepest Anglo-Saxon penetration, Offa's earthwork runs at a distance of some fifty miles from the Severn – an ineffaceable piece of evidence in the twentieth-century landscape of the successful and rapid expansion of the West Midland kingdom more than a thousand years ago.

It is hard to date the earliest incursions of Mercian settlers into the lands beyond the Severn, just as it is equally difficult to be certain about the numbers of colonists moving westward, the nature of relations between Saxon and Celt, or even the trails followed by the migrants from the heart of the Midland kingdom. The westward advance of Mercia was probably heralded by the Battle of Chester in A.D. 614, fought against that powerful northern rival among the kingdoms of the Anglo-Saxon heptarchy, Northumbria. Graham Webster has suggested that the final abandonment of Viroconium as a settlement probably took place after the Battle at Chester. The poem of Llywarch Hen, with its references to Pengwern and the death in battle of the hero Cynddylan, described events in the same period early in the seventh century. The Dark Age kingdom of Powys was about to lose its rich base in the middle basin of the Severn at the expense of an expanding Mercia.

The westward growth of Mercia is recorded in the formation of a transitory buffer state, Magonsaete, in the middle Marchland. The kingdom of Magonsaete appears after the middle of the seventh century as an Anglian principality ruled over by Merewalh, third son of the pagan king of Mercia, Penda. Merewalh also has a place in the historical record because of his conversion to Christianity in 660 by the Northumbrian missionary, Eadfrith, and as the founder of the church at Leominster. Leominster (SO 4959) probably lay close to the core of Merewalh's buffer state, Magonsaete. The name, when it first appears in the records in 811, refers to the Magonsaetan, meaning the people who dwelt around Magana. The form of that place-name takes the mind back to late Roman times. Place-name studies have equated Magana with Maund (SO 5650), a quiet hamlet among the orchards of the Lugg valley seven miles below Leominster. The Magonsaetan have long been considered as a thrusting band of Mercian settlers, perhaps thousands strong, who took over a territory stretching from the Wye to the Wrekin and westwards to the wilderness of Radnor Forest. In this view of seventh-century Mercian expansion, the Wreocensaetan formed another powerful group of colonists clearing the forests around the Wrekin while the Pecsaetan were members of another wave of Anglian settlers who colonised the Peak District. But it may be equally argued that the Magonsaetan were in truth a Celtic people, descendants through the two post-Roman centuries of the Iron Age tribes in this region.

The present-day place-names of Herefordshire provide a clear pointer to the Celtic ground base of the territory of the Magonsaetan. Dinmore (SO 4850), for instance, barely conceals in its anglicised form an older Welsh form, Din Mawr. Treville (SO 4232) contains the Celtic element 'tref', while Mordiford is compounded from the Anglo-Saxon 'ford' with the older Welsh elements, 'mawr' and 'ty'. The lands of that other mysterious Saxon state of the Welsh borderland in the seventh century, the kingdom of the Wreocensaetan, extending from the region of the Wrekin into north Shropshire, reveals a similar surviving Celtic element in its place-names. Ercall, Hodnet, Lizard and Prees (SJ 5533) all hint at an older Celtic ancestry before this territory assumed a high strategic importance as a buffer zone to Penda's Mercia. Additional evidence from the original Celtic character of these territories is provided by the dialects of Herefordshire and Shropshire with their suggestions of descent from Welsh speakers. Again, the land-holding system of the Celtic world with its scattered and fragmented pattern of territorial units as opposed to the compact and integrated lands of the Saxon manor may be discerned in the Domesday Book folios for Herefordshire that deal with the former territory of the Magonsaetan. Domesday Book's account of the great manor of Leominster reveals something of the territorial organisation of the Lugg valley before the Saxon settlements. There, Leominster appears as one of the largest manors of late eleventh-century England. It consisted of eighty hides when the estate passed from Queen Edith to William I, and it was divided into sixteen scattered manorial units, some of them forming completely isolated segments encompassed by the properties of other landlords. Leominster is a typical example of the 'discrete manor', the divided, fragmented estate that was characteristic of the Celtic west.

Leominster probably holds the key to the mystery of 'who were the Magonsaetan?' The head of this huge and complex Domesday manor has strong claims to be the centre of the territory of the Magonsaetan. An earlier form of the place-name is Leen Minster, and Leland, in his great topography written in Henry VIII's reign, claims that the original name of the town, a Welsh one, was Llanllieny, 'the church of the rivers'. Leominster's seventh-century importance is suggested by the foundation of a church there in 660 by the recently converted Merewalh, prince and ruler of the Magonsaetan. Leominster housed the relics of a saint, Ethelred, and was the ecclesiastical centre of the Herefordshire plain before the removal of the seat of bishops to Hereford.

One other important clue remains to be considered in an attempt to trace the evolution of the territory of the Magonsaetan. The core of this post-Roman tribal area seems to be focused on the Lugg valley below Leominster if one is to judge from the history of the name *Magana* and its survival as Maund in Maund Bryan, Maund Common and Rosemaund (SO 5648). The countryside of the Maunds is dominated by one of the most impressive of the Iron Age forts of the borderland, Sutton Walls (SO 5246). Archaeology has recently proved its continuous occupation over hundreds of years from the early Iron Age until late Roman times. It seems highly likely that Sutton Walls might have been the focus of organisation for one of the tribal territories of the Celtic Iron Age – a territory that perhaps coincided with that of the ancestors of the Magonsaetan. By the end of the sixth century, if not earlier, Sutton Walls had been abandoned for a site in the marshy valley of the Lugg where five brooks and rivers converge. Llanllieny, 'the church of the rivers', was chosen as a residence and seat of government, the place where Merewalh lived and ruled, in the seventh century as Mercia expanded its influence westward through the creation of a chain of border kingdoms.

The entry of Mercia into the Welsh borderland in the seventh century, an entry of an alien, non-Celtic people, represents the first phase in the development of the region's marchland character. One can only speculate about the nature of the Mercian colonisation of the March at this time. Was it aggressive and warlike, involving large bands of settlers, or was it largely a peaceful penetration of the long-settled plains and valleys beneath the centuries-old forts of the Iron Age? Opinion leans to the view that this was a piecemeal and mainly peaceful settlement of tracts that had been cleared and farmed since the prehistoric centuries. The distribution of the earliest Saxon place-name elements in the Marches leads to the latter conclusion.* Names with the primary elements of *ing* and *ham*, and those involving the combination of *ing* with *ham* or *ton* are scarce indeed. There are only two in Herefordshire – Bullingham and Ballingham (SO 5731) – close by the Wye below the county town. Again, Shropshire has only two – Uppington (SJ 5909) and Atcham (SJ 5409) – and both lie in a long-settled region close to the chief waterway of the northern March, the Severn. The marks left by the Mercians in the form of place-names in the present landscape point clearly to their settlement in the plains of the main rivers such as the Wye and its tributary the Lugg about Hereford. The hilly western fringe of the Marches was probably rejected until the next century when Mercia reached the peak of its political power and a frontier was established by King Offa that, in parts, still forms a dividing line between Welsh and English.

The hills that project far to the east in south Shropshire, and whose last outpost is the vast hump of Brown Clee, were also neglected in the first phase of Mercia's impact in the marchland. Much of this country was forested and even after the Norman Conquest it passed under the Welsh name of Y Coed, the wood. Mercian and Celt probably mingled over the years, a process suggested by the ancient place-names that have come down to us distorted by Saxon modes of speech. Perhaps a long, subtle and unrecorded take-over of the lands of the Celt is remembered in that poem of Llywarch Hen whose events are set in the seventh century. In one place he recalled:

> Mae Wyn, when I was of thy age
> No one trod on my mantle,
> No one without bloodshed ploughed my land.

A later reference in the same poem may tell of the annexation of land in the Golden Valley by a small band of marauding Mercians, when the bard bewails that 'a gift has been stolen from me, from the valley of Mafwrn'.

*D. Sylvester, *The rural landscape of the Welsh borderland* (London, 1969).

99

The expansion of Mercia into the Welsh borderland quickened in the years after 700. Under her eighth-century kings, Mercia became the most powerful among the Anglo-Saxon states. In 731, Aethelbald of Mercia was recognised as the overlord of the whole of England south of the Humber, and later still Offa, the builder of the great marchland earthwork, was reckoned by the Emperor Charlemagne among the princes of Europe. The first half of the eighth century probably witnessed an active colonising movement by Mercia deep into the Celtic hill country of the western March. The remote pioneer fringe of this wave of settlers can probably still be traced in the pattern of English place-names to the west of Offa's Dyke. This linear earthwork – a frontier on the ground for all to see – was thrown up between the years 757 and 796. As Dorothy Sylvester has claimed of Offa's Dyke in her detailed analysis of settlement problems in the Welsh Marches, 'it defined the then accepted bounds of Mercian settlement'. But in four areas along the course of the dyke we find clusters of Anglian place-names well to the west of the frontier earthwork. Two lie among the interlocking hills and valleys of the Middle March between the Severn and the Wye. A number of places in the Severn corridor between Welshpool and Montgomery – Forden (SJ 2201), Edderton (SJ 2302), Leighton (SJ 2405) and Buttington (SJ 2408) – all lie to the west of the dyke. No historical record exists of the making of these settlements with English names deep in the lands of Powys. The most likely explanation is that they belong to a westward thrust of Mercian colonisation in the years about A.D. 700. Half a century later, when Offa's Dyke came to be constructed, the course laid out for the earthwork, high on the steep western slopes of Long Mountain in Leighton Park, suggests the aban-donment by Mercia of any claims to the outlying English settlements on the valley-floor of the Severn. A similar and even more striking pattern of settlements with names of English origin may be observed in the sheltered lowland, enclosed on every hand by wooded hills, to the south of Radnor Forest. Here, Offa's Dyke follows an exposed line across the slopes of hills facing steeply westward across the little plain of the Summergil Brook towards New Radnor. There is little doubt that this tiny lowland with its spread of light fertile soils has long been occupied by man. The unusual number of standing stones and Bronze Age burial sites, as well as the massive Iron Age entrenchments of Burfa Camp (SO 2861), suggest that the Mercian colonists may only have taken over a favoured and early-settled tract of the borderland. Their mark has remained in the place-names around New Radnor. Walton (SO 2559), Womaston (SO 2660), Harpton (SO 2359) and Kinnerton (SO 2463) could belong to almost any part of the West Midlands, but here we find them to the west of Offa's Dyke. Even Burlingjobb (SO

2558), amidst a cluster of Welsh names in the headwaters of the River Arrow, is undeniably English.

The history of the English settlement of the Radnor basin and of the upper parts of the Lugg and Arrow valleys westward of the great eighth-century linear earthwork has gone without record. There is no literary source from which this period of border history can be reconstructed. All that we have is the silent evidence of the place-names and the kind of speculation that arises from an investigation of the objects in the present landscape. Two possible interpretations of the surviving evidence can be made. The English settlement of the Radnor basin could have been completed before the building of Offa's Dyke. If this view is correct, the making of the earthwork must have entailed political negotiations with the Welsh that ended, at least here in the Middle March, in the loss of territory by Mercia. On the other hand, the English place-names may record an expansion of control from the east at some time between the building of the dyke in the late eighth century and the making of Domesday Book in 1086. Several of the names are recorded in the Domesday folios, for instance Burlingjobb appears as *Berchelincope*, and this is undoubted proof that they were in existence by the end of the eleventh century. Thus, it has been proposed that these most westerly settlements of the English in the Middle March were made in the years before the Norman Conquest, a confused time of warfare between the Welsh and the Saxons and Normans, involving the son of Earl Godwin, Harold, and the forces of Norman lords already established in the Marches before 1066. In the 1050s the power of the Welsh stretched far to the east. An Anglo-Norman army was

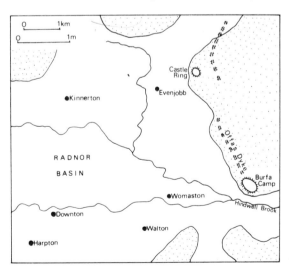

10. *A pocket of Saxon settlement left outside the frontier of Offa's Dyke when this political boundary was drawn at the end of the eighth century.*

defeated at Leominster in 1051 by the troops of Gruffydd ap Llewellyn, the ruler of Gwynedd and Powys. Another raid of 1055 reached the outskirts of Hereford. But in 1062 Harold Godwinson's campaign in Wales reversed the fortunes of the Saxons and pushed the fluctuating frontier of political influence far to the west. The Vale of Clwyd was reached and Gruffydd's castle at Rhuddlan was burnt; in the Middle March much territory that lay to the west of Offa's Dyke passed into the control of the English. The fruits of this campaign for Harold Godwinson seem to be recorded in his possessions at the time of the Norman Conquest when he held fifty manors in Herefordshire alone.

Eighteen of Harold Godwinson's manors lay in north-west Herefordshire, including Eardisley, Kington, Huntington, Titley, Presteigne and Old Radnor. Old Radnor (SO 2459) must be one of the quietest and most peaceful places in Britain, secluded on a lane that climbs across the ridge separating the Hindwell and Arrow valleys. But the landscape round about still bears the marks of the uneasy politics of the Middle Ages. A ruined castle mound and moat stands close beside the fifteenth-century church of St Stephen. In the plain below, beside a brook that idly meanders towards the Hindwell, are the earthworks of Castle Nimble (SO 2459), a circular mound and ditch as well as rectangular enclosures whose history is anything but clear. Only a mile to the north-east lies another defended site, a large castle mound and moat at Womaston (SO 2660), commanding the narrow gap between Burfa Camp and Rushock Hill where Offa's Dyke descends to cross the Hindwell valley. Although the later decades of the twelfth century saw the raising of many military earthworks in the Marches, it has been argued that at least one of the sites around Old Radnor must belong to the pre-Conquest years when Harold Godwinson inherited the spoils of warfare on the western frontier.

Earl Harold's military successes in the Marches in the years before the Norman Conquest seem unlikely to be the primary cause of the establishment of English-speaking settlements to the west of Offa's Dyke. The two decades that passed before the making of the Domesday Survey seem too short a time for the shaping of the mature communities recorded in 1086. In fact, most of them appear in Domesday Book as units of assessment in the time of King Edward the Confessor – *tempore regis Edwardi* – which means that they were in being before Harold entered his possessions in the western March. One important piece of evidence in the solution of this problem can be read from modern large-scale maps of the region. An examination of parish boundaries in this part of Radnorshire shows that Offa's Dyke was rarely used to define the limits of the parish or of manorial estates. The conclusion seems inescapable that the great earthwork, snaking across the hills of Radnorshire and north Herefordshire, could not have been there at the time of the English settlements in the Radnor basin, as well as at Kington (SO 2956), Huntington (SO 2453) and Staunton-on-Wye. If these remote Mercian colonies predate the making of the dyke, they must belong to the period of expansion in the early years of the eighth century when the consolidation of this West Midland state brought about the political extinction of the territory of the Magonsaetan. If this view of the Mercian settlement of the Radnor basin is correct, then the delineation of the English–Welsh frontier in Offa's Dyke represents an abandonment of the lands of these most westerly outliers of pioneer farmers. That the English sounding place-names have survived and that Radnorshire was to evolve as a non-Welsh-speaking county within the limits of Wales is a tribute to the active anglicization of the Middle March in the later Middle Ages.

In one other part of the Welsh borderland the pattern of English place-names on the map suggests a transgression of the late-eighth-century frontier as defined by the course of Offa's Dyke. At its southern extremity Offa's Dyke ends abruptly on Sedbury Cliffs (ST 5592), cutting across the low peninsula that separates the estuarine Wye from the wider Severn. To the south and west, where the ever broader Severn begins to look like a sea separating Wales and England, the low Welsh coastal plain reveals a succession of settlements with names of Anglo-Saxon origin – Nash (ST 3483), Goldcliff (ST 3683) and Bishton (ST 3887). There is no historical evidence to explain the time or nature of this colonisation of the coastal fringe of the Severn shore in South Wales. Most likely these places represent one of the earliest incursions of the Anglo-Saxons into the Marches, perhaps about the year A.D. 600, soon after the Battle of Dyrham had opened up the lower Severn valley to the expanding Saxon kingdoms.

Of all the relics of the Saxon centuries in the landscape of the Marches at the present time, without doubt the great linear earthwork attributed to King Offa is the grandest. So many features of the dyke, as one traces its course between the Dee and Severn, lead the mind to speculate upon the motives and intentions of the politicians and engineers who determined and plotted its location. Its relation to the eternal topographical features of the borderland, the high plateaus deeply dissected by eastward-flowing rivers and the wide plains of Wye and Severn, provoke thoughts that cannot be checked against any documentary record. Perhaps even more fascinating is the connection between the dyke and the man-made objects that were already present in the landscape of the late eighth century. For instance, in the section of the dyke above the Radnor basin the massive Iron Age earthwork of Burfa Camp is incorporated into the line of the Mercian frontier. Farther

103

16. *Offa's Dyke, the earthworks of Mercia's western frontier, thrown up in the eighth century, forms a barrier across the plateau between the deeply entrenched valleys of the rivers Clun and Teme.*

north, in the unlovely landscape of the coalfield near Ruabon, Offa's Dyke crosses a tract of low ground to the east of a prominent hill crowned by the Iron Age fort of Pen-y-gardden (S J 2944). If the rules of strategy, the securing of strong positions with westward outlooks, had always prevailed in the alignment of the dyke, one would have expected Pen-y-gardden to have been absorbed into the Mercian structure. Here, it has been argued, the hill-fort site remained in Welsh hands as a result of negotiation at the time when the western limits of Mercia were determined.*

Even more fascinating speculations about the purpose and origin of Offa's Dyke arise when one considers the earthwork in relation to similar linear banks and ditches in the Welsh borderland. The hardest problems surround any interpretation of the relationships between Offa's gigantic earthwork and the more modest feature, Wat's Dyke, that runs roughly parallel to its more famous neighbour in the northern Marchland. Wat's Dyke lies to the east of the Offan earthwork, following a course through generally lower country. It stretches from the Dee estuary, in the neighbourhood of Flint, to the Morda Brook (S J 3027), a tributary of the Vyrnwy river. The most critical section for the understanding of Wat's Dyke probably lies at its southern end. The Morda Brook may seem to be of little topographical importance, but this pleasantly dull part of the Shropshire plain to the south of Oswestry and within sight of the Breidden and the Montgomeryshire hills may have been an area of considerable political importance in the Dark Ages. Here the vast multi-ramparted Iron Age fort of Old Oswestry is incorporated into the line of Wat's Dyke and the earthwork itself ends at Maesbury (S J 3025), the ancient core of a Saxon hundred and the forerunner of Oswestry. Somewhere in this district the Battle of Maserfelth was fought in the year 641, a battle between Mercia and Northumbria as part of the struggle for the control of the north-west Midlands. Penda of Mercia defeated Oswald, the ruler of Northumbria, and Northumbrian ambitions in the northern borderland were extinguished. Henceforward the Mersey was to be recognised as a frontier between the two Saxon kingdoms.

The building of Wat's Dyke probably took place at some time between the Battle of Maserfelth, a battle whose very location hints at the importance of this tract of the upper Severn plain for the expanding Mercia, and the middle of the eighth century when the grander and more westerly earthwork of Offa shows that the influence of the Midland kingdom had pushed westward into the hills of Powys. No documentary clue survives to tell of the making of Wat's Dyke. History is completely silent about this low grassy bank, here

*C. Fox, *Offa's Dyke* (London, 1955).

and there marked by gnarled and lonely trees, that twists its way through the pit-heaps and glaring red-brick terraces of the Wrexham coalfield. We have only the name as evidence. It has been argued that Wat descends from the Old English personal name, Wada, and that he, unknown as any specific person in the records of Anglo-Saxon England, was the Mercian who constructed the dyke. L. F. Chitty, the eminent Shropshire prehistorian, in an important summary* of the county's archaeology, believed that Wat's Dyke was a Mercian earthwork of an earlier date than King Offa's frontier. Wat's Dyke may well belong to the time when Penda created those shadowy buffer kingdoms of the Magonsaetan and the Wreocensaetan in the Marches.

If doubt exists about the origin of Wat's Dyke, there is an equal uncertainty, in some places, about its course on the ground. At its northern end the earthwork fades in a wooded dingle above Flint and in several places the line of the earthwork has been erased completely. One of the most striking sections of Wat's Dyke survives in the gentle pastoral scenery of the Alun valley between Mold and Hope (SJ 3058). Here the earthwork always lies in the meadows and woods on the lower eastern flank of the valley; to the west, with the hills of Wales beyond, winds the river like some natural defensive line reinforcing the man-made frontier, if such it is. South of Hope, a planned town of the fourteenth century, a dramatic change comes over the landscape. The Alun plunges into a narrow wooded gorge before breaking north-eastwards towards the Dee. At the entrance to the gorge, on its eastern flank, stands the site of an Iron Age camp, Caer Estyn (SJ 3157). An even more splendid ramparted earthwork (SJ 3353) of the Iron Age occupies the tight loop in the Alun to the north of the outskirts of Wrexham where the river turns back on itself. Wat's Dyke, in this section through the gorge and between the two hill-forts, reminds one of Offa's earthwork in its exploitation of the established features of topography. For instance, the two hill-forts appear to have been deliberately incorporated in the line of the earthwork, providing a clear hint that the dyke post-dates these earlier objects of the landscape. The deepest part of the Alun gorge, at Sydallt (SJ 3155), presents a difficult problem in speculating about the history of Wat's Dyke. The site itself reminds one of the course of Offa's Dyke from Monmouth southwards, where it runs high in the woods above the deep winding gorge of the Wye. This section of the Alun might be the lower Wye in miniature, for Wat's Dyke seems to follow the crest of the wooded cliff above the river. The Ordnance Survey have confidently mapped the line of the earthwork in this position, on the sharp edge of the miniature escarpment

*L. F. Chitty, 'An introduction to Shropshire archaeology', *Archaeological Journal*, 113 (1956).

that beetles above the river. Fieldwork, however, shows no clear evidence of the dyke in this position. The original surveyors of the ordnance map seem to have mistaken the weathered crest of the escarpment for the stony rubble of a Dark Age earthwork. Nevertheless, given the clearly established sections of Wat's Dyke to the north and south of the Alun gorge and its incorporation of the strong points of the Iron Age camps, it seems that the eastern flank of this deeply cut section provided a natural, clearly demarcated element of the earthwork. Just as Sir Cyril Fox in his detailed analysis of Offa's Dyke was led to believe that sections where the earthwork is missing from the land-scape, near Welshpool and for many miles of the Wye basin in Hereford-shire, are places where it was never constructed, so one may believe that the builders of Wat's Dyke were prepared to use a natural feature to define the course of their boundary line.

Apart from the borderland's two great dykes that seem to be attributable to Mercian engineering, the landscape still bears the marks of other more mysterious ditches and banks with a linear form. A puzzling collection of such features, earthworks of scarcely more than half a mile in length, lies scattered about the Kerry Hills. The Cross Dyke (so 1185), made up of three short sections, straddles the highest tract of open moorland between the headwaters of tributary streams flowing towards the Wye and Severn. Farther east, across a flattened ridge of Clun Forest, we find Upper Short Ditch (so 1986) and Lower Short Ditch (so 2288). The common topo-graphical relationship of these earthworks, separated from each other by some half-dozen miles, is that they all lie to the west of Offa's Dyke and that they are joined by an ancient ridgeway – a track that can still be followed for many miles through scented, close-growing plantations or else across remnants of open heather moor, but always far removed from the sounds and stink of motor cars. The Kerry Hill ridgeway is one of the centuries-old routes between Wales and England. The abundance of prehistoric finds from its vicinity in Clun Forest suggests that it was a means of Bronze Age trade; and it was followed by the cattle drovers of the later Middle Ages. The building of the short dykes at several points across the ancient ridgeway hints at some purposes related to the control of trade or warfare. Nothing is known of the date of their construction, but it has been suggested that they functioned as outliers of Offa's Dyke in this late eighth-century effort to organise the frontier zone between Mercia and the Welsh. Not only may the ditches have been outliers of Offa's Dyke, but perhaps they were forerunners in time of the great linear earthwork. The Kerry Hill and its ridgeway, in this view, formed one of the most vulnerable lines of approach from Wales into the West Midlands. The ditches laid across the upland track may have served some useful purpose in establishing the strength of Mercia among the hills and deep valleys of the Middle March. In this view, the idea of the linear earthwork and whatever functions it performed in the state of Mercia were enlarged in the reign of Offa to a scale that was to encompass the whole western border of the kingdom.

Sir Cyril Fox's research on Offa's Dyke, the result of several summers' field-work in which he tramped every mile of the earthwork, were finally gathered into a monumental volume.* He not only provided a close description of the dyke, section by section, in relation to the changing topography of the marchland, but he also established from the field evidence some of the broad general principles that governed its construction. Fox's work has shown that the strongest and best constructed parts of the earthwork are to be found on the floors and slopes of each of the main eastward-draining river valleys. Again, it forms a prominent, carefully engineered feature across the high plateaus of the Middle March in Shropshire and Radnorshire that are traversed by the much older ridgeways. Elsewhere, Fox showed that Offa's Dyke was more roughly constructed, little more, perhaps, than a visible line through the forest. There are notable differences in the pattern that the dyke makes on the ground. In some sections the line of the earthwork maintains an arrow-straight course; in other places it is gently winding. It has been suggested that these important differences in the plan of the earthwork might tell us something about the presence or absence of woodland at the time when the Mercian engineers marked out the land for the army of diggers who must have been employed in cutting the westward-facing ditch and raising the rampart of earth and rubble. The longer straight sections suggest country – usually on the higher hills and the plateaus of the Middle March – that had already been cleared of forest. Here the surveyors were able to take long clear sightings and to maintain a directness in the line of construction. The gently curving sections of the dyke, on the other hand, suggest that here it was originally laid down through woodland where the determination of the course of the earthwork between distant strongpoints and critical topographical features became more difficult.

Despite the scale and fertility of ideas in Fox's pioneer research on Offa's dyke, much still remains to be discovered. For instance, no account or documentary reference has come down to us that throws any light on the making of the earthwork. Fox was sure that the grand design emerged from the mind of one person, probably the historical Offa of Mercia himself. As Fox has written, 'the scale of the work suggests the power of a ruler that went

*C. Fox, *Offa's Dyke* (London, 1955).

unchallenged through the Midlands'. But of the labour force that undertook the task, of its organisation and the time taken over the making of the earthwork, nothing is possible beyond speculation and intelligent guesswork. In north-west Shropshire, in the borderland hills between Oswestry and Chirk, Fox felt that the earthwork 'was built under the direction of men trained in a military tradition'. Were they units of the military forces whose energies had shaped the expanding state of Mercia over the previous half-century? Or, as one suspects without any firm evidence of proof, were the skills of the marchland folk, descendants of the builders of the scores of Iron Age forts, mobilised for the construction of this the grandest of Britain's earthworks that is outstripped only by the architectural splendour of Hadrian's Wall?

The way forward towards a fuller understanding of Offa's Dyke and its origins must lie through archaeological excavation at places along the earthwork. At present, a narrow ribbon of the Dark Age marchland landscape, more than a hundred miles long, lies preserved beneath the earth that was raised in the late years of the eighth century. One section of the dyke, taken at Ffrith (SJ 2855) in north-east Wales, shows the potentialities of detailed archaeological investigation for increasing our knowledge of the earthwork and its construction. There the topographical relationships of the linear earthwork seem to abide by the general principles exhibited at so many places along its course. For two miles to the north of this little industrial hamlet it has followed the eastern bank of the River Cegodog, occupying the middle and lower slopes of a steep westward-facing escarpment. At Ffrith the dyke crosses the Cegodog in a typical location just above the river's confluence with its tributary from the deep wooded valley of Nant Ffrith. This place was the site of a small Roman station and the cottages of the present hamlet are built on the bank of the Mercian earthwork. Here a section across the dyke has revealed the older land-surface beneath. It shows a core of water-worn boulders used by Offa's engineers in the foundations of the earthwork as well as quantities of pottery, tile and glass of Roman origin, suggesting that Roman rubbish dumps were used in providing material for the Dark Age frontier-line. A post-hole was discovered in the foundations of the dyke and it is likely that here we are presented with a clue to its design and construction. It seems possible that lines of posts were driven to show the alignment of the earthwork to the gangs engaged on excavating the ditch and raising the rampart. This solitary detail of what lies beneath the dyke at Ffrith points the way to a much more secure knowledge of the date and means of its building. At present the ascription of the dyke to King Offa rests on the fact that *Offedich* was a name current in the Middle Ages for the central portions of the earthwork. Again, Asser's *Life of King Alfred*, written within a century of the supposed raising of this linear earthwork, says that the building of the dyke was ordered by King Offa. But a more exact archaeological proof of its date is still wanting. The suggestion has also been made that in parts Offa's Dyke incorporates sections of earlier earthworks, for instance in its course across the hills above Selattyn in north Shropshire. This view of the making of Offa's Dyke contends that among the older parts of the earthwork, if such are ever firmly proved, some sections could date back to the Iron Age and the Romano-British marchland.

5

The Medieval Marchland

The character of the country that extends between the estuaries of the Dee and Severn as a border region, a marchland, is at no time more clearly revealed than in the centuries between the Norman Conquest and the creation of the Tudor monarchy. Place-names and relict features in the present landscape still recall those years from the eleventh to the sixteenth centuries when the Marches were a border zone of conflict between two peoples and two cultures, the Anglo-Norman and the Celt. This conflict was not only a competition for the possession of the land, particularly the rich valley plains between the uplands, but also a conflict of languages, legal systems, of ways of cultivating the land and of the relations between men in the local community. The years of conflict are still written on the landscape in hundreds of lonely castle mounds and the crumbling walls and keeps of border fortresses, in the proud Norman place-names such as Caus and Montgomery that speak of the pleasant far-away landscapes of northern France, and in the surviving Welsh names that become ever more abundant as one travels westward across the marchland shires.

The closing decades of the eleventh century witnessed the making of a new political order in this critical border territory with the creation of scores of Marcher lordships (the exact number is still a topic of debate). The Act of Union in 1536 that brought the centuries of border warfare and conflict to an end mentions 136 lordships, but other calculations have found a total of 143. The lordships represented the territorial estates of the great Marcher families, the Mortimers, de Says, Bohuns, Corbets, Lacys, Clares and Bigods, to mention only a few of the names that colour the pages of every local and county history of the region. The medieval political history of the Marches is an ever-changing, kaleidoscopic pattern, a pattern determined by family relationships and rivalry expressed through marriages and warfare. Superimposed upon the endless mutations of local politics in the borderland were the frequent incursions of armies from the Welsh heartland with their raids on upland pastures, the burning of farmsteads and churches and the long sieges beneath the walls of the stone-built fortresses that formed the strong-points of the Anglo-Norman occupation of the Marches.

After the creation of the mosaic of Norman lordships in the years about 1100, the next important stage in the political evolution of the borderland is marked by Edward I's conquest of Wales between 1272 and 1284. The Treaty of Rhuddlan that concluded this successful military campaign profoundly modified the political geography of the northern March. A new county, Flintshire, was created and four new lordships, after the earlier Anglo-Norman pattern, came into being. Out of the old Welsh territory of Perfeddwlad, the Treaty of Rhuddlan demarcated the new lordships of Denbigh, Ruthin, Bromfield and Yale, and Chirk. But, as one of the great historians of Wales, William Rees, has remarked, the conquest of Edward I proved to be the prelude to the conquest of the March. As the power of the king expanded, so the privileges of the Marcher lordships became more restricted. The final stage in the evolution of the political geography of the Marchland is marked by the Act of Union with Wales in 1536. A range of new counties was then created along the mountainous western border of the March in Denbighshire, Montgomeryshire, Radnor and Brecon. The intricate frontiers of the hundred and odd lordships were transformed into a meaningless memory of the Middle Ages.

The Anglo-Norman contribution to the shaping of the landscape of the border counties was far more lasting than the mosaic of tiny states that must have seemed the strongest representation of power in those distant centuries. Markets and urban communities gathered beneath the walls of their castles. The founding of monasteries was to lead to economic growth and extensive woodland clearance upon the properties of the great houses such as Tintern, Abbey Dore and Valle Crucis. Wherever we view the lovely and varied landscape of the Marches we can trace features of the present scene that owe their origin to the medieval centuries between the Norman Conquest and the final Tudor Act of Union that was to bind together the separate histories of Wales and England.

If we make our way northwards along the ancient track that follows the high backbone of the Longmynd, as we reach All Stretton and Woolstaston the land begins to fall away to the plain of the middle Severn. Eastward a barrier of low hills points towards the wooded cone of the Wrekin, and in between the plain that spreads at our feet owes so much to the later Middle

Ages in the shaping of its countryside. The ground plan of settlement in this countryside dates back to the Roman period. There, close beside the Severn, stood Viroconium, ranking with Caerleon and Caerwent among the chief Roman towns of the Marches. Romano–British farms have been located here in this countryside, and roads joined Viroconium to Chester, the military settlements of the West Midlands, to Kenchester and the Roman sites of the southern March. The prehistoric and Roman pattern of settlement and communications has been overlaid and nearly obliterated by man's exploitation of this rich landscape through the medieval centuries. The Roman road that connected Viroconium with the lead mines in the western hills has been lost among a network of medieval lanes by Longden (SJ 4406), Exfords Green and Condover (SJ 4905) Similarly, Watling Street west, the grand route through the Marchland hills from the Severn to the capitals of the Usk, can be traced today through Acton Burnell (SJ 5202) and Pitchford (SJ 5303) only as a disjointed succession of minor roads, rough cart-tracks and footpaths that wander along ancient hedge-lines. The medieval centuries have imposed a fresh pattern of communications – the winding lanes connecting villages and hamlets that still serve us in our own day.

The greatest achievement in changing the face of the Marches after the Norman Conquest was the clearance and colonisation of extensive tracts of woodland. Domesday Book and numerous medieval records make it clear that the Severn plain was widely and densely forested eight centuries ago. Southwards from Condover (SJ 4905) across the winding valley of the Cound Brook stretched Buriwood, a tract of woodland covering several square miles. During the twelfth century the records show that Buriwood was a royal forest, but by the close of the thirteenth century it had become common to all the tenants of Condover manor and was open to clearance. Over the next three hundred years Buriwood gave way to new farms, roughly carved out patches of pasture, as well as intakes for extensions to the open fields of border settlements such as Great Ryton (SJ 4803). By 1545 only four hundred acres of Buriwood were left and before the end of that century most of the timber had been cleared. This story of woodland clearance, perhaps the most striking change during the medieval centuries in the parish history of Condover, is repeated at several places in the plain of the middle Severn around Shrewsbury. Lythwood reached to the south of Bayston Hill (SJ 4809) across the sharply etched ridge of Lyth Hill. The records that have come down to us from the later Middle Ages contain references to frequent grants of timber from Lythwood for fuel and building purposes to Shrewsbury Abbey, to churches and friaries in the town of Shrewsbury as well as to the castles there and at Bridgnorth. The final clearance of the last patch of primitive woodland in Lythwood did not happen until the middle of the eighteenth century. Its site is still preserved for us on the maps of the modern landscape by the place-name Old Coppice (sj 4607).

When we look down from the hills and moorlands of the Welsh Borders to the enclosed plains and valleys, we are viewing landscapes that have undergone two important phases of evolution towards the shaping of the scenes that we know today. In the plain of the middle Wye about Hereford, in the fertile basin of Brecon, as in the middle Severn valley, the skeleton plan of settlement and communication outlined through the long centuries of prehistory has been overlaid, obliterated, distorted and, above all, elaborated in the years after the Norman Conquest. The power politics of the Marcher lordships are long forgotten, but the life and work of the late medieval centuries is commemorated in the living landscape of today, in the sites and names of hamlets and lonely farms carved out of the medieval woodlands, in the intricate pattern of lanes and footpaths that has served to gather communities together, at least until this present age of the trunk road and motorway, in the sites of towns and markets, and in the innumerable patches of coppice and woodland, all that remains of the vast tracts of forest that filled much of the landscape of the marchland a thousand years ago.

Towards the end of William I's reign, the king ordered the making of the Domesday Survey. Within two years, by 1086, the factual information had been collected and collated, manor by manor, to form the first general review of the resources of the greater part of England. Domesday Book speaks of plough-teams and ploughlands, of tracts of woodland and the fisheries and water-mills of England's rivers. It counts, not with the thoroughness of later population surveys, the more important members of villages and towns, but above all it is a survey for taxation purposes placing a fiscal valuation upon the mosaic of estates and properties that the Normans took over from Saxon England. Through the clipped phrases and telegraphic sentences in medieval Latin that characterise the style of this vast factual notebook about England between 1066 and the 1080s, the modern geographer* has been able to discern, however dimly, something of the geography of those times. For instance, the Domesday folios that concern the Welsh border country reveal immediately the uncertain political state of this frontier land where the Norman aristocracy was still carving out the shape of its Marcher lordships and pressing an Anglo-Norman frontier ever westwards into a Celtic land. Herefordshire reveals the uncertainties about the shape, extent and political

---

* See H. C. Darby and I. B. Terrett, *The Domesday Geography of Midland England* (Cambridge, 1971).

control in the Marchland counties. Some places surveyed in the pages of Domesday Book now lie beyond the present border of the county in Wales. On the other hand, two tracts of Herefordshire, to the south-west across the Wye and on the fringes of the Black Mountains, were still dominantly Welsh in the eleventh century. Archenfield, occupying the broken hilly country between the Wye and Monnow, still observed Welsh laws and custom in 1086. Ewias was a newly conquered territory between the Golden Vale and the sombre frowning scarp of the Black Mountains controlled from the castles of Ewyas Harold (SO 2838) and Longtown (SO 3229). The Domesday statistics from both Ewias and Archenfield are far from complete in Domesday Book, suggesting territories that still remained beyond the full reach of the English realm.

If Domesday Book points to the uncertain nature of the political frontier between English and Welsh in the Marches, it leaves us in no doubt about the settlement pattern in the long-occupied tracts of lowland – the Hereford plain, the smiling vales between the Clee Hills and the Longmynd, and in the low country that stretches beneath the face of the Welsh hills from the Severn to the Dee estuary. When we consider the Domesday folios that cover the modern area of Shropshire, we find that 437 places are named there. Again, there are more than three hundred place-names in the Domesday Book for Herefordshire, while the entries for Cheshire that survey the Vale of Clwyd and the hill country of north-east Wales name a hundred places in what was to become the county of Flint at the end of the thirteenth century. Most of the places that have served as the cores of parishes down the succeeding centuries are there in Domesday Book, but several that must have been in existence are unaccountably missing. Presteigne (SO 3164), for instance, that was to emerge as the county town of Radnorshire, is absent from the pages of the great survey. But a settlement must have been in existence in 1086. The name in its medieval form, *Prestehemed*, means the 'the household of priests'. This tells us that there was an early church at Presteigne, probably a community of priests gathered in an enclosure, the *llan*, serving a wide tract of country after the manner of the Celtic church. The existence there of a settlement and a religious community before the Norman Conquest is also implicit in a reference to *Prestehemed* – its first occurrence in the documents – in a survey of Herefordshire made between 1160 and 1170 known as the Balliol Herefordshire Domesday.

Apart from the focal points in the pattern of rural settlement, the villages and parishes that are named in Domesday Book, many of the places are recognisable now only as hamlets or isolated farms. Some of the names tell of places that have since been erased from the map of settlements, deserted sites whose misshapen grassy mounds are the sole evidence on the ground of living communities that were extinguished in the post-Domesday centuries. A residue of Domesday names remains unidentified after all the labours of modern research. For instance, in Herefordshire some twenty-eight names are still without a certain place on the ground. Some of the lost settlements of the Domesday record give rise to intriguing speculations. *Sargeberie*, for example, seems to refer to Sawbury Hill (SO 6255) in Bredenbury while *Bageberge* (SO 5838) may describe a similar kind of site near Mordiford. The 'bury' elements in both names most probably refer to the presence of prehistoric earthworks, ramparted enclosures of the Celtic Iron Age, on the hill tops. Backbury Hill still bears the remnants of an ancient earthwork on its wooded summit above the rich red earths and hopyards of the Frome valley. Is it possible that this Domesday reference to active settlements at these hill top sites with their prehistoric earthworks means that we have here some slender proof of the continuing social and economic functions of the Iron Age camps of the Marches into the years after the Norman Conquest?

A close study of the content of Domesay Book by geographers over the past twenty-five years, involving the mapping of its incomplete and controversial data, has revealed regions of prosperity, well populated and economically developed, contrasted with poorly settled areas exposed to the raids of Welsh tribesmen, valueless as sources of tax. The richest part of Shropshire certainly lay in the Severn valley between Welshpool and the Ironbridge gorge. Here the record shows the thickest distribution of settlements and a modern analysis of the Domesday statistics calculates a population of six per square mile, reckoning only those mentioned in the eleventh-century survey – perhaps a quarter or a fifth of the real population. The plain of north Shropshire emerges as a different place in the Domesday record, as it is in its topographical and geological make-up. Northwards of Shrewsbury the rich lands of the Severn give way to a landscape of confused drainage, the remnants of extensive meres and peat-bogs, intractable glacial clays and an island-like ridge of tiny sandstone hills. North Shropshire contained only a third of the Domesday population recorded in the plain of the middle Severn, some two per square mile. Herefordshire similarly reveals a well-settled regional core. There in the eastern parts of the county, particularly in the middle Wye around Hereford and along its tributary the Frome, the density of population as recorded in the survey reaches eight per square mile. To the west and north-west, in what later became Radnorshire, the figures drop to between three and less than one per square mile.

The picture of the Marches in the eleventh century presented by Domesday Book shows a countryside prepared for the centuries of medieval development. The cores of settlement in the river plains inherited from prehistory become the cradles of the great regional capitals, Chester, Shrewsbury and Hereford. In the west, among the hills and in the extensive woodlands, lie large tracts of country that are to be opened up to colonisation in the ensuing centuries. Until long after Edward I's conquest of Wales, much of this territory was insecure, politically uncertain, sometimes under the control of Welsh princes and at other times part of a Marcher lordship. Just occasionally the Domesday record provides a vivid snapshot of this kind of territory whose taming was to be the great achievement of the medieval centuries. Of eleven manors in Radnorshire that had become the property of Osbern Fitz Richard, we read: 'on these waste lands have grown up woods in which Osbern hunts, and thence he has whatever he can take. Nothing else!' The stark language of Domesday Book suggests the wilderness that awaited reclamation, and much there was of it. For Minton beneath the Longmynd the Book says 'wasta fuit et est', 'waste it was and is'.

Objects and patterns in the English landscape reflect the changing economy and social organisation of the peoples of these islands over the centuries. Patterns of ridge and furrow imprinted in the stiff clay soils of the English Midlands recall the forgotten economy of the medieval open fields. The ordered landscapes of our great country parks remember the powerful aristocratic families of Georgian England. From the medieval centuries the hundreds of mottes and castles in the Welsh Borders recall the political disorder and social unquiet of this region. Territory among the 143 marcher states was only secured and perilously held through the building of elaborate defences and strong-points. The focus of each of the Marcher lordships was a castle, raised, as a rule, at some strategically central place. The lordship of Brecon turned towards the motte- and-bailey castle that had been established at the junction of the Usk and Honddu (SO 0428) before the end of the eleventh century. Bernard de Newmarch advanced on the ancient Welsh princedom of Brycheiniog, a political entity that had been in existence for almost a thousand years, from his base at Hereford. In his choice of Brecon as the core of the new lordship that came to replace Brycheiniog, Bernard de Newmarch followed the topographical patterns of the earlier organisation of society in the Usk valley. Brecon castle was placed not only at the most important river junction in the basin beneath the Brecon Beacons, but it lay close to the Roman roads that served to guide the path of the Norman invader into the region. Scarcely two miles to the west of Brecon at another strategic river junction of the Afon Yscir with the Usk had been established the major Roman fort of Y Gaer (SO 0029). On the hills around, even closer to the

Norman castle town, are the sites of three hill top enclosures, settlements or defensive works from the late Iron Age or the Dark Age centuries. The Norman lordship of Brecon was a repetition of earlier topographical expressions of political power in the basin of the Usk.

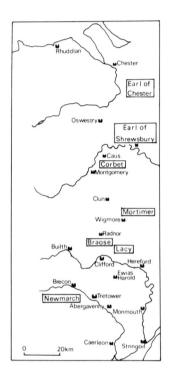

11. *Castle centres of the Marcher lordships.*

Not only the extensive territories of the most powerful among the Marcher lords – the earls of Chester, Shrewsbury and Hereford – found their focus in fortresses located in the emerging regional capitals, but the property of almost every minor landowner sought the security of a defensible motte or stone castle in those uneasy centuries before the Tudor peace. The followers of Bernard de Newmarch whose troops secured the conquest of Brycheiniog were themselves rewarded with estates in the newly won territories. For instance, the valley of the Rhian goll and a part of the Vale of Usk around Crickhowell (SO 2118) comprised one of the ancient territorial units within the Welsh kingdom of Brycheiniog. It was known as Ystrad Yw, and at some time before A.D. 1000 had been divided into two, Ystrad Yw Uchaf – the lower plain of the Rhian goll centred on Tretower – and Ystrad Yw Isaf,

118

focused on the Usk valley at Llangattock and Crickhowell. One of the followers of Bernard de Newmarch, Picard, was given Ystrad Yw Uchaf. By about 1100 he had raised the first castle at Tretower (SO 1821), a motte-and-bailey earthwork after the manner of so many castles that mark the Norman penetration of the Marchland. Over the centuries the defences of Tretower were to become much more elaborate. At some time in the second half of the twelfth century the first stone building was raised in the form of a small keep on the flat summit of the motte and a residential block composed of a hall and kitchen within the bailey. Later still, between 1230 and 1250, Tretower was extensively redesigned with the construction of the great stone tower whose walls are three yards in thickness and which rises through four stages above the original Norman mound. This final shaping of the castle at Tretower in the thirteenth century was a product of its times, an age of warfare when for a decade and a half the Marcher lordship of Brecon was returned to Welsh rule after the successful campaigns of Llywelyn ap Gruffydd.

The other part of Ystrad Yw, Ystrad Yw Isaf, was given to another of the Norman followers of Bernard de Newmarch who helped in the establishment of the Lordship of Brecon, Robert de Turberville. The main lines of the motte-and-bailey that he raised at Crickhowell in the early years of the twelfth century are still discernible. There a huge earth mound, some fifty feet in height, was placed on the edge of a river terrace that falls steeply to the flood plain of the Usk. The uneasy history of the lordship of Brecon in the thirteenth century, the time of the Welsh resurgence, illustrates the need to strengthen the chief centres of English settlement with impregnable stone castles and numerous outlying mottes that could act as strongpoints against invasion from the west. A contemporary account of the campaign of Llywelyn Fawr in the 1230s reveals the uncertainty of life on the western frontier of the medieval Marchland. 'He proceeded to Brycheiniog and destroyed all the castles and towns of the country, ravaging and despoiling every place . . . and he fought against the castle of Aberhondi [Brecon] for a month with missiles and engines and in the end desisted after reducing all the town to ashes.' At such times the power of the Marcher lord scarcely reached beyond the curtain wall that surrounded his castle bailey.

Beside the high earth mounds, the mottes, that represent the first stage in the evolution of the major marchland castles, at the cores of the lordships and their sub-territories, we come across in many parts of the borderland a much more humble kind of earthwork in the form of a simple grassy hummock, often crowned by a spindly cluster of trees. The Ordnance Survey maps recognise these primitive mottes with a label in gothic script of *tomen*, *motte* or *motte and bailey*, *castle mound* or even *tumulus*. Perhaps the most remarkable concentration of such earthworks occurs on the borders of Montgomery and Shropshire in the wide corridor to the south of Long Mountain occupied by the Camlad and the Rea Brook. The Rea-Camlad depression forms one of the critical topographical features in the history of the Welsh Borders. It was used as a major line of movement between Shrewsbury and the upper Severn. The western end of the corridor leads to one of the historic crossing places of the Severn, Rhydwhyman, close by the important site of the Roman fort of Forden Gaer (SO 2098). Rhydwhyman lay on the medieval boundary between England and Wales and it was the place where truces were signed in the years of smouldering medieval warfare. The western mouth of the Camlad-Rea depression is blocked by Offa's Dyke, the Dark Age frontier of Mercia. In the lee of the dyke, on its English side, we find a dozen sites of simple castle mounds. All but one of the castle mounds now has a farm close by or attached to it. At Brompton (SJ 2593) the motte stands on the line of Offa's Dyke behind a small farm beside the Caebitra Brook. Until recently this was a mill site and a pond fills the shallow ditch in front of the small crescent-shaped bailey. The castle mounds of Wilmington (SJ 2901) and Marton (SO 2902) face each other across the narrowest part of the corridor on the watershed between the Rea and Camlad. At Wilmington (SJ 2901) the motte overlooks a large farm, the lonely survivor, as in so many settlements of the border country, of what was once a hamlet. Marton's motte and bailey and the shape of the latter enclosure suggests an important change in the local topography at some time since the construction of the earthwork in the twelfth century. Some hundreds of yards from the earthwork across a level, muddy field we find Marton Pool. At the time of its building it seems that the castle was located on the edge of a larger pool and an extensive marsh. Drainage and reclamation have erased from the landscape a strategic feature that must have been important at the time of the building of Marton's castle.

The close network of castle mounds and their related farms is suggestive of their origin. They must belong to some phase of organised settlement in this insecure land on the dangerous western frontier of the Marches. Unfortunately no document exists that tells of their making. As with so many features of Britain's landscape, the documents that could contribute the evidence for the unravelling of their history are either lost or, as is most likely, have never existed. The first reference to the farmyard castles of the Camlad lowland appears at the time of the raising of Montgomery Castle (SO 2196) in the 1220s. The founding of the new town at Montgomery and the building of its castle are documented in some detail among the Crown records. For 30 May 1225 we find an Order of Henry III to Godescal de Maghelins who was directing affairs at Montgomery. It says: 'We command you that on our behalf you straitly charge all those who have mottes in the Vale of Montgomery, that without delay they have their mottes defended with good bretasches [wooden towers], for their own safety and defence and that of those parts.' Here is handed down to us a precise description of the purpose of these scattered mounds, and also the document provides proof that they were already in existence by the first quarter of the thirteenth century with a clear hint that they were for the security of the settlers in this troubled land. The most likely years for the raising of the mottes and the throwing up of the shallow earthworks around their tiny baileys must have been at the turn of the eleventh century, perhaps in the decade after the Domesday Survey, which makes no mention of them. The design of the earthworks points to a Norman inspiration, for the high castle mound and its enclosed courtyard seem to represent a style of military architecture that evolved in northern France in the early years of the eleventh century. Was this part of a planned settlement of the western borders of Shropshire under the Earl of Shrewsbury at a time when the neighbouring earls in the Palatinate of Chester were engaged in colonising their western flank along the Dee? Is it possible too that Roger Corbet from his great castle at Caus (SJ 3307) overlooking the plain of the Rea Brook was also collaborating with his overlord of Shrewsbury in the settlement of a class of military tenant farmers on this frontier beneath the Celtic hills?

The association of the great castles of the marchland with powerful Anglo-Norman families and the knowledge that so many sites were established about the turn of the eleventh century leads to the mistaken view that this particular feature belongs only to the Norman Conquest and the period of the creation of the Marcher lordships. The establishment of a Norman aristocracy on the soil of the Welsh border had started before William the Conqueror and his massed army made their landings in Sussex. Edward the Confessor had already introduced the Normans to the west to counter the Welsh and to offset the powerful English earls, Leofric of Mercia and Godwin of Wessex. For instance, Ralf the Count of Vexin Normand was granted the *comitatum* of Hereford before the year 1050 and it seems that the first earthworks of the castle there were in existence by 1055. Farther north, Richard le Scrob, another pioneer of the new Norman order, had built his castle of *Auretone*, as Orleton (SO 4967) appears in the Domesday Survey, before the Conquest. Today Richard le Scrob is remembered in the place-name of Richard's Castle (SO 4870) and the motte, raised in this earliest phase of castle-building, can be found in the dark green shade of a wood that climbs

17. *Richard's Castle; Richard le Scrob was given land here before the Norman Conquest; a castle was raised and early in the twelfth century a town had been founded.*
  (a) *The church of St Bartholomew, built about the time of the town's foundation.*
  (b) *A lane leads out of the former market-place of this 'failed town'.*

the hillside above the church and former market-place of the forgotten borough.

Castle-building began not only before the Norman Conquest but it continued for several centuries later as the unstable peace of the Marches demanded. For instance, the castle at Montgomery, ranged in a series of three wards along a narrow rocky spur, was not founded until the first quarter of the thirteenth century. Henry III's castle, built at the time of Welsh resurgence under Llewelyn the Great, took the place of the earlier motte and bailey of *Hen Domen* (SO 2198), known as Old Montgomery, a castle from the earliest years of the Conquest that is already mentioned in the Domesday Survey. At an even later date, in the closing years of the thirteenth century, the Edwardian campaigns in Wales gave rise to the last great epoch of castle-building. A few hundred yards downstream from the Norman motte at Rhuddlan (SJ 0277), Edward I ordered the laying out of a new castle site in the November of 1277. A few years later Henry de Lacy, Earl of Lincoln, began building one of the most dramatic castles in the British Isles on the crest of a limestone ridge at Denbigh (SJ 0565). Elsewhere, as at Builth, military works arose on the ruins of castles that had been founded two centuries earlier in the first phases of the Norman Conquest.

Although the techniques of castle-building and the basic plan of motte and bailey were originally brought from northern France, it is also evident that Welsh princes quickly adopted many ideas from the east, and it is among the hills of the Marches that we find several examples of earthworks that follow a Norman pattern. Such a site hides among the secluded hills to the west of Oswestry. The castle of Sycharth (SJ 2025), whose flat-topped mound spans almost a hundred feet, housed the court of Owain Glyndwr at the turn of the fourteenth century. A contemporary document in the form of a poem written about 1390 by Iolo Goch, the court poet to Owain Glyndwr, has preserved a rhapsodical description of the royal residence with its great hall and the buildings lying in the shelter of the bailey:

> This is its manner and appearance, in a fine
> circle of water within an embankment
> Is not the court splendid, a bridge over the moat,
> and one gateway through which a hundred loads could pass.
> There are crucks, they are the work of joining;
> each arch joined with the other.
> It is of foreign workmanship; like the bell tower
> of St Patrick, joined together pliantly like the
> cloisters of Westminster.

Iolo Goch goes on to describe the deer park that adjoined the motte-and-bailey castle at Sycharth, the fishpond 'which is necessary for casting nets where pike and fine salmon are found oftenest', an orchard and a vineyard as well as 'fair meadows of grass and hay, corn in well-tended fields'. Some of the elements in the topography of this Welsh court of the medieval centuries we can still trace in the landscape today. There are the empty grass-grown fishponds in the valley floor, and the wooded escarpment that overshadows the valley plain of the Cynllaith from the east is still known as Parc Sycharth, the place no doubt where Owain Glyndwr's deer wandered.

Sycharth was a focus of Welsh power in the Marches in the fourteenth century when the motte was occupied by a great timbered hall of cruck-frame construction and the bailey was filled with a collection of wooden buildings. But a great deal of uncertainty still surrounds its origins despite the long, if florid, contemporary poem and a recent excavation of part of the site. One view claims that the motte was raised in the early years of the Norman advance into the Marches towards the close of the eleventh century. Even today Sycharth Castle lies scarcely a mile from the English border. In the eleventh century, the valley of the Cynllaith formed the core of the commote of Cynllaith for which territory this castle acted as the strongpoint and administrative centre. Cynllaith became an early object of Norman aggression and Domesday Book shows that by 1086 it had been annexed to the fief of Oswestry by Rainald the Sheriff. A Norman castle mound may well have been raised in the first years of the advance into the hills from the Shropshire plain. By the middle of the twelfth century the resurgent Welsh kingdom of Powys had recaptured Cynllaith, and it is not unlikely that this Norman castle may have been made the centre of Welsh control until Sycharth was burnt and finally deserted in 1403. Of the latter event there is clear evidence in a letter written by Prince Henry to his father, Henry IV, in May of that year describing the campaign of the English against the forces of Owain Glyndwr. He tells of how they marched to 'Saghern, Glyndwr's principal mansion', and of how it was burnt to the ground. The excavations at Sycharth Castle in 1962 and 1963 have cast some doubt on the theory that a castle built by the Normans, perhaps under the direction of Rainald of Oswestry, was later taken over by the princes of Powys. Very little pottery was found and all of it has been dated between the late thirteenth and late fourteenth centuries. One coin alone was discovered, a silver penny of the 1350s. The total absence of finds from the eleventh and twelfth centuries chimes in with the line in Iola Goch's poem that refers to the beginnings of Sycharth. Did the Welsh rulers in Cynllaith employ foreign, probably

French, military architects in the building and design of Sycharth at some time in the thirteenth century?

If the abundance of castles and the complexities and mysteries of their building history suggests something of the uncertainties of the political life of the Marchland over more than five centuries, we find that another contribution of the Normans to the life and economy of the region, the founding of a succession of great monasteries, reflects the long, silent struggle against the wilderness, the pressing forward of the frontier of settlement through the creation of new farms, and the raising of the commercial potential of the borderland through the organisation of the wool trade. In the pre-Norman centuries monastic communities had flourished in the Marchland, but the great period for the establishment of monasteries came after the Norman Conquest. The earliest foundations, belonging to the Benedictine Order, were in existence by the beginning of the twelfth century. They include St Werburgh's at Chester, the abbey at Shrewsbury whose site and lands still form a distinctive quarter of the town, the priory at Monmouth and the community of Augustine canons at Strigoil, that ancient, romantic and long disused name of Chepstow. All of these communities served the long-settled hearts of the Marchland. They were located in places that were to emerge as important towns before the end of the twelfth century. The religious order of the Cistercians revived among its basic tenets the fundamental ideas of monasticism that the religious life could be pursued only in lonely and desolate places away from the life and works of ordinary mankind. The earliest English foundation that owed allegiance to the mother community of Citeaux was founded in 1128; the first of the great Cistercian houses in the Marchland appeared with the establishment of Tintern (SO 5300) in the deep wooded gorge of the lower Wye in 1131.

Cistercian foundations followed through the middle years of the twelfth century. Abbey Dore (SO 3830), whose patron was Robert, son of Harold of Ewyas, was established in 1147 at the mouth of the Golden Vale. The plain words of the medieval record of the monastery begin with the phrase 'in 1147 was begun the abbey of Dore'. One of the daughter houses of Citeaux, Morimond the founder of eighteen other monasteries, sent a party of white monks from France to the Golden Valley. Within thirty years the first monastic buildings had been completed. Grace Dieu, whose site is not exactly known and which is remembered by the survival of the name Parc-Grace Dieu (SO 4412) in the valley of Monmouthshire's River Trothy, was established in 1226 as a daughter community to Abbey Dore. Among the richly endowed Cistercian monasteries of the northern March we find Basingwerk Abbey (SJ 1977) in a secluded place above the marshes of the Dee

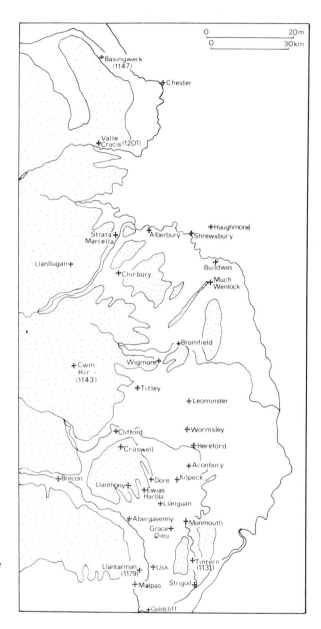

12. *Monastic centres of the border country. Dates of foundation are given when precisely known.*

Basingwerk
(1147)

Chester

Valle
Crucis (1201)

Haughmond

Strata
Marcella

Alberbury

Shrewsbury

Llanllugan

Chirbury

Buildwas

Much
Wenlock

Bromfield

Cwm
Hir
(1143)

Wigmore

Titley

Leominster

Clifford

Wormsley

Craswell

Hereford

Aconbury

Brecon

Llanthony

Dore

Kilpeck

Ewias
Harola

Llanguan

Abergavenny

Monmouth

Grace
Dieu

Llantarnam
(1179)

Usk

Tintern
(1131)

Malpas

Strigoil

Goldcliff

0   20m
0   30km

126

estuary. Apart from the magnificent remains at Tintern, Basingwerk survives as one of the most substantial fragments of monastic building in the border region of Wales. Its site, within earshot of the busy trunk road and main-line railway into north Wales, conveys little of the original remoteness and seclusion that must have belonged here eight centuries ago. A mill chimney, as derelict as the monastery now, protrudes above the trees and the floor of the adjacent valley is filled with abandoned mill-ponds fed by the healing waters of the springs of Holywell.

The Marcher lords were not the only ones who planted the Cistercians in their territories; Welsh princes too encouraged the settlement of the white monks. The earliest of the Welsh Cistercian houses and mother to several later foundations was made in Whitland, in the far west of Carmarthenshire, in 1140. Three years later followed the establishment of Cwm Hir (SO 0571) among the remote hills that lie between the upper Severn and Wye, on the western fringe of Radnorshire. In 1170 the ruler of Powys, Owain Cyfeiliog, invited the Cistercians to build a monastery in the Severn valley where the river widens into the Shropshire plain beneath the precipitous flank of the Breidden. The buildings of Abbey Marcella have vanished completely and nothing now remains in the landscape to locate what must have been one of the greatest monasteries of the marchland. After the Reformation and Henry VIII's destruction of the monasteries, the scattered early industrial settlement of Pool Quay grew up on the site of Abbey Marcella (SJ 2510). The charcoal iron industry there was developed by Roman Catholic recusants who seem to have continued the industrial traditions of Strata Marcella. Nearby at Severn weir, very close to the assumed site of the abbey, was the greatest water-power source in the whole of southern Britain, and among the wooded hills of the upper Severn lay a rich source of charcoal. Both resources, water-power and charcoal, were most likely marshalled in the late medieval centuries by the monks of Abbey Marcella. Madoc ap Gruffydd endowed another Cistercian house in the Vale of Llangollen at the opening of the thirteenth century. Valle Crucis (SJ 2044) was established there by pioneering monks from Strata Marcella. Even today, when the week-end day trippers in cars and coaches form an endless snake of traffic over the Horse Shoe Pass, one can still recapture much of the original feeling of Valle Crucis. There still stands a substantial building where the short Eglwyseg river tumbles through the woods towards the Dee. Behind the ruin a pool shaded by tall trees is the fishpond that fed the monastery. This deep valley completely encircled by slate mountains and heather-purple moors is closed to the north-east by the precipitous white wall of the Eglwyseg Mountain. What better place could those unknown and forgotten planners of Cistercian fortunes have chosen than this remote basin among the hills of eastern Wales, at one remove only from paradise if one's first intentions were set on prayer and the rearing of sheep.

In one sense the monasteries were rich corporations exploiting the resources of the countryside with much greater effectiveness than the manorial peasant. At the time of the dissolution of the monasteries, Tintern was the wealthiest in the Welsh Marches. Its properties comprised a dozen

18. *Valle Crucis, a Cistercian monastery established by a Welsh prince early in the thirteenth century in a secluded tributary valley of the Dee at Llangollen.*

estates, several of which are still recognisable by the survival of the place-name element 'grange' in their title. On the rolling plateau westward of the deep trench of the Wye we find Rogerstone Grange (SJ 5096) and Trellech Grange (SO 4901). The scattering of grange farms in the country north of Chepstow made the abbey one of the greatest landowners in this region. The records of Tintern Abbey, incomplete as they now are, cast a light into the darkness of medieval social and economic history that shows up, in detail, the secular activities of a religious community. For instance, we are told that Rogerstone Grange was received as a gift from William Marshal the Younger so that a lamp might burn perpetually in the abbey at the tomb of his mother, Countess Isabel of Pembroke. William Marshal's grant also confirmed in 1224 some of the other important resources of the abbey when it specified the gift of 'all things needful for the abbey, and the grange of Trellech, and stone for building and other needs in the forest of Wyeswood, as they have had hitherto'. Some of Tintern's granges lay much farther afield. In the Usk valley they owned a grange at Monkswood (ST 3402), and southward, within sight of the wide Severn estuary, there were estates at Merthyrgeryn and Moor, now known as Upper and Lower Grange. Upper Grange (ST 4288) lay on the edge of the foothills near Magor; Lower Grange (ST 4285) stands enmeshed by the channels and drainage ditches of the Caldicot Level, a former coastal marsh whose reclamation owes much to the work of the Cistercians.

The estates of Abbey Dore were even more extensive than those of Tintern. Their properties included seventeen granges, of which nine were in the Golden Valley. It is evident that this fertile corridor, isolated from the Wye valley by a broken wooded sandstone ridge and screened to the west by the lowering plateau of the Black Mountains, owes the sketch-plan of its present rural settlement to the pioneering activities of the Cistercians in the twelfth and thirteenth centuries. Some of the granges of the Golden Vale are hard to recognise today, but they include Morehampton Park Farm (SO 3734), a moated site close beside the river Dore, New Grange (SO 3834), Blakemore Grange (now Blackmoor Farm, SO 3934), Whitewall Grange (SO 3435), Hollings Grange (SO 3631) and Bacton Grange (SO 3632). Another group of farms belonging to Abbey Dore was engaged in pioneer development in the gentle hilly countryside of north Monmouthshire, a land of many brooks and quiet secluded valleys leading towards the Monnow and the Trothy. Here was Llyncoed Grange (SO 3622), known as Great Compston and Cold (SO 3822), a name perfectly descriptive of a new farm hacked out of the circle of woodland above Grosmont. At Llanfair Grange (SO 3919), in the same part of Monmouthshire, the remains of a chapel suggest the medieval links with the monastery at Abbey Dore. Even farther from the parent abbey lay the outlying estates in Breconshire, huge sheep farms in the western tributaries of the Wye that drain the flanks of Mynydd Eppynt. One of these distant granges, Gwenddwr (SO 0643), still forms the only core of settlement in a deep valley whose slopes climb steeply to the open moorland of Waun Hirwaun where the valuable harvests of wool were taken by Abbey Dore. A famous account of the medieval wool trade, *La Pratica della Mercatura*, reveals that wool from Abbey Dore commanded the highest price among all the English fleeces. Another source, the *Taxatio Ecclesiastica* of 1291,

129

suggests something of the importance of wool production to this monastery with its record of flocks of almost three thousand sheep.

The surviving monastic records show that the establishment of the monastic farms involved considerable woodland clearance. When Walter de Clifford granted lands at Gwenddwr to the monks of Abbey Dore, it is on record that they were allowed 'to till, assart, enclose and deal with at their pleasure'.

19. *Tintern Abbey, the earliest of the great Cistercian monasteries of the Welsh Marches, founded in 1131 in the deep wooded gorge of the lower Wye.*

The cartulary of Tintern Abbey contains many references to the clearing of woodland as well as hinting at the uses for which timber was required. For instance, in 1411 there is mention of payments made for the felling of timber. Robert Smyth, we are told, 'received 8d for wood-felling and his servant, William, 6/3d for making wheels and other things'. Tintern's constant demand for wood was for building, the making of fences, fuel and the production of charcoal, as well as more specialised tasks such as the building of weirs across the Wye. Over the five centuries between the Norman Conquest and the Tudor dissolution of the monasteries extensive clearings had appeared in the forest wilderness. By the first decades of the fourteenth century the monks of Tintern had created a new settlement on their manor of

Plataland. It lay in the belt of medieval woodland that stretched from Chepstow across Wentwood to the valley of the Usk. Today we know it as Newchurch (ST 4597), a name that hints at a history of deliberate forest clearance in the Middle Ages with the creation of a new parish.

The *Annales Dorenses* contain some of the most specific references to woodland clearance by the Abbey of Dore, references that allow us to see the advance of the frontier of farming into the wilderness. In 1216, for instance, King John handed over to the monks *Trivel Wood* with permission to *assart*, that is to make clearances. We can still explore this particular piece of the Herefordshire countryside and reflect on the succession of landscape changes that followed the granting of rights of development to Abbey Dore; until that date Trivel had been preserved for the huntsman under the forest laws. Now we know this former deer forest as Treville (SO 4232), lying to the north of Kilpeck and St Devereux beyond the Hereford–Abergavenny road. Treville contains a country house and it is even now extensively wooded. Big Wood (SO 4132) straddles the ridge that separates Treville from the Grey Valley and the outlying grange farms of Abbey Dore to the south-west. Here one suspects woodland has always existed, woodland that has evolved through many stages from the raw wilderness haunted by the red deer to the managed plantation that we see today. One suspects that Abbey Dore's assarts in Trivel were made on the lower ground where the country house and its enveloping park now lie. One more reference in the medieval record hints at the location of the monastic improvements. In 1216 King John allowed the monks to enlarge and raise a mill-pond in Trivel Wood. Was this perhaps the forerunner of the ornamental lake that fills the floor of the shallow valley on the edge of Whitfield Park (SO 4233)?

From many parts of the border country there is evidence of the role played by the monasteries in woodland clearance. Shrewsbury Abbey was active in the fourteenth century in the development of Lythwood, a medieval forest that lay to the south of the county town. In 1346 Lythwood was granted to the abbey and the first extensive clearances soon followed. By 1365 there is a report of complaints about the extensive decimation of the woodland. It was alleged that half the wood had been devastated and that 'divers men had been given licence to make assarts there'. The work of the monasteries in creating new farms out of the woodland wild was not universally applauded in medieval society. Even a churchman, Giraldus Cambrensis, Archdeacon of St David's, had some harsh things to say about the economic activities of the monasteries when he wrote about his tour of Wales in the closing years of the twelfth century. He accused the monks of 'changing an oakwood into a wheat field'. Giraldus believed that Abbey Dore's explanation of the clearance of a tract of woodland because it was 'wild and rough and offered secure refuge to the Welshmen and robbers' was nothing more than a lame excuse. And the medieval topographer from St David's, writing our earliest description of Wales, quotes a contemporary proverb about the Cistercians: 'they are bad neighbours, just like the white monks'. It seems that economic change and its impact on the landscape has been able to arouse a conservationist opposition centuries before our own age of the industrial estate, the motorway and large-scale exploitation of oil wells beneath the North Sea.

The castle ruins and roofless monasteries of the Welsh borderland remind us of the alien elements in the medieval society of the region. But the landscape also contains reminders of the work and lives of other classes in society beside the Marcher lords and the abbots of great monastic houses engaged in the organisation of the wool trade with the distant textile centres of Flanders and northern Italy. Timbered, black and white farmhouses in the hidden lowlands among the Montgomeryshire hills tell of a rural middle class that began to emerge towards the end of the fifteenth century. Ancient, half-forgotten lanes that lead one to the airy summit plateaus of the Longmynd and Black Mountains recall the lost custom of driving cattle and sheep to the summer pastures in the month of May. Again, patchworks of tiny fields and a disorderly scatter of cottages record the squatters of the seventeenth and eighteenth centuries.

Early in the twentieth century the researches of economic historians into the rural management of medieval England had established a model of the manor and its landscape in which the lord and his villeins lived in a compact village dominated by the manor house and church, working the strips of three great open fields that encircled the settlement. In recent years local research in many parts of England has elaborated and corrected this picture of a rigid, unchanging medieval society bound to the rules of a three-field system. From all over the Welsh borderland we have evidence of a varied and evolving society through the medieval centuries. New settlements come into existence long before the end of the Middle Ages, especially in tracts of active woodland clearance. Of late, the sites of deserted villages have come to light in Herefordshire and Shropshire, and there is abundant proof that many hamlets have degenerated, particularly between 1500 and 1800, into single isolated farms. Field patterns and structures too are far more complex than the early elementary models ever allowed. New open fields were often added to settlements in the course of the Middle Ages. It is not unusual to find villages and hamlets that were once surrounded by half a dozen or more open fields. On the western fringe of the Marchland, in the hill country of central

Wales, there is abundant proof in the meaning of place-names of the transformation of temporary summer farms on the edge of the high pastures into
permanent residences.

Shropshire's medieval records contain many hints of the quiet creation of
fresh farms and hamlets in the centuries after the Norman Conquest. In
1334, for instance, at a time when a newly founded market town was in the
course of development at Ruyton (SJ 3922), we find a reference to the 'new
vill of Acton near Ruyton'. Most likely this new settlement, carved out of the
woodland, was Shotatton (SJ 3622), a tiny hamlet on the western fringe of
the parish. The medieval history of Condover provides several examples of
the making of new farms and hamlets. As we have already seen, to the south
of the Cound Brook there lay an ancient tract of woodland that was slowly
cleared through the late medieval centuries. Between 1377 and 1500 the
court rolls record sixty-two licences to hold assarts in severalty. This means
that clearances from waste and woodland, mainly in Buriwood, had been
made and that these nameless pioneers of the local wilderness had then been
given permission to farm the new land as they wished – the rules that applied
to the ownership and working of the land in the open fields around the old
nuclear settlement of Condover did not apply to the new clearances.
Wheathall (SJ 4903) and Berrywood Farm (SJ 5004) are descendants of
settlements made in the medieval clearances. Wheathall seems to have come
into existence in the late twelfth or early thirteenth century; it is first
mentioned in the records in 1209. The documents of the fifteenth century
suggest that the settlement comprised eight farmsteads around a green that
was itself hemmed in on three sides by woodland. Wheathall, like many
hundreds of places in the marchland, has shrunk since the eighteenth century. Today, and ever since the 1840s, it has consisted of only two farmhouses.

Medieval colonisation took place not only at the expense of the primitive
woodlands, the hunting preserves, in the lowlands, but was also active in the
wilder and less fertile uplands. Through the records of the *Survey of Oswestry*
made in 1577 it is possible to trace in some detail the making of a new
township in the hill country that rises suddenly to the west of the borough.
Here two rivers, the Morda and the Cynllaith, flow close together in deeply
entrenched valleys. On the hilly plateau separating the valleys that reaches to
more than a thousand feet above sea level a scattered settlement of upland
farms, Cynynion (SJ 2430), was carved out of the waste. No date is firmly
known for this colonisation of a tract of upland common, but the *Survey of
Oswestry* makes it clear that the new township of Cynynion was in being by
the latter half of the sixteenth century. The Survey tells how the settlers won

the possession of their new lands after they had been released from servile duties to cart stone and lime for the upkeep of the castle and the wall at Oswestry.

> Kyninion is the Lords and at the beginning was enclosed out of the commons, The Lord did enter; whereupon the tenants were contented to carry stone and lime to mayntayne the castle and walls of the town and there upon they had freedom in towne and the Lord gave them the said land.

Another reference to Cynynion a few years later, in 1585, shows that there were seven farms there and also that the working of the land had been organised through a system of two open fields. One farmer, according to the 1585 account, had twenty-four parcels of open-field land and meadow to his name. The farms of Cynynion were scattered and one of the common fields bore the name Town Field, a name that frequently provides a clue to the presence of former open-field farming when almost all other evidence has disappeared. The other field has almost entirely Welsh names for its different elements and the appearance of the term *quillet*, an arable strip, among its names leaves incontrovertible proof of a former open-field economy at Cynynion.

The history of the making of the township of Cynynion is an example of the provocative and often startling evidence that can be thrown up by the researches of the local historian. Here is a community in the process of colonising a patch of sterile commonland, probably about the turn of the fifteenth century, but they adopt a social organisation and system of land-use in two open fields with shared and intermixed strips of arable and meadow – a pattern for the taming of new land that would seem utterly anachronistic by the beginning of the Tudor period. Moreover, the names in the southern field, as recorded in the document of 1585, suggest that a goodly number of the pioneer farmers at Cynynion were Welshmen. One cannot resist the conclusion that this little community comprised two clear social elements, one Welsh and the other English, and that each group managed one of the common fields.

An important line of research that has changed our view of medieval landscape history of recent years has been the discovery of hundreds of deserted village sites in lowland England. In Yorkshire, Leicestershire, Lincolnshire and Warwickshire the abundance of deserted settlements has shown that the medieval settlement patterns were anything but stable and unchanging. But until lately it was believed that the great economic and social upheavals that led to desertions in the Midlands had scarcely touched the Marchland to the west – a region where the long established pattern of settlement involved innumerable isolated farms, scattered hamlets and somewhat rare clusterings in villages. Of late years, the discovery of a number of deserted villages and hamlets and the realisation that perhaps hundreds of isolated farms occupy places where hamlets flourished scarcely more than two centuries ago has shown that change was also an important element in the shaping of the landscape of the medieval marchland.

In the late 1960s S. C. Stanford, an archaeologist who has enunciated so many original ideas upon the Iron Age forts of the borderland, communicated the results of two excavations at deserted settlements in Herefordshire and Shropshire. The Shropshire site, near Detton Hall (SO 6679) in the parish of Neen Savage, belongs to the rich, broken countryside to the east of the Clee Hills. It is a district of remote, scattered hamlets, lonely farmsteads at the end of deep lanes and quiet brooks that once powered a long-vanished iron industry. Detton Hall, a stone farmhouse of the early seventeenth century, is one of the many survivals of the great age of rebuilding in the Midland countryside. Nearby, in Chapel Meadow, we find the evidence of a former settlement with deep holloways and earthworks that suggest the foundations of simple buildings. The line of a main street runs from east to west with the foundations of dwellings on either side, each in its own rectangular shaped croft. Parallel to the street and running behind the crofts is the impression of a characteristic back lane. At the west end was the site of a manor farm and, as the field-name still implies, there was a chapel at Detton, traces of which survived into the nineteenth century. Pottery from Dr Stanford's excavation revealed a time-span from the early twelfth to the second half of the thirteenth century. At its best this was a tiny settlement, perhaps with a population of no more than fifty, but it seems likely that there were many such hamlets among the valleys of the eastern Marchland.

Dr Stanford's excavation at a deserted settlement on the edge of the Dittonian sandstone upland of north-east Herefordshire suggested a longer and somewhat more complex history than that of the Shropshire hamlet. Hampton Wafer (SO 5757) appears in Domesday Book as a manor held by Roger de Lacy. In this Herefordshire countryside of steep slopes and deep valleys, settlements are attracted to the ridge-tops and spurs. Here the dominant feature is three holloways, and there is evidence that a considerable part of the site was covered by buildings. The limited excavations at Hampton Wafer showed that one of the buildings had gone through a complex structural history of five phases of rebuilding, first in timber and later in stone. The pottery from Hampton Wafer showed that a village was established there shortly before the Norman Conquest and that its full development was reached in the twelfth century. Domesday Book, at a

135

slightly earlier date, provides documentary proof of a flourishing settlement. Its value at the time of King Edward the Confessor was 40/- and by 1086 Hampton Wafer was assessed at 30/- and 'there was one plough in demesne'. Not all trace of farming with the plough, some thousand years ago, has completely disappeared from the present landscape for the field pattern of earthworks and three holloways gives way to the characteristic broad ribs of medieval ridge-and-furrow. Hampton Wafer became extinct at some time in the fourteenth century. The last evidence of pottery there dates to about 1330 and the final reference to a chapel in the Registers of the Bishop of Hereford comes in 1378. The reason for the desertion of Hampton Wafer remains completely obscure. It certainly happened in the century of the Black Death, but there is nothing to associate this depopulation with the plague. In fact, the last ceramic date would place the decline almost two decades earlier than the striking of the Black Death. S. C. Stanford* has argued that the ill-fortune of Hampton Wafer must be related to the interests and policies of the manorial lord. In 1330 the manor passed from the de Mortimers to the Fitz Allens, who turned their energies to the development of their properties in the Lugg valley at Hampton Court (SO 5252). It is not impossible, although a fanciful suggestion, that the population of the tiny isolated hill settlement was transferred to the sheltered, richer lands of the Lugg.

Many other places in the marchland pose the kind of problems suggested by the recent investigations of obscure earthworks and faint markings in the fields of Shropshire and Herefordshire. Along with the publication of his findings at Hampton Wafer, Stanford printed a list of twenty-one places in different parts of Herefordshire where the evidence of earthworks in the present landscape points to the decay and dissolution of former villages and hamlets. For instance, he notes the extensive low earthworks to the north of the church at Kilpeck (SO 4430); and at Much Dewchurch (SO 4831) fields contain hints of extensive settlement to the east of the castle mound, at least a quarter of a mile from the present village. Stanford has been led to the view that the settlement patterns of Herefordshire have been far from stable and he concluded that 'the disruption of many Herefordshire hamlets and villages occurred between Domesday and the fifteenth century'. These plain words challenge views about the history of settlement in the border country that have long been held. Since settlement studies took on a scientific form at the close of the nineteenth century, the belief has been that the primary pattern in much of western upland Britain, and this includes the Welsh Marches, was one of scattered, isolated farms and tiny hamlets. Nucleated

---

*S. C. Stanford, 'The deserted medieval village of Hampton Wafer, Herefordshire', *Trans. Woolhope Nat. Field Club*, 39 (1965).

villages were rare and the lonely parish church, devoid of any other buildings except perhaps a manor farm, seemed to typify these parts of Britain. The earliest thinking on the subject associated the dispersed patterns of settlement with Celtic peoples and their pastoral ways of life. Although ethnic theories of settlement origins were to fall into disfavour, the great antiquity of the patterns that man has inscribed on the border landscape has never been in doubt. The organisation of the economy and social life of the borders in small and isolated units seemed to date back at least to the Dark Ages and even perhaps to the later epochs of prehistory. Now it is becoming evident that an important reshaping of the man-made elements of the border countryside took place in the centuries after the Norman Conquest.

If the Middle Ages were the time of radical changes in the landscape through colonisation, woodland clearance and the extinction of scores of smaller settlements, so they saw the beginning of revolutionary transformations of the rural economy. Perhaps the most striking of the ancient ways of rural life, and also the most romantic as we look back into the past, was the migration of flocks and herds as well as the temporary removal of households to the high summer pastures from the beginning of May until the end of September. The conversion of the summer pastures to permanent farms was already taking place before the end of the Middle Ages, and the process gathered momentum in the sixteenth and seventeenth centuries. By 1800 the practice of transhumance, the grazing and settlement of the high upland pastures through the summer months, was all but extinct. It seems strange that little is now known about the nomadic pastoral ways of life in the hills of the borderland when they must have formed an essential part of the economy and society of so many communities for an untold length of time. The origins of this nomadic pastoralism go back into the depths of prehistory. The movement from lowland to upland pastures for three or five summer months depended on the simple climatic facts of the environment. The Black Mountains and Brecon Beacons, the heights of the Berwyn and the summit plateau of Radnor Forest all reach levels where the winter climate is both severe and long-lasting. Particularly in the frequent cold springs of Atlantic Britain, temperatures in the uplands are slow to reach the figures necessary for plant growth. There, all is concentrated into the three months of the long hours of summer daylight. Lately, it has been argued that the organised migration of man and his domesticated animals to the upland pastures may have started more than five thousnd years ago. Neolithic farmers were perhaps first led into the uplands along the trails followed by wild animals to their natural summer grazing grounds in the high country. As D. P. Webley has written in an important article on prehistoric farming in

137

the southern Marches, 'if Neolithic peoples are allowed astro-mathematical abilities, it is not too much to assume an awareness of the biology of the world around them'.*

If the beginnings of transhumance in the marchland hills seem to be lost in prehistory, it is surprising that so little survives from contemporary records of this way of life and of the location of the summer settlements. The most detailed literary record, and one much quoted, appears in Pennant's description of Llanberis towards the end of the eighteenth century. By then the old ways to the hill pastures had become largely abandoned and Snowdonia was the last refuge of a way of life that had been rapidly forgotten. As the Welsh topographer wrote,

> this mountainous tract scarcely yields any corn. Its produce is cattle and sheep, which, during summer, keep very high in the mountains, followed by their owners, with their families, who reside in that season in *hafodtai*, as the farmers of the Swiss Alps do in their *sennes*. These houses consist of a long low room, with a hole at one end, to let out the smoke from the fire, which is made beneath. Their furniture is very simple: stones are the substitute of stools; and the beds are of hay, ranged along the sides. . . . During the summer the men pass their time either in harvest work, or in tending their herds: the women in milking, or making butter and cheese. . . . Towards winter they descend to the *hendref*, or old dwelling, where they lead, during that season, a vacant life.

Pennant's description of farming in Llanberis with its two dwellings, the old farm or *hendref*, and the temporary upland home of the high summer months, the *hafod*, provides the chief clue whereby one can now recognise the former extent of transhumance in the Marches. Medieval documents and the literary record are practically silent about this part of the ancient economy, but the abundance of *hafod* elements in the countryside suggests the true extent and great economic importance of the former summer pastures. Another name, *lluest*, was also used to describe the summer farm. Today it is particularly found among the place-name elements of central Wales. Where the journey from the *hendref* or *hendre*, the winter home, covered several miles and a considerable range of altitude, a temporary resting-place was established to provide a period of pasturing before the completion of the migration to the higher pastures. It was known as the *meifod*, the May house – a name that we still find in the little former market town of the Vyrnwy valley that was perhaps the Dark Age residence and capital of the princes of Powys. The *hafod* element is especially common

*D. P. Webley, 'How the West was won: prehistoric land-use in the southern Marches', in A. C. Boon and J. M. Lewis (eds), *Welsh Antiquity* (Cardiff, 1976).

among the place-names of the sombre moorland plateaus that enclose the valley of the upper Severn and its tributaries above Newtown. High on the steep slopes above Carno in the headstreams that feed the Afon Garno we find a farm with the simple name of Hafod (SN 9495), lying beneath the rim of the extensive moorland pastures. Again, if one follows the steep lane that climbs northward out of Trefeglwys to the same moorland tract of the Waungarno one passes first through a scattered, untidy squatter settlement of the eighteenth century – small, inadequate farms in a patchwork of misshapen fields that were quietly and illegally carved out of the common pastures. The last farmstead along this lane, before the track peters out into a path across the high spur of open moorland, is called Hafod (SN 9793). This house, in a hollow some distance below the headsprings of the Colwyn Brook, was the site of a temporary summer farm that was transformed into a permanent residence with the great advance of the frontier of farming that began before the end of the Middle Ages.

If the documentary evidence about the life and economy at the summer pastures remains scanty, the same may be said of the objects that survive in the landscape from the centuries of transhumance. Where the *hafod* was converted into a permanent farm, nothing remains of the original primitive

20. *The valley of the Afon Cownwy. Among the hills of western Montgomeryshire an abandoned farmhouse represents a cycle of evolution from medieval* hafod *to permanent occupation in the nineteenth century, to dereliction in our own times.*

139

buildings that were used by the summer migrants. At higher and bleaker sites, such as the north-facing spurs of the Brecon Beacons or in the remote valleys of western Montgomeryshire, low grassy mounds and the simple foundations of rectangular houses buried in heather indicate *hafotai* that were abandoned as the common pastures fell out of use. One such summer settlement was investigated on the face of the Brecon Beacons in the 1960s. Two summer houses occupied a natural platform that breaks the long northern spur, Cefn Cwm-llwch (SO 0123), extending from the highest summit of the Brecon Beacons. Each *hafod* was surrounded by a number of fallen flagstones that once formed pens for sheep and cattle. The simple rectangular outlines of the houses were marked by broken foundation walls, scarcely more than a foot in height and composed largely of rubble. C. B. Crampton,* who investigated this summer settlement, was able to find little documentary evidence that could throw light on its history. The tithe maps of the 1830s, such a valuable source of information on forgotten elements of the countryside, show no summer farms in the Brecon Beacons. By that time they must have been abandoned and forgotten. The only literary reference to the *hafotai* of the Brecon Beacons comes from a local scholar of the sixteenth century, Sion Dafydd Rhys, who mentions a summer farm in the recesses of Cwm-Llwch as 'under the trees at the foot of Pen y Fan'. It is evident that the summer trek to the high pastures was still part of the way of life in the Usk valley in the sixteenth century.

The three centuries that followed the political union of England and Wales were a time of immense change in the countryside. As we have seen, an archaic way of life with its roots in the dark past of prehistory vanished with the abandonment of the summer pastures. Today we can only sense this aspect of the marchland economy in the flotsam of place-names on the modern map or by following the ancient roads that led to the common pastures, lanes known as *outracks* that take one up into the Clee Hills or by steep twisting spurs to the space and silence of the Longmynd plateau. Many forces, both social and economic, were active in the disintegration of the medieval way of life. The expansion of sheep-rearing after the seventeenth century, itself following on the growth of the wool trade, gradually took the place of cattle-raising on the high pastures. Sheep did not demand the daily attention of cattle for milking and the tasks of the dairy; one man could look after the flock on a mountain range. The hunger for land that accompanied a steadily rising population in the eighteenth century was reflected in the quiet enclosure of patches of common by squatters. But this was only a quickening

*C. B. Crampton, 'Hafotai platforms on the north front of the Brecon Beacons', *Archaeologia Cambrensis*, 115 (1966).

of a process that had been going on quietly and unrecorded since the late medieval centuries. Many of the upland farms of Montgomeryshire with their small, irregular-shaped fields and high earth banks had been carved out of the common lands before the end of the Middle Ages. But perhaps the most striking changes in the rural economy and on the face of the landscape were to result from the social and legal changes that followed the Act of Union in 1536. Most important was the abolition of the ancient Welsh laws of inheritance. The complex rights of all the offspring were replaced by the law of primogeniture that allowed an estate to pass intact to the eldest son. Again, the Tudor period brought an expansion of trade, a greater use of money in society, and also a belief that the only secure wealth lay in the possession of land. In a word, estate-building was to have an immense influence on the very appearance of the landscape by the end of the eighteenth century.

Estate-building, the accumulation by individuals of property in land, was a potent force in the disappearance of the common open fields that were part of so many marchland settlements. In turn this process caused the extinction of scores of hamlets, tiny communities of up to half a dozen farmsteads that were replaced by single isolated farms. The rich countryside around Shrewsbury abounds in lost hamlets that had given way to single farms at the close of the eighteenth century. The local history of the large parish of Pontesbury (SJ 4005) contains several examples of shrunken settlements and the accompanying consolidation of estates. In the east of the parish we find a cluster of settlements that suffered in this way. Arscott (SJ 4307) was a considerable village in 1308 when twenty-one tenants are recorded there. By the opening of the seventeenth century the settlement had been reduced to a hamlet of six farms. Between 1777 and 1822 the estate-building activities of the Harries family bought out the remaining farmers and by 1840 the hamlet of Arscott had been reduced to its present shape of two farmhouses, Arscott House and Arscott Hall, a large brick building dating from the late eighteenth century. Scarcely a mile from Arscott Hall is Sibberscote Manor, a sixteenth-century timber-framed house on the lands of a medieval hamlet. Sibberscote remained stable through the Middle Ages; the records show that four tenants held land from the thirteenth until the beginning of the seventeenth century. The shrinkage to one manor house took place in the seventeenth century.

The same story of the extinction of clusters of farmers who shared the resources of the common fields around their hamlets applies to the history of the parts of Pontesbury lying to the north of the Rea Brook. There, out of twelve nucleated settlements that existed in the Middle Ages, only one, Asterley (SJ 3707), survives as a village of moderate size. For the rest,

Malehurst (SJ 3806), Newnham (SJ 4109) and Polmere (SJ 4109) have shrunk to single farms and seven other settlements contain only two or three houses. This fragment of the Shropshire landscape shows that changes in settlement patterns have been going on ever since the Norman Conquest. The ambitious estate builders of the Stuart and Hanoverian decades are part of a centuries-long process that also includes the desertion of villages and hamlets in medieval times.

The long-settled tracts of the Welsh Marches, in particular the lowlands that encompass the regional capitals, were undergoing a marked modification of their settlement patterns and a depopulation of their hamlets between late Tudor and Georgian times. Over the same period, population in general was on the increase and one might ask how the displaced and increasing numbers were accommodated. Of the rising numbers of people, local evidence leaves us in no doubt. Church Pulverbatch had a population of 260 in 1676, and by 1801, the time of the first census, 439 inhabitants were recorded. Compensation for the development of larger and more efficient farms and private parks was found in the growth of squatter settlements on the edges of the dwindling commons. To return to the huge Shropshire parish of Pontesbury, we find that while the hamlets and holdings of small tenant farmers were being extinguished on the rich terraces of the Rea Brook, new squatter settlements were coming into existence in other parts of the township. Squatters were taking in land at Ford Heath (SJ 4011) on the northern boundary of the parish from the early years of the seventeenth century. Nox (SJ 4110) was one such pioneer development, named after the owner of an alehouse, built there by Richard Nock about 1650. The two hills that loom over the parish church and mother village from the south, Pontesford Hill (SJ 4005) and Pontesbury Hill (SJ 3905), were the scene of squatters in the seventeenth and eighteenth centuries. The first mention of a cottage on Pontesbury Hill comes in 1615. The manor court rolls in subsequent decades tell of the problems of illegal settlement there when a number of persons was fined, late in the seventeenth century, for 'inhabiting cottages on Pontesbury waste'. By 1810 there were twenty-six cottages on Pontesbury Hill and by 1842 the number of squatting families had risen to about a hundred. The rapid growth of this settlement in the early years of the nineteenth century was related to lead mining in the surrounding hills. The vestry minutes of Pontesbury throw some light on the character of the squatter village. In 1836 there is a reference to 'huts wherein several men, women and children are all living together in one room whereby the morals of many children are corrupted and vice and immorality encouraged to a great extent'.

The squatter hamlets and villages of this period are recognisable by their disorderly patterns. Pontesbury Hill's history shows that they went through marked stages of development. The first cottages were huts built of turf. They suggest the rootless character of their owners, the anxiety to find a place of shelter. By the 1850s all the huts had been replaced by single-storey stone cottages. A community had shaped itself at Pontesbury Hill based on long and dangerous hours of work in the mines and at the lead smelters of the White Grit Company in Pontesford, Malehurst and Pontesbury. This mining community too was distinguished by its religious allegiances; it was solidly nonconformist. Since the end of the last century and after the collapse of lead mining in the hills about Snailbeach, Pontesbury Hill has experienced a steady fall in population. Cottages have been left empty and today few of the buildings that were there a century and a half ago remain standing.

The forms of the Marchland countryside – the arrangement and layout of fields, the size and shapes of settlements, reflect the organisation of society in past centuries. One of the most detailed records of social change that we can find in the landscape is that preserved for us in cottages, farmhouses and the mansions of the gentry and landed aristocracy. They reflect the changing taste and fashions as well as the distribution and accumulation of wealth in the Marches since the Middle Ages.

When the scientific study of vernacular architecture, of the buildings of the common people, began early in this century, it was soon recognised that the long house is one of the oldest types of farm-building. In the medieval long house the dwelling quarters of the farm and the byre were all accommodated under one roof. As a rule, a cross passage from one long wall of the house to the other separated the living quarter from the cattle. The origins of the long house as a design for living and working the land are very obscure. Peate in his pioneer study, *The Welsh House*, believed that this was 'an ancient form rooted in Welsh medieval history'. It is not unlikely that this earliest of farmhouse types first evolved in prehistoric times.

The problems associated with the unravelling of the origins of the long house were highlighted in the 1960s with the excavation of an Iron Age hill-fort at Coed-y-Bwynydd (SO 3606), a multiple ramparted structure on a wooded sput above the Usk. The use of a soil detector had suggested the presence of a rectangular-shaped feature within the interior of the fort and excavation showed the foundations of a long house, probably of medieval date. Also no Iron Age material was found in this excavation of Coed-y-Bwynydd. The neat time-scales of our textbooks appear to be disrupted by this hill-fort above the Usk – one of so many sites that await investigation in the Marches. Its history suggests that a recognised style of Iron-Age

143

earthwork was being thrown up in the early Middle Ages, while at the same time it seems to contain the relics of an early long house. Two disparate periods of history are brought together at one site with a strong hint that the word 'continuity' provides a valuable clue to the evolutionary pattern of the Marches.

The long house remained the basic model in the layout of rural building until the end of the Middle Ages and many examples, modified in the great age of reconstruction of the seventeenth century, have survived until the present day. They are particularly abundant among the farms of the western uplands of the Marches. One reliable clue in the recognition of an original long house, despite subsequent modifications, is an alignment down-slope. The upper end with the dwelling quarter may be built into a hollow hewn out of the hillside; at the lower end the byre was located. One of the earliest houses of north Breconshire, at Llanwrthwl (SN 9763), illustrates these features. Here Llanerch-y-cawr is aligned down a steep rocky hillside. The house probably dates from the fifteenth century, but the timber-framed walls were rebuilt in stone at about the middle of the seventeenth century. Two of the cruck roof-trusses from the medieval house still survive within the stone rebuilding and the long slabs of the seventeenth-century reconstruction contrast with the megalithic foundations and footings that remain from the earlier house.

The decades of social and economic change that began at the turn of the sixteenth century are reflected in the buildings of the Marchland. House plans began to evolve away from those of the long house and the medieval hall. By the end of Elizabeth's reign most new houses were built with two storeys; fireplaces and chimneys replaced the central hearth, the cross-passage began to disappear and there was a much greater use of glass. Above all, new building materials were taking the place of medieval timber and wattled frameworks with plastered surfaces; the seventeenth century was the age of the great rebuilding in stone, and bricks were coming into wide use. Two houses in Radnorshire, perhaps the greatest in the county and among the finest buildings of the whole of the Marchland, display in their design and construction the great leap forward from the Middle Ages to the Renaissance. The older house, Bryndraenog (SO 2078), lies in the remote upper part of the Teme valley in Beguildy parish. It is a timbered medieval hall-house, built in the fifteenth century. As H. Brooksby has written in his study of *The Houses of Radnorshire*,* 'the carpentry is of the finest order ... but the final result, with open fires and shuttered windows, must have been somewhat

*H. Brooksby, 'The houses of Radnorshire', *Radnorshire Soc. Trans.*, 40 (1970).

21. *Monaughty, one of Radnorshire's finest houses, in the Lugg valley, belongs to the great age of rebuilding in stone in the first half of the seventeenth century.*

uncomfortable compared with the arrangements at Monaughty, one of the first large houses of Radnorshire to be built in stone'. Monaughty (SO 2368) stands in the Lugg valley close beside the main road from Knighton to Rhayader. A stone date-tablet of 1638 inscribed with the initials of James Price, as well as two shields of the Price family, show that the house belongs to the early years of the seventeenth century, the great period of rebuilding in stone. Monaughty is fully storeyed, all the windows were glazed and each important room was built with a fireplace.

Perhaps the most revolutionary change in the building materials of the great age of reconstruction was the introduction of bricks. Building in brick appeared in the middle of the sixteenth century at the northern limit of the Marches in the Vale of Clwyd. There in the 1560s Sir Richard Clough, a native of Denbigh who rose high in the service of the Tudor monarchy as the factor to the Royal Agent in Antwerp, built two houses that used brickwork in their construction. Clough's long service in Flanders influenced the life-style that he established in his native Vale of Clwyd. Flemish architects were employed on both houses and the bricks themselves may have been imported. Bachegraig (SJ 0771) alas no longer stands; only the gatehouse and some outbuildings that were intended as a warehouse have survived the demolition in the early years of the nineteenth century. The site of Bachegraig lies in the valley floor of the Clwyd some three miles above St

145

Asaph. Thomas Pennant's description of the house published in the second volume of his *Tours in Wales*, printed in 1781, leaves us in no doubt about the grandeur and strange incongruity of Sir Richard's mansion, the premises of a rich Flemish merchant planted amid the woods and meadows of the Clwyd. Pennant describes its pyramidal shape rising through six storeys whose 'windows of painted glass depict *armes* of the knights of the holy sepulchre, of his great partner Sir Thomas Gresham, and of several kingdoms with which these munificent merchants traded'. Bachegraig 'was built with a view to commerce' as another topographer of the Welsh landscape Richard Fenton,* makes clear. Sir Richard Clough designed Bachegraig as a depot for the import of luxuries from overseas and a canal was to connect the house with the navigable estuary of the Clwyd at Rhuddlan. Sir Richard's plans were cut short by death; if they had come to maturity, the Vale of Clwyd could have boasted a canal long before the age of the Industrial Revolution.

Sir Richard's other house, Plas Clough (SJ 0567), still stands on the outskirts of Denbigh. Its stepped gables display the Flemish tastes of its founder. Both houses, in their histories, show that the introduction of bricks and brick-building techniques depended on the wealth and whims of a single person, one whose horizons of experience had been extended far beyond the hills and secret valleys of the Marchland. Where external influences were slow to penetrate, we find that traditional materials and familiar architectural ideas persisted. For instance, the survival of black-and-white timbered buildings forms one of the visual strands in the personality of the border region in the wooden farms and mansions of western Montgomeryshire, in the former merchants' houses of Shrewsbury, or the glare of white-washed plaster in summer sunshine that one remembers from the villages of the Hereford plain. Nowhere in the Marches is the history of building in timber better displayed than in the upper Severn valley beyond Newtown. This remote district, the medieval Welsh cantref of Arwystli, is isolated to the south and east by the long ridges of the Kerry Hills; westward the tributaries of the Severn lead to the high mist-bound moorlands of Plynlimmon. Arwystli shows the strength of regional forces in the design and building styles of earlier centuries. For instance, the great age of rebuilding in the English countryside when the medieval timbered hall-house was generally replaced by Renaissance styles in stone is widely dated to the period 1540 to 1640. In this part of the upper Severn there is no evidence of rebuilding before the Civil War. Here the yeomen farmers reconstructed their houses through the decades after the Restoration, in the latter part of the seven-

*R. Fenton, *Tours in Wales*, 1804–14.

22. The medieval techniques of building in timber lingered until the eighteenth century in the remote valleys of Montgomeryshire as illustrated by this 'black and white' farmhouse in Cwm Nant-y-meichiaid.

teenth century and into the beginning of the eighteenth century. The date of the great rebuilding is not only late, but a conservatism of taste and outlook predominates. The ancient medieval building materials, timber, wattle and plaster, remained in use and in several of the rebuilt houses the old principles of design prevailed with the use of up-and-down hill sites and the placing of windows only in the long walls. The evidence of local history alone can place the grand themes of our national history in their true proportions. The landscape of Arwystli today reminds us of the strength of the locality in times past when a man's world was comprehended within the range of his own vision. The solid, black-and-white yeomen farms of Trefeglwys (SN 9790) and Carno (SN 9696) are a testimony to the harmonious relationships that prevailed between men and their natural environment in those centuries before the Industrial Revolution widened the horizons of that restricted world, bringing the garish, mass-produced bricks of Ruabon among the grey-green hills of the upper Severn.

147

6

The Industrial Imprint

Though the Welsh Borders is not now thought of as one of the industrial regions of present-day Britain, this was not always the case. In earlier periods, especially the seventeenth and eighteenth centuries, what is now a quiet countryside resounded to the noise of the forge hammers or felt the belching smoke and ruddy glare from furnaces and kilns. There were local entrepreneurs who became national figures of the so-called Industrial Revolution. Some of the early industrial sites still survive to give a direct link with the past but in many cases time and changing economic bases have led to complete abandonment. Only the painstaking research and interpretation by the industrial archaeologist will allow the few tangible remains to yield up their secret past. In the case of mining, the scars in the present landscape can often give a clear lead but, in many parts of the Welsh Borders even this has been denied as nature has once again taken control of the site. Then the attempted reconstruction by the archaeologist becomes more difficult and he has to combine the most fragmentary field evidence with any available documentary records. Nevertheless there is considerable scope for this type of past reconstruction and it is surprising how rotten timbers, disintegrating footings of former buildings, silted ponds and barely discernible tracks can be brought back to life and used to recall the past.

Many parts of the long corridor of country between the Dee and Severn have never experienced industry and so have retained their natural setting throughout history. But if water power or ample supplies of timber were once available then it is probable that there was a phase of industrial activity, however brief, in the past. A drive through the Montgomeryshire (Powys) lanes can reveal, from a single isolated mill or even a place-name, a past history of industrial enterprise which is entirely unexpected in the absence of

148

other tangible remains or even documentary records. Sites which initially had the same natural advantages for industrial growth as Birmingham or Manchester are now submerged amidst the rich greenery of the Welsh countryside. There are instances of continuity over the centuries where, perhaps for human rather than natural reasons, industry has survived though not always in its original form.

One area of industrial continuity is the belt of country fringing Deeside and particularly the valley running inland to Holywell (SJ 1876). There were two reasons why this area should have had a relatively early start. First, there was a plentiful supply of water which could be harnessed for power and secondly, local mineral resources, mainly lead, from the Haklyn Mountain. Added to this, its geographical position near the Dee estuary and the main route along the north coast were also helpful. It was the availability of water above all else that was its most valuable asset, especially in the steeply falling valley running down from Holywell to the coast. The relatively small stream is fed with a constant supply of water from a copious spring at St Winifred's Well, for long a place of religious pilgrimage. Provided the water could be stored in artificial ponds and the head of water harnessed by means of a wheel, a number of industries could benefit at different points down the valley. The earliest use of water power recorded was for the corn mill built by the abbots of Basingwerk Abbey in the thirteenth century. It was not until much later that the full potential of the stream was fully realised and when the local writer and traveller, Thomas Pennant, wrote his history of the parishes of Whiteford and Holywell in 1796, he noted that 'the spring never floods or freezes and discharges 25,000 gallons a minute'. To make full use of it, numerous dams were thrown across the valley floor, creating a string of artificial paternoster lakes, each with a mill sited on its lower side. Most of the mills have now become ruins but the ponds have survived and indicate how the same water was recycled time and time again in the one-mile length of valley floor. From many points of view the Holywell valley today represents a relict industrial landscape with the lush vegetation making it more and more difficult to unravel its past glories.

Like so many similar sites based on water power, the Holywell valley has seen a succession of industries over the centuries. After the monks of Basingwerk had built their medieval corn mill and showed the great value of water power, metal-working industries, textiles and paper mills all came into the valley, often re-occupying sites vacated as an earlier industry died out. At the outset of the Industrial Revolution there was a wire-drawing mill using a technique going back to Tudor times. A generation later, when Dr Johnson visited the Holywell district in 1774 as part of his grand tour of North Wales, the wire mill was still working. Lower down the valley at Greenfield (1977) he was shown a tilting mill where iron bars were slit and then beaten by large hammers driven by water power. Higher up the valley the other mills were producing paper. This was a manufacture which had come to the area relatively early for in 1690 the powerful local family of the Grosvenors had taken over an old copper forge. Not only did it have water for power but also its necessary purity for the manufacturing process. Since its early beginning the industry has undergone many changes but in spite of this it still exists in the Abbey Paper Mills at Greenfield. Originally rags were used as the basic raw material but from the mid-nineteenth century onwards wood pulp and esparto grass have been used. Fortunately the site is sufficiently close to the small port of Mostyn for these to be imported without difficulty. In addition, as the changeover from water to steam power took place, there were ready supplies of coal from the Point of Ayr colliery (1283).

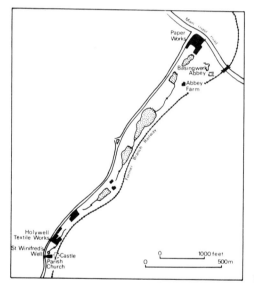

13. *Holywell valley with its relict industrial sites.*

The copper industry of the Holywell valley had its beginnings in the mid-eighteenth century and arose as the result of a decision in 1761 that the hulls of naval vessels must be sheathed. Copper was not found locally but could be easily imported from the Parys Mountain mines in Anglesey. A local man, Thomas Barker, who owned the tilting mill at Greenfield, saw the possibility of smelting copper and became the principal shareholder of the Cheadle Brass Company. The industry quickly established itself and

150

benefited from the boom which occurred at the time of the American Civil War in 1775 and also the discovery of exceptionally rich ores in Anglesey. Thomas Williams, the manager of the Parys Mining Company, saw the great potential of the Holywell valley for metal manufacture and in 1780 he built a copper forge, wire and rolling mills so that he could take advantage of both the water power and nearby coal. A few years later he bought out the Cheadle Brass Company and so obtained control of virtually the whole range of copper manufacture from brass plates, copper bolts, cylinders for muslin printing, copper pans and other household utensils right down to gaudy brass ornaments. A fleet of nearly fifty vessels was constantly plying between the Anglesey port of Amlwch and Mostyn bringing in the raw material. So great was the demand that copper was also brought from Cornwall and even overland from the Duke of Devonshire's mines in the Peak District. This alternative supply was fortunate, for when the Anglesey copper began to run out, the Holywell industry was able to continue. The works were severely damaged in a storm of 1821 but continued in a reduced state until about 1840 when the copper industry finally left the valley because of competition from South Wales.

The collapse of the copper manufacturing industry was disastrous for local employment for it came at a time when the textile industry was undergoing a similar decline. It too had been initially attracted to the valley by the plentiful supplies of water as well as coal from the nearby Flintshire coalfield. John Smalley, a liquor merchant and house painter from Preston and an early associate of Richard Arkwright, was responsible for bringing cotton manufacture to Holywell. He had moved from Lancashire to Derbyshire with Arkwright when the famous mill at Cromford was established but quickly left following a disagreement. Holywell was a satisfactory alternative and in many ways an even better site than Cromford, for not only did it have the necessary water power but a much easier means of importing the raw cotton. With the help of a local man, John Chambers, Smalley acquired the old coarse paper mill (itself on the site of the original Basingwerk Abbey corn mill) and then built a new three-storey mill using great sandstone blocks from the now-ruined abbey. Although Smalley lived for only another five years, the whole enterprise was taken over and run by his son. Fortunately the cotton trade was booming at the time and Christopher Smalley was able to build two further mills, known as the Upper and Lower, in the Holywell valley in 1783 and 1785. A fourth mill, the Crescent, was built in 1790 after Smalley had taken a Lancashire businessman, John Douglas, into partnership. The new company, which became known as the Cotton Twist Company, was now employing well over a thousand people, most in the valley

151

mills but also a considerable number in outlying villages like Newmarket (0979) and Ysceifiog (1571) as well as farther afield in Denbigh. Thomas Pennant, who visited the mills in 1795, has left us a contemporary picture of textile manufacturing when the industry was at its height in the closing years of the eighteenth century. He was conducted around the mills by Smalley himself and shown the manufacture of cotton twist which in turn would be used for making a whole range of cloth, from gingham to calico. The strength of the industry is shown not only by the concentration of four mills in the valley but in its ability to withstand a succession of difficulties and economic problems brought about by the American War, the post-war depression, severe floods in the valley in 1821 and an attempted arson of one mill in 1822. The changeover from water to steam power was carried out smoothly in 1835 and with coal nearby the future seemed bright. But in a matter of six years the whole enterprise collapsed because of the great countrywide cotton slump. By 1841 only fourteen people were employed at the mills, and with no prospect of improvement the Cotton Twist Company went into liquidation shortly afterwards. The amazing change of fortune in less than a decade is truly remarkable and indicates how vulnerable the industry was to economic circumstances because of its somewhat isolated situation away from the mainstream of activity in Lancashire. A contributory factor may have been the lack of family control – for Christopher Smalley had died in 1829 – and with it the personal interest and involvement that could weather such storms. Fortunately the demise of the cotton trade coincided with the rise of the woollen industry so that although there was a period when Holywell became a ghost town of empty houses, the valley mills were ultimately taken over by a Newtown man, John Jones, who promoted flannel weaving. This was something of an experiment, for it was the first time that the power loom had been used in the Welsh woollen industry. Although there were initial problems, the power loom in time fully justified itself and led to the industry surviving here long after mills in the more traditional areas had been forced to close down. Working mills still exist in the valley making traditional Welsh cloth which finds a market both in the home tourist industry and abroad.

The main manufacturing activity has, however, moved from the narrow valley floor with all its limitations on factory layout, to the more spacious sites of Deeside. Viscose rayon is the principal product. The industry is dominated by one firm, Courtaulds, with their Greenfield works at Holywell (2077) and the Aber and Castle mills at Flint (2473). No direct link with the past exists, save perhaps the existence of a pool of labour and the common need of energy supplies. The enterprise had its beginning early in the present century when a German firm started a factory at Flint in 1908 to make artificial silk. Within a few years the plant had changed over to making viscose rayon, the patent for which was held by Samuel Courtauld. Ultimately he took over the works and in the 1920s built the additional factory which became the Castle Works. The site at Greenfield was not developed until 1934, advantage being taken of the cheap, flat land for the spacious layout and the good communications offered by the railway alongside. The choice of the site was also influenced by the availability of large supplies of pure water, not from St Winifred's Well but from old lead workings on Halkyn Mountain which a mineral company was anxious to drain. The rayon industry is at present undergoing great competition from other man-made fibres and its prospects have changed dramatically in the last few years. The closure of the Castle Works at Flint in January 1977 could mark the beginning of the complete eclipse of the industry on Deeside. In an area of already high unemployment this could lead to the same situation as followed the collapse of the cotton industry in a brief space of a few years in the 1840s.

Even when the Holywell mills were in full production in the first half of the nineteenth century they could not compare, either in size or output, with the industry of the Middle Marches centred on the towns of Newtown, Welshpool and Llanidloes. Here it was woollen manufacture rather than cotton and so its basic raw material was closer at hand. The history of manufacture goes back to Elizabethan times when it was a cottage industry which formed a valuable supplement to farming. The numerous fast-flowing streams and rivers provided ideal sites for fulling mills and the Welsh word for them, *pandy*, is still fairly common as a place-name element. Often, in the absence of buildings or other remains, it is the only indication of past industrial activity. The scattered character of the industry has meant that production was never great, though marketing of the finished cloth was well organised by the Shrewsbury Drapers Company who had a virtual monopoly of sales for about two hundred years. Oswestry became a great collecting centre and involved a long journey for many workers who travelled on foot with the finished cloth on their backs.

In the last quarter of the eighteenth century the flannel industry became established in its own right and not merely as an adjunct to farming. Marketing was now in the production area after the establishment of a fortnightly flannel market in Welshpool in 1782. Fifty years later it moved to Newtown after an imposing market hall had been built on the banks of the River Severn. By this time the production of flannel was almost entirely in factories which used water power and later steam power to drive the looms. Tall three- and four-storey buildings made their appearance in the towns of Newtown and Llanidloes and some of the weaving shops still survive. By the early nineteenth century Newtown, in particular, had been transformed from a small market town into an urban complex of flannel mills on the banks of the Severn and weaving shops in nearly every street. Its population grew rapidly from about 800 in 1771 to over 4,500 sixty years later. The arrival of a branch of the Shropshire Canal in 1821 gave a tremendous fillip, for it allowed the bulky cloth to be transported more easily and cheaply. A few years later a

23. *A former flannel factory in Newtown with the upper rooms of the three-storey building used as shops.*

regular service to Manchester had developed while the opening of a road across to Builth gave access southwards to the valuable markets of South Wales. By 1833, according to Lewis's *Topographical Dictionary*, there were fifty factories in the town and its immediate neighbourhood. At first the mills depended on water power and had to be sited on the banks of the Severn. The same was true of the other mills of Montgomeryshire so that every sizeable stream had its grouping of small factories. For a time it seemed that the prosperity of the industry, both in town and countryside, was assured. The changeover to steam power inevitably led to a concentration in those areas where coal could be readily imported, at first by the Shropshire Canal and then after 1860 by the Cambrian Railway. New mills sprang up by the dozen in the favoured area of Newtown between 1855 and 1865 while there was an alarming contraction in rural areas, especially in Llanbrynmair well to the west. A single new factory like the Cambrian Mills at Newtown had as many as 250 power looms working in 1870. Fire, however, was a constant hazard and the Cambrian Mills suffered badly in 1875 and again in 1912, after which it was never rebuilt.

The revival in the fortunes of the flannel industry in the 1870s led to speculation that Newtown was destined to become the 'Leeds of Wales'. But the prosperity proved short-lived, largely because of inherent geographical and commercial disadvantages stemming from its situation in a relatively remote part of the Middle Marches. Although the Cambrian Railway passed through the town it was a west-coast route and did nothing to help capture the lucrative markets of the industrial towns of South Wales and the Midlands. There was also the difficulty that the local area could not produce sufficient capital and when outside financial help was sought in England, this area had to take second place to Lancashire. By the turn of the century, outside competition was proving too great and even the larger mills were becoming uneconomic and an embarrassment. Although the industry struggled on until the 1950s, largely processing local wool, it has now finally died out. At Newtown and to a lesser extent at the smaller centre of Llanidloes, the past is represented only by red-brick buildings often given over to other uses. Fresh industries have been encouraged to move into the area and a new industrial estate has been built on the outskirts of Newtown, largely through development grant aid and other artificial stimuli.

In the countryside the impact of the former woollen industry is now felt even less than in the towns for little by way of tangible remains are now to be seen. Buildings have either been altered for other purposes or simply pulled down. In the case of mill sites it is often only the weir across the stream or river and the race running from it that once fed the mill with power which have survived. In extreme cases the only hint of past activity is in the name.

When we come to examine the other great industry of the past which affected the border country, namely lead mining, the remains are much more substantial if only because of the vast heaps of waste which were the inevitable by-product. When the industry was at its peak, whole areas were sterilised not only by the mining itself but also from associated activities like smelting. Though it is many years since large-scale mining died out, the

155

effect is still visible in the present landscape, for even nature has failed to reclaim the derelict lands in many cases. One area of intense lead mining where the remains are all too clearly visible is the Halkyn Mountain, now part of Clwyd. Over several square miles of the limestone plateau top the rumpled ground, old fenced-off mine shafts and the surviving head-gear at New Halkyn mine (sj 1972) all point to a past when the bowels of the earth were made to yield up their treasures. Interest in the area dates from Roman times and although the exact sites are unknown, there is other evidence which

24. *Surviving head-gear of the former New Halkyn mine, the last of the lead mines to operate in the area.*

makes the early working undisputed. From time to time great pigs of lead, each weighing about 170 pounds, and with the distinctive marking ASCANI, have been found, and these point to a Flintshire source. It is also probable that the Romans had a smelting site on the Dee shore at Pentre Ffwrdan (2572) from where the concentrated pigs were sent to distant parts of the Empire. The final departure of the Romans from Britain – in the early years of the fifth century – ushered in a period which has left no records, either in lead pigs or workings. This period spans several centuries and it is not until almost 1300 that we again have real evidence of large-scale lead mining. At this time Edward I was making a determined bid to contain the Welsh princes and lead was a prized metal, especially for use as a roofing material for his string of castles in North Wales. In 1304, for example, fifteen cartloads of lead were needed to roof the great tower of Flint Castle. The sheet lead was also needed by the abbeys, manor houses and even the salt pans of the region. One of the privileges given to the English burgesses of the town of Flint was the right to go outside the bounds to search out lead veins and also cut down timber for charcoal in order to smelt the lead. It was the lack of extensive woodlands that brought about a temporary setback for the industry and even in Tudor times there was no great activity.

The large-scale exploitation of the lead ores came only after about 1660 when local families like the Myddletons and Mostyns saw it as a means of quickly acquiring wealth. The main driving force at this time was the chartered company of the Royal Mines Copper. From similar operations in the Pennines, this company had acquired considerable expertise in exploiting lead veins and it was not long before their Halkyn Mountain operations were in full swing, even though problems of mining rights often brought them into conflict with the local and powerful Grosvenor family.

The mining of lead on a large scale made it necessary for the Royal Mines Copper to establish a smelt. This they did at Gadlys (2174) which was close to their Halkyn Mountain operations as well as serving other interests in areas farther west. The site chosen was a level one on the edge of the low plateau overlooking Bagillt and therefore in easy reach of the Dee estuary. Mill pools were dug out and used for power supplies. For smelting, a refining furnace and a slag hearth were built at an estimated cost of £225 and both were ready for the opening of the works in 1704. The Gadlys complex quickly justified itself, for not only did it use the local ore but also began to smelt silver-lead from other parts of Wales. Unfortunately, after the works were closed the main buildings were pulled down so that it is only the site that is of interest today. The mine manager's house, with its date and company crest, still survives as a farm and the former ponds are just discernible amidst the pastures. They give little true indication of the importance attached to Gadlys by the London Lead Company who were the successors of the Mines Royal.

While the ores were near the surface and rich veins were being discovered, the Company naturally flourished. As other mining firms moved in and obtained leases so competition increased. All went well until the working out of the richer veins brought pressure on the Company whose fortunes began to wane some time after 1730. Deeper mines were then dug but this inevitably led to problems with water. In part this was solved by installing pumping engines and the London Lead Company had the foresight to purchase the latest Newcomen engine for use at Trelogan as early as 1731. Even this did not solve the problem of drainage in many of the deepest mines on Halkyn Mountain and unfortunately it was these that were tapping the richest veins. A particularly rich vein was discovered near Holywell in 1774 and this led to a new approach being tried to unwater the mines. An underground canal, wide enough to take barges, was built running in from the coast. This would not only carry away the water but also allow any ores to be removed using water transport. Little success followed the driving of the Holywell tunnel but it set a precedent that was followed in the nineteenth century when other rich veins were discovered. Unfortunately the London Lead Company never really solved the problem of unwatering its deeper mines and it was this fact that finally brought about its withdrawal from Flintshire in 1792, including the selling of the Gadlys smelter.

For the Halkyn Mountain lead industry this was only the end of a chapter. In the early nineteenth century Cornish mining expertise was introduced and almost immediately it brought success with further discoveries and increased output. A new drainage level was started in 1822 but soon abandoned. When reopened in 1838 it immediately struck a rich lode of solid ore about nine feet wide. The new company promoted to exploit the lead ores quickly found that its £50 shares were worth £1,900. Flooding still remained a problem in many areas, so it was decided to extend the Halkyn Deep Level farther inland. This brought about yet another enormous rise in production and in the last decade of the nineteenth century the Flintshire mines were yielding high profits. By now all the known lead veins were becoming exhausted and after 1909 the output began to fall off dramatically. Even the 1914–18 war did not improve fortunes and although the industry lingered on during the inter-war years, production was now centred on only one area around the New Halkyn mine (1972). This, too, closed in 1958, though its head-gear and winding equipment is still maintained for drainage purposes. Many have predicted that there is still valuable ore to be exploited but it seems unlikely that Halkyn will ever again witness the activity of the last century.

Halkyn Mountain and its surrounding area was but one of the number of lead-working areas in north-east Wales. Close to Wrexham lay the Minera mining complex (2651) which saw the main period of activity after 1792, the date when the London Lead Company withdrew completely from North Wales. Over the next fifteen years the Minera mines produced over 5,000 tons of ore, largely the result of the efforts of John Wilkinson, the ironmaster who became a lessee. The main veins were located in the Minera valley and the adjacent edge of the Esclusham Mountain. For a time this was the scene of intense activity with mines and galleries penetrating the hillside while the smelters were grouped along the valley floor. A new lode discovered in 1853 brought profits well in excess of £½ million over the next twenty-five years and employed well over a thousand men. The final closure of the Minera mines did not come until 1914 and even then activity did not completely cease, for the waste tips were re-worked right up to 1950. Today the valley still retains old ruins which recall the past, while on the hillside the rows of cottages of the settlement which the miners called New Brighton provide a further link.

The Middle March, too, had its share of the prosperity which the lead mining industry brought to the borderland countryside in the nineteenth century. Even the quiet valleys of Montgomeryshire reverberated to the sound of hammers in the dressing sheds and felt the full impact of pollution from the acrid smoke of the smelters. The area centred on The Van (SN 9487) (an anglicised version of the Welsh Y Fan) was the richest lead field with a number of lodes running across the area from south-west to north-east. The existence of lead had been known for a considerable time and sporadic working had taken place at various points, although without ever making a rich strike. The situation was to change dramatically in 1862 when the chance discovery of an exceptionally rich ore-bearing section led to an era of great prosperity. Ore was found at a depth of only 200 feet on the south-east side of Van Farm and immediately the whole paraphernalia associated with mining – a dressing plant, washing launders, water-wheels and settling pits – began to alter the character of this rural backwater. In April 1855 the Van mine began despatching the first of its many loads of lead ore. A contemporary print gives a good impression of the scale of the whole enterprise which was by far the largest in Wales at the time. Those lucky to have bought shares for £5 at the outset now found that their capital had increased twentyfold.

The first phase of prosperity was to last for just over a decade until in 1878 a world-wide slump brought about a reduction in output from the Van mine. Production had been averaging between 4,500 and 7,000 tons of dressed ore a year but after 1880 the working out of the richer deposits and competition from abroad started a decline from which the Van never recovered. Even fresh discoveries in the late 1880s failed to increase production to former levels so that by 1890 only 500 tons were leaving the mine. The steady profits of previous years were now replaced by considerable operating losses and by 1891 the mining company was £3,000 in debt. This rapid change of fortune is a familiar occurrence in the history of all metalliferous mining, so the Van was following a set pattern which was not entirely unexpected. For miners who had benefited from rich pickings only a few years previously, there was now little employment and many were forced to leave the area. The Van mine, which earlier had been synonymous with wealth, was now almost abandoned and the ownership changed hands frequently as successive

25A. *The Van lead-mining area as it appeared when working was at its peak in the 1870s.*

25B. *The same scene today with its air of dereliction and abandonment.*

160

operators tried and failed. The end finally came in 1921, since when the area has become derelict.

In the decade of 1870 to 1880, when production was at its peak, the Van valley must have presented a very different appearance to the solitude of today. The clatter of the crushing plant and the thick pall of smoke which hung over the area on still days was completely out of character with the rural surroundings. The mine also disrupted the social life of the valley for when fully working no fewer than five hundred men and boys were employed.

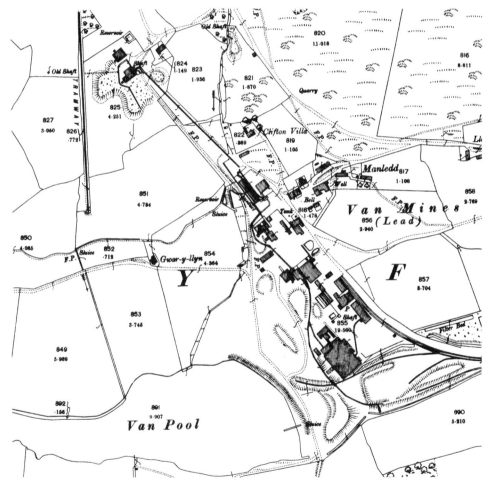

14. *The lead-mining site of the Van when it was working at full capacity at the end of the nineteenth century.*

161

Many were drawn in from the surrounding hamlets and from the nearby market town of Llanidloes but there were large numbers of 'foreigners' who were willing to work long hours and reap the rich reward that was there for the taking. The continued prosperity of the Van mine was such that it did lead to some permanent settlement around, unlike many other ventures elsewhere. The mining company built rows of cottages amidst the existing farms and started a school for the community. Lower down the valley the company also built a group of eighteen terrace cottages close to the railway which connected the mine to the Cambrian Railway at Caersws. For the first few months the railway carried only ore trains but pressure from the local community led to the provision of a rudimentary passenger service. It never paid its way as a passenger line and by 1879 the mining company was only too willing for the Cambrian Railway to take it over completely. It was as part of this bigger network that the branch line to The Van survived long after the mines closed and it was not until 1940 that the track was taken up. Little remains today, though the route is still easy to follow through the pastures of the Cerist valley.

It is now over fifty years since lead mining ended at The Van but there is still plenty to see in the vicinity of the old mine workings. Like all similar sites it has an untidy air, as though when the last ounce of ore was hauled to the surface everyone vanished overnight. Great spreads of grey waste lie in heaps on the valley floor, though recently these have begun to disappear as bulldozers have made deep inroads. Van Pool, probably created as a result of the damming of the valley floor by the waste tips, also survives and makes a pleasing addition to the landscape. Few of the actual mining buildings remain much above ground level but the storage bins and the brick supports for the washing troughs are still to be seen. Higher up the hillside, above the conifer plantation, are the remains of the mine shaft with its two ruined chimney stacks, now in a state of advanced decay. The actual shaft is largely filled in with rubbish and parts of the original winding gear have fallen into it. It was from here that the lead ore was taken down to the dressing sheds in the valley below by two inclined tramways to await processing prior to loading into the trucks of the Van Railway. Water power from the hillside streams was used extensively and a contemporary print of 1870 shows a giant water-wheel alongside the main mine buildings. Although there is desolation around, a hamlet of a few cottages has managed to survive as a quiet successor to the once thriving miners' settlement.

With so many former lead mining sites like the Van falling into ruin, it is pleasant to record that one, Bryntail, not far away, has been selected to become the first industrial monument in Wales to come under the care of the

26. *Clwyedog dam and the site of the Bryntail lead works which the Department of the Environment is restoring as a monument of industrial archaeology.*

Department of the Environment. It is located three miles north-west of Llanidloes at the foot of the Clywedog Dam (915868). With its crumbling crusher house and water-wheel pit, ore-dressing sheds and floors, mine shaft and pumping house, it is a typical mid-nineteenth-century mining complex. Like so many other lead mines its main period of activity was between 1845 and 1867. Later the upper part of the mine was worked for barytes and this led to the building of the incline to the valley crushing mill. At present the whole site is being reconstructed so that in time the visitor will be able to appreciate the impact which the metalliferous mining industry made on this and other quiet backwaters of the borderland.

The lead mining and smelting industries, though of great importance in certain localities, have not had the continuity or impact which the iron and steel industry has enjoyed over the centuries. With present-day production of the latter now concentrated on the coalfields, it is perhaps natural to assume that this has always been the case. The movement of the industry to this source of power is, however, a development of the last two hundred years. Prior to about 1770, iron manufacture was much more dispersed and could be found where water power and charcoal, its two basic needs apart

163

from the iron itself, were available. In some cases the iron ore was transported over relatively long distances to the furnace, which would be sited on or near the banks of a stream in an area where ample supplies of timber existed for making charcoal.

There have been two distinct stages in the history of iron making, the initial water-power/charcoal phase and then the later coal/steam-power phase. The Welsh Borders can provide examples of both, although in terms of natural resources it was better endowed to participate in the earlier period.

27. *The former factory at Dolobran which over the centuries has seen a succession of uses as various industries have made use of its water-power resources.*

Remote country districts with wooded valley slopes where a constantly flowing stream could be harnessed to provide power for both furnace and forge, were sought out by the early ironmasters. One such site was Pool Quay (SJ 2511), where the Earl of Powys owned mills by the banks of the Severn, probably the successors of the corn mills of the nearby Strata Marcella Abbey. Here both furnace and forge were active in the seventeenth century and although very large by contemporary standards, little trace of them has survived save for some stonework around the banks of the Severn and some possible remains of the weir thrown across the river. The Earl of Powys also owned the mill at Mathrafal (124119) by the side of the River Vyrnwy and this became a forge in 1651 when it was operated by the Myddleton family of Chirk. It later came into the hands of the Lloyd family whose estate of Dolobran was close by. Charles Lloyd was one of the great figures of this formative period of the iron industry, a man of great energy and skill with a wide range of interests. He came here in 1698 and immediately became involved in the iron industry while his younger brother, Sampson, went off to Birmingham to accumulate considerable capital and ultimately found Lloyds Bank. Sampson Lloyd also owned several forges in the Wednesbury area where he made rod-iron for the nail industry and was thus intimately involved in the fortunes of the Black Country. While Sampson was succeeding in the Midlands, his younger brother Charles at Dolobran continued to expand production at his Mathrafal forge. In 1736 it had an output of 100 tons, although its potential capacity had now risen to about twice that amount. The Dolobran works probably continued until 1789 when it was turned into a flannel factory by Joseph Jones of Welshpool. This was not uncommon, for while the iron industry was coming to the end of the water-power/charcoal phase, flannel manufacture was growing rapidly. It is the flannel factory that occupies the site today, a tall three-storey building now standing rather isolated in the fields of the Vyrnwy valley with its leat running in from the river.

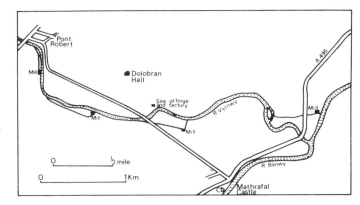

15. *The mill sites of the middle Vyrnwy valley centred on the Lloyd home of Dolobran.*

Long before the Dolobran forge became a flannel factory, the Lloyd family had widened its interest in the iron industry by building a new blast furnace at Bersham near Wrexham (SJ 3049). The choice of site must have been determined by the availability of water power, charcoal and iron ore, for it was a long way from Dolobran as a producer of the pig iron needed for the forge there. Accounts show that it cost Charles Lloyd thirteen pence a ton to transport the pig iron from Bersham to Dolobran. In time, Bersham was to replace Dolobran as the major centre of the early iron industry in the border country, for it had the advantage of a nearby supply of coal from the Denbighshire coalfield. In December 1721 Bersham ceased to use charcoal and substituted 'coked' coal for smelting in the casting of pots. It seems probable that the Lloyd and Darby families, both Quakers, were working together at this formative stage. Ultimately they were to revolutionise the whole industry. The early experiments at Bersham using coking coal must have been partly successful for three years later Charles Lloyd bought the nearby colliery of Rhos. Although there are records of coal being taken from here to the forge at Dolobran, the main fuel used in the making of bar iron continued to be charcoal. For a while this was quite successful and the bars were taken by road to be loaded into barges at Llanymynech (2620) and then carried into the Severn waterway system to reach places as far away as Bewdley. With the long distances involved, both in the gathering of some of its raw materials and the export of its products, Dolobran Forge was clearly at a disadvantage compared with many of its competitors, especially those located on the coalfields. Even the Bersham works was not an unqualified success, perhaps because it was largely experimental in its use of coal. Ultimately Lloyd sold it to pay off some of his creditors and after a succession of different owners it came into the hands of perhaps the best-known of the early ironmasters, John Wilkinson. After acquiring Bersham in 1761, Wilkinson immediately tried to diversify the works and produce largely specialist wares using precision engineering. Coal finally replaced charcoal in the foundries and the prosperity of the works was assured after a boring mill was built and used for making cannon. A new Boulton and Watt engine was designed in 1782 and in its development the Bersham works played a leading role. The rather enclosed nature of the site in the valley bottom prevented much expansion and it led Wilkinson in 1792 to purchase the nearby Brymbo Hall estate. It was from this early beginning that the present highly specialised Brymbo steelworks grew up, the only surviving link in the border country with the original iron industry. Bersham has now fossilised and the farm which occupies the site does not have the appearance of a past industrial working, though a corn mill (with large wheel in place) and a curious octagonal building give a hint of a hidden, illustrious past waiting to be fully investigated.

Another site of the early iron industry of which little now remains is at Mostyn (SJ 1580) on the marshland bordering Deeside. Until a few years ago the traveller on the Chester to Holyhead railway could look out on the rusting remains of the former ironworks, an intricate assemblage of pipes, boilers, cylinders and a blackened, scarred furnace. Coastal sites like this at Mostyn could take advantage of flat land and in later works, like that at nearby Shotton, this became even more important. The history of the Mostyn Iron and Steel Company goes back to the early nineteenth century when armaments were needed during the Napoleonic Wars. Apart from the advantage of the waterside location, with Mostyn Harbour close by, there was coal, clay-ironstone and limestone available in the vicinity. By 1840 a foundry and shipbuilding yard alongside the harbour had been built as part of the industrial complex. Even when the local clay-ironstone ran out, the port enabled the easy import of haematite from Cumberland. Unfortunately the Dee estuary could not handle big ore carriers, so Mostyn was forced to specialise in manganese steel. Modernisation of the works took place after the 1939–45 war but economic pressures ultimately brought about its closure in 1964. Mostyn

28. *Brymbo, one of only two remaining steelworks in the borderland area.*

steelworks were dismantled shortly afterwards, leaving only Brymbo and Shotton as the survivors of a traditional industry of the northern Marches. Even Shotton has a question mark hanging over its future, for unless the Dee approach channels are improved, the works cannot compete on equal geographical terms with works like Margam in South Wales.

While the charcoal iron industry was at its height in the marchland countryside of Montgomeryshire and Denbighshire, there was considerable contact across the border with Shropshire and the West Midlands. As with the Dolobran forge on the Vyrnwy, local families often played a major role in

167

establishing the industry in a particular locality. One site which developed in this way was in the Downton gorge where the Teme had broken through the limestone rim of the Wigmore Dome. The Bringewood Forge (SO 4575), as it became known, was to bring considerable wealth to the Knight family and enabled them to build their Gothic castle in 1774 overlooking the Teme gorge. The ruin of the former forge still survives downstream close by an elaborate stone bridge which spans the gorge. Although now overgrown, it is not difficult to appreciate the layout of the former works with its leat bringing water from the Teme. Charcoal was readily available in the woods around while the iron ore was brought by packhorse from the Clee Hills. Bringewood Forge and its association with the Knight family has a history typical of many of the borderland ironworks. The early period, when charcoal and water power were the two most important assets of any site, was a time of great prosperity and led local landowners with the necessary capital and energy to become very wealthy in a very short time. Once steam power took over, waterside sites like Bringewood could not compete and therefore went out of production almost as quickly as their meteoric rise. Very little now remains save for the occasional hint, like the iron gravestones in Burrington churchyard (4472), to indicate a past interest in iron manufacture.

In some ways the southern Marches could point to more natural advantages than areas farther north when it came to establishing an iron industry. Not only was the area endowed with the usual swift streams, woodland and a major river (in this case the Wye) to act as a transport artery, it also had a rich supply of iron ore from the Forest of Dean. Not surprisingly, the Wye valley region became a primary iron-producing area in the seventeenth century. The presence of ironstone in the limestone rocks of the western margins of the Forest of Dean plateau had been known since Roman times. Rich pockets of haematite ore occurred near the surface and were easily reached by shallow pits, each with a narrow opening at the top but gradually widening below ground. These bell pits were an effective means of recovering large ore bodies quickly and cheaply. The main effort in Roman times was probably in the area known as The Scowles (SO 6004), although this is not certain in view of the later medieval working which has effectively removed all trace of any Roman mining. Today The Scowles bear the scars of centuries of primitive mining for amidst the coppice woods the rumpled ground represents the remains of the collapsed bell pits with their rim of excavated debris around. The Romans probably took the ore to the northern fringes of the Forest of Dean for smelting. Recent excavations at Ariconium (SO 6423) show that this site was once a major industrial town with furnaces and smithies and it is more than likely that some of the ore used came from The Scowles. A stretch of Roman road, with its carefully laid stones channelled by the wheels of carts, has been uncovered at Blackpool Bridge (6508).

It is quite clear from sites like The Scowles, Ariconium and Lydney Park (where there is an undoubted second-century iron mine) that the Romans looked upon this corner of the southern Marches as an important iron producer. With their departure, however, little is heard of any mining until medieval times. The Scowles pits were then opened up again and considerably extended. It was to the Wye valley and its many tributaries that the iron manufacturers turned when seeking suitable sites for their works. Only a handful of these early water-power sites are now known with certainty from actual remains of buildings. One, recently investigated by Dr Tylecote at Coed Ithal near Llandogo on the west bank of the River Wye (SO 527026), dates from 1651 and had a furnace capable of producing eighteen tons of pig iron a week. The furnace site, with about twenty feet of its sandstone walls still standing, depended on a small stream for the power to work its bellows. In design it was similar to many of the seventeenth-century furnaces which once flourished in this area. Another lies only a few miles to the west at Woolpitch Wood (487048) near Trellech. It is now very much overgrown but the square base to the former furnace can still be recognised. Like many similar buildings it was sited on rising ground to allow recharging with ore from above. The ruins of a large storehouse survive close by.

In these abandoned sites at Coed Ithal and Trellech we are seeing the sole remains of the early creative stages of the iron industry. Increased demand left them unable to cope with much larger tonnages so they quickly went out of production. Unlike at Bersham there was no family of local ironmasters who were ready to expand the works. Only one enterprise, wire-making at Tintern, was able to change with the times and thus survive right up to the present century. The side valley of Angidy Brook, which runs westwards into the plateau edge from Tintern, contained a sizeable industrial complex in the seventeenth and eighteenth centuries, with its specialisation in bar iron and wire drawing. At one period there were three blast furnaces and as many as six forges in a short stretch of valley. A succession of ponds made the greatest possible use of the water provided by a relatively small stream as it tumbled down the steep valley floor to join the River Wye. Many of the ponds still exist, and below the dam of the upper one a forge known as Pont Saeson formerly existed. The main ironworks lay farther down the valley in a section which is now crowded with cottages and bungalows. Although time has taken its toll of the early buildings, which are only known in detail from documents and water colour paintings, it is believed that a Forestry Commission building (527001) on the right bank of the Angidy Brook was once part of the Lower Wireworks. Throughout its long history the wire industry had to face periods of depression and often sought protection from foreign competition. By the end of the nineteenth century the difficulties of operating an industry not actually on a coalfield meant that it suffered in competition over prices and although a last attempt was made in 1884 by the Tintern Abbey Wire and Tinplate Company to make it viable, the end was now in sight. Apart from the ponds, little now remains of the industry itself, though the valley still has the air of a former industrial hamlet. One can only turn to the writings of Lord Byng who visited the area in 1782 to catch the atmosphere of former days when 'the incessant thump of the furnace hammers' made itself felt throughout the narrow valley.

The most remarkable thing about the Tintern wireworks was that it managed to survive so long. Even at the time of Lord Byng's visit he was told that the iron now had to be brought in from Lancashire. By now the main centres of the industry were moving away from these rural valleys to the coalfields and those fortunate to survive did so as a result of industrial inertia. One of the new sites on the south Wales coalfield was at the lower end of the Clydach valley close to its confluence with the Usk at Gilwern (SO 2313). Here the first works had been established in the water-power era as early as 1606 with the Worcester family of Hanbury very much to the fore. It was under this same family that the works were later to make the successful transition to steam power. Coal was available on the spot and the adjacent hillsides were riddled with levels which followed the outcropping seams. Limestone was also close at hand so it was only necessary to import iron ore for the industry. There was a forge lower down the valley nearer to Gilwern. Nothing now remains, though a terrace row of cottages is still named Forge Row. Today the scene has once more reverted to one of relative tranquillity and it is only the traffic on the new 'head of the valleys' road which is likely to disturb the peace. The adjacent hillside still bears the scars of past coalworking but once above these and on to the limestone plateau top the scene is close to that which must have once characterised the area before the impact of the Industrial Revolution began to make itself felt. The tide of industrial working has now swept over this region and worked its way farther south nearer the coast.

7

Communications of a Corridor

Very few parts of Britain have such a network of roads which carry so little traffic as the Welsh borderland. Once away from the A49 trunk road, which runs the length of the border corridor, there is a vast complex of lanes which are sheer delight to the unhurried traveller. Coming from the snarled up urban highways of the West Midlands, the country roads of west Shropshire, Montgomeryshire and indeed the whole of the Middle March, are more reminiscent of conditions of the 1930s when only the most venturesome motorist penetrated the area. In many ways the present picture is even brighter, for what were mere upland dirt tracks, especially those along ridgeways, have been metalled in the last twenty years, largely to provide access for the milk lorries to outlying farms. There are still plenty of 'green' roads and ridge tracks remaining, as well as the recently designated Offa's Dyke Path which runs the whole length of the border from the Dee to the Severn. Although the path has to depart from the actual line of the eighth-century dyke in a number of places, it seems destined to become increasingly popular with walkers seeking wider horizons. But even the less adventurous can sample what the borderland countryside has to offer on foot, for many tracks of long-forgotten railways now provide easy routes.

When were the first tentative steps taken to establish the present closely knit pattern of roads, lanes, tracks and paths? Archaeological evidence has provided at least a partial answer, especially in the central section in the upper headwater region of the Clun and Teme drainage systems. Here a detailed examination of the distribution pattern and nature of archaeological finds has convinced Miss Lily Chitty that some of the ridge-top routes came into being in the early Bronze Age, some time between 2000 and 1500 B.C. There were two main tracks in use to link the hill country of Wales with the English lowlands to the east. One ran along the tops in order to avoid the damper Clun valley and the lowlands which had once been occupied by glacial lakes (see pages 44–8). The other led off from the Kerry Hill ridgeway at Cefngolog (SO 1887) and then ran southwards past the present Anchor Inn until it reached the watershed separating the Clun and Teme valleys. Both routes are well defined in their western sections where they form almost straight tracks linking the hill tops. Here they can be traced as

29. *The narrow road running along the top of the Kerry Hills and following the line of the prehistoric track.*

footpaths in the Kerry Hills (1285). This section is known, perhaps significantly, as Yr Hen Fford (the old road). Farther east it runs through a recent plantation and is known as The Sarn (causeway). Here, and for many miles as it makes its way towards Bishops Castle, it forms the boundary between Shropshire and Montgomery, perhaps yet another sign of its antiquity. The southern route, the Clun Trackway, is equally well defined in the present landscape by a minor road which runs from the Anchor Inn by way of Bettws y Crwyn (2081) and then along the length of Spoad Hill, keeping to the crests until it makes the descent down a long spur to Twitchen and the river crossing at Clungunford (3978).

Once in this hill-basin province of the Marches the exact courses of these prehistoric trackways are less easy to follow. Prehistoric man himself might have had difficulty in tracing and maintaining a route through an area that was heavily forested at the time and in great contrast to the more open country of the ridge tops. The focusing point of both the Clun and Kerry Hill ridgeways would seem to have been the upstanding Titterstone Clee (SO 5977), with its dolerite capping giving it a distinctive and easily recognisable outline. While making his way eastwards along the ridgeway, the Clee top must have stood out as a homing beacon for Bronze Age man. Once past Clee there was a fairly direct route to the Severn near Bewdley and after this was reached the waterway gave access to regions both north and south.

In trying to understand why Bronze Age man was anxious to carve out east–west routes running for scores of miles across the borderland region, archaeology provides at least a partial answer. The valued commodities of prehistoric time included certain types of rock which could be fashioned into axe and hammer heads. Few rocks have the necessary qualities needed for shaping and usually they are distinctive in appearance and easily recognised from chance finds. One such rock is the Hyssington Picrite which outcrops on the southern slope of Corndon Hill (3194). It is an igneous rock which is peculiar to this particular locality and yet it has been found in barrows at such distant places as Avebury and Stonehenge. This suggests that it was a commodity much sought after and traded in the Bronze Age. Although the exact site of the Hyssington axe factory, where the rock would have been roughly hewn, has not been found, the outcrop of the picrite is only a few miles north of the ancient Kerry Hill trackway. It seems likely, therefore, that traders would use the upland route in making their way to the Severn and thence by rivers to Salisbury Plain. The presence of the Hyssington Picrite would not, in itself, account for the making of the Kerry and Clun ridgeways. In the fields alongside the route, archaeologists have from time to time turned up thousands of flint implements and associated fragments. The parent material must have come from a distant chalk outcrop, the nearest of which is the Marlborough Downs over a hundred miles away. This suggests that during the Bronze Age there was a two-way trade between this part of central Wales and southern England. The routes could have an even wider significance for they offered an alternative means of reaching the shores of Cardigan Bay and the Irish Sea, in preference to the more circuitous way northwards through the borderland using the Severn and Dee and thence along the north coast of Wales. The inland route was certainly used by travelling Irish bronzesmiths on their way to southern England. Its importance was to decline in late Bronze Age times when the climate began to deteriorate and bogs and peat formed on the higher tops. Clearly the route was not completely obliterated for it was later to serve as a boundary and to meet the needs of the cattle drovers from Wales, ever anxious to avoid the toll roads of the lowland valleys. Perhaps it is because of the drovers that we owe the chance survival of the routes today when, for different reasons, we can appreciate their usefulness as arteries of solitude. With so little traffic, the passing traveller has time to grasp the essential ingredients of this still largely unspoiled countryside.

There were other early ridgeways apart from the Clun and Kerry Hill routes. This is true of North Wales where the productive Craig Llwyd axe factory near Penmaenmawr distributed its wares widely in much the same way as the Hyssington Picrite. The main alignment was again west to east, indicating trading contacts across the border zone from the Welsh uplands to the English lowlands. This was a pattern of traffic movement which was to persist throughout prehistoric time and even when the ridgeways fell into temporary disuse, their valley counterparts, using the river basins of the Clun, Teme, Vyrnwy, upper Severn and Dee, continued the dominant west-to-east alignment.

The situation was to change dramatically with the arrival of the Romans, who substituted a predominantly north-to-south line of communication throughout the border country, mainly in response to defensive needs. The Roman incursions into the foothills of Wales began less than a decade after their landing on the Kent shores in A.D. 43. They were met with stern resistance by the powerful Iron Age tribes of the Silures in the south and the Ordovices in the north. It was not until the campaigns of Agricola in A.D. 74 to 78 that Wales really felt the stranglehold of Roman subjugation. The lines of communication in this conquest phase probably followed both the major river valleys into the interior and some of the existing tracks across the uplands. Many of the isolated marching camps established at this time were only occupied for a short period, though pollen analysis has shown that there was a considerable forest clearance taking place and this would suggest more permanent settlement. Once Agricola had achieved his main objective of subduing the local Celtic tribes, the marching camps lost much of their significance and many never became incorporated in the main communication network which the Romans were to establish in the next century.

The cornerstones of Roman military rule were the legionary fortresses of Deva (Chester) in the north and Isca (Caerleon) in the south and therefore the main road linking them ran almost the entire length of the borderland. Although it made use of existing tracks over limited stretches it was mainly a newly engineered route with a prominent agger or embankment raising it above the adjacent lands. This was very important in certain areas like the

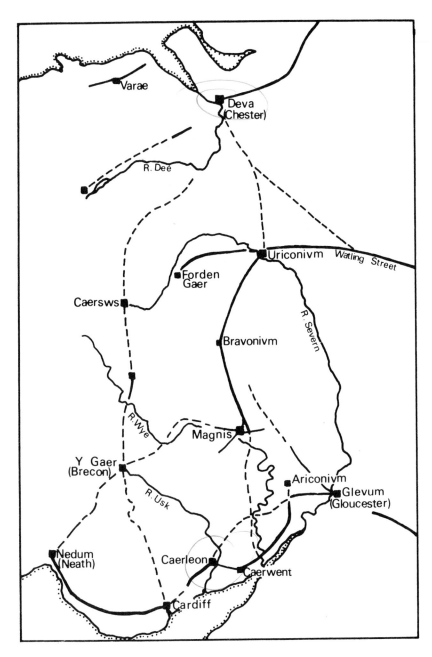

16. *Roman road system through the border corridor and adjacent regions.*

lowland basins – some sites of former lakes – through which it ran, for it made it a relatively dry causeway. The agger varied in height and width and was sometimes simply an earth bank although often it was constructed of carefully laid layers of stones. In the case of the Chester-to-Caerleon road there are few remains because modern roads have been built over it and the centuries have taken their toll. In many parts only the line of the road is known as it corresponds with a continuous field boundary or minor track. The antiquity is undisputed when it forms a parish boundary for this indicates that it existed in Saxon times when the parishes originated.

In the borderland the topography imposed some degree of control over the exact lines followed by the major north–south road, sometimes known as Watling Street West. There are many straight stretches across lowland basins or along river valleys but in order to negotiate the hilly terrain of south Shropshire it twists and curves in relation to the topography. Occasionally it has to seek out gaps like the gorge at the southern end of the Church Stretton trough (SO 4489) or at Aymestrey (4264) where the road breaks through the southern rim of the Wigmore Dome. In the section south of the Roman settlement at Leintwardine (Bravonium) (4074) the early road follows a very different route from that of its modern successor (A4110). The Roman method of crossing the low ground of the Wigmore lowland was a direct one while the present road clings to the lower slopes of the surrounding hills. Although no longer in use, the course of the Roman road can be clearly made out for it is followed in part by a footpath and rough lane. In places the agger has survived as a turf bank about two feet high and about thirty feet wide. The re-routing obviously poses the question as to the reason for adopting a more circuitous course for the later road. In part the answer might be found in the fact that today in the lowest part of the vale there is a tendency to flooding in the winter months and so, at an early date, opportunity was taken to fashion a better route. Another possible influence was that the Mortimer family, one of the great Marcher lords, had their castle at Wigmore and it would therefore be natural for the main borderland road to pass through the settlement which had grown up around. The fact that the former section of the Roman road does not form any boundary suggests that it was abandoned at a relatively early date, in which case adverse physical conditions, namely danger from flooding, would seem to be the principal reason.

The use of a former line of a Roman road as a major boundary in the present-day administrative pattern can be clearly seen where it crosses the north Herefordshire plain west of Leominster. From Mortimer's Cross to Stretford (4455), a distance of five miles, the former Roman road is followed by parish boundaries though it is now little more than a footpath. The name

Stretford is also significant and indicates that when the first Saxon settlers moved in the area the road was still in being. Many Saxon settlements were named in this way by incorporating the element 'stret', for example Stretton Sugwas, north-west of Hereford and Church Stretton amidst the Shropshire hills.

In the section from Caerleon to Viroconium near Shrewsbury, the Watling Street West was a typical borderland route making use of river valleys and lowland basins to ease construction. North of Viroconium, however, the final section of the road to the fortress of Chester ran unimpeded across the lowlands of north Shropshire and therefore, both in situation and character, it is not a true border road. It is curious that there is no Roman road much closer to the Welsh hills, perhaps along the line connecting the present-day settlements of Wrexham, Chirk and Oswestry and thence into the upper part of the Severn valley where there was a Roman fort at Forden Gaer (SO 2098). The recent discovery, as a result of air photography, of a major Roman site close to the Dee at Rhyn Park, covering approximately forty-eight acres and halfway between Shrewsbury and Chester, must renew speculation that there was once a road hugging the edge of the Welsh hills, with possible offshoots into major valleys like the Vale of Llangollen.

Undoubted Roman roads using valley routes into the interior plateau country of Wales are known from a number of places in the Marchland. The starting point is usually the main north–south route of Watling Street West. In some cases the penetrating valley routes westward were connected with mineral workings for lead and silver but usually they originated as connecting links to another north–south route much farther west across the interior plateau. This ran from Dinorben in the Vale of Clwyd through Caersws (SO 0391) in the Severn valley and then southwards towards Brecon Gaer, across the Brecon Beacons to Gelligaer, Caerphilly and ended at Cardiff. It is significant that all these place-names preserve the element 'caer' in their present-day designation. The line of this heartland road is not so well known as the truly borderland route in the east, for long sections have never been traced on the ground and we have to rely on other inferences in projecting a possible route. This is particularly true in the north, where there is little direct evidence, apart from near Caersws where there is a distinct agger traceable for several miles. The disappearance of large sections of this central upland route is not unexpected, for it was probably abandoned as the Roman grip on the interior lessened after the initial conquest period. The temporary nature of this line of communication, built to serve a particular need at a certain moment of time, is perhaps shown by the section of route in the vicinity of Castell Collen near Llandrindod Wells. This isolated area must have been difficult to hold and pressure elsewhere must have led to the withdrawal of the military garrison located here for long periods.

Although the major elements in the Roman road network in the borderland has been known to archaeologists for some time, new discoveries of some of the lesser routes are made from time to time. It is a field where the amateur can participate alongside the professional. Because of the directness of the Roman roads, there is plenty of scope for mapping out possible routes connecting new sites which the archaeologist or the air photograph is continually bringing to light. Although fascinating, the mere drawing out of possible former roads on a map is not constructive and the would-be investigator must be prepared to go into the field and search for the tell-tale agger or use an auger to drill at selected points for a buried metalled surface. Many unsuspected Roman roads have been found as a result of this method of approach. A route in the Golden Valley, possibly making for the fort at Clyro, was discovered in this way and part of it is now exposed in the former station yard at Abbey Dore (3830). Perhaps the finest section of Roman road uncovered is found in the Forest of Dean at Blackpool Bridge where the blocks of limestone of the foundation make an impressive feature (see pages 168–9).

By the time of the Saxon settlement of the border region many of the original Roman roads had already been lost and thus never became part of the system of later centuries. The role of the Saxon as road-builder has claimed only scant attention, largely through a lack of documentary and field evidence. With so many new settlements being founded during the period of Mercian supremacy in the eighth century, culminating in the making of the political frontier of Offas's Dyke, a supporting road system must have come into being. Perhaps for the first time we are seeing in these Saxon centuries the genesis of a road pattern, large parts of which still exist today. The dominant north–south alignment of major routes through the borderland corridor was further reinforced as the area enjoyed a period of relative stability following the building of Offa's Dyke. After the Norman Conquest the creation of the Marcher lordships led to a slight shift from a national to a more local emphasis and this would have helped the creation of many minor routes, often the quiet, leafy lanes of today. Newly created towns like Ludlow and Richard's Castle inevitably brought new roads in their wake. Where the planted towns were successful, a radiating road system was created and became superimposed on the earlier pattern.

Prior to the formation of the turnpike trusts, which ushered in a long-overdue period of road improvement, many of the roads in the border country as well as most of Wales were in a deplorable state, perhaps the worst

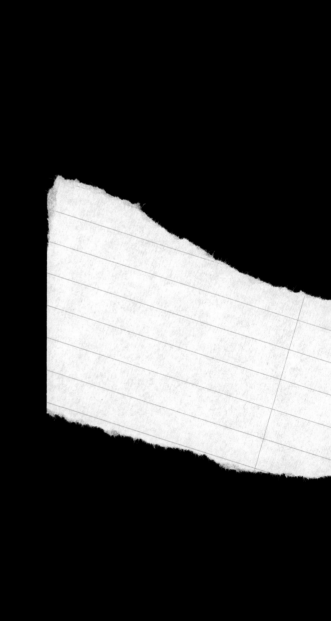

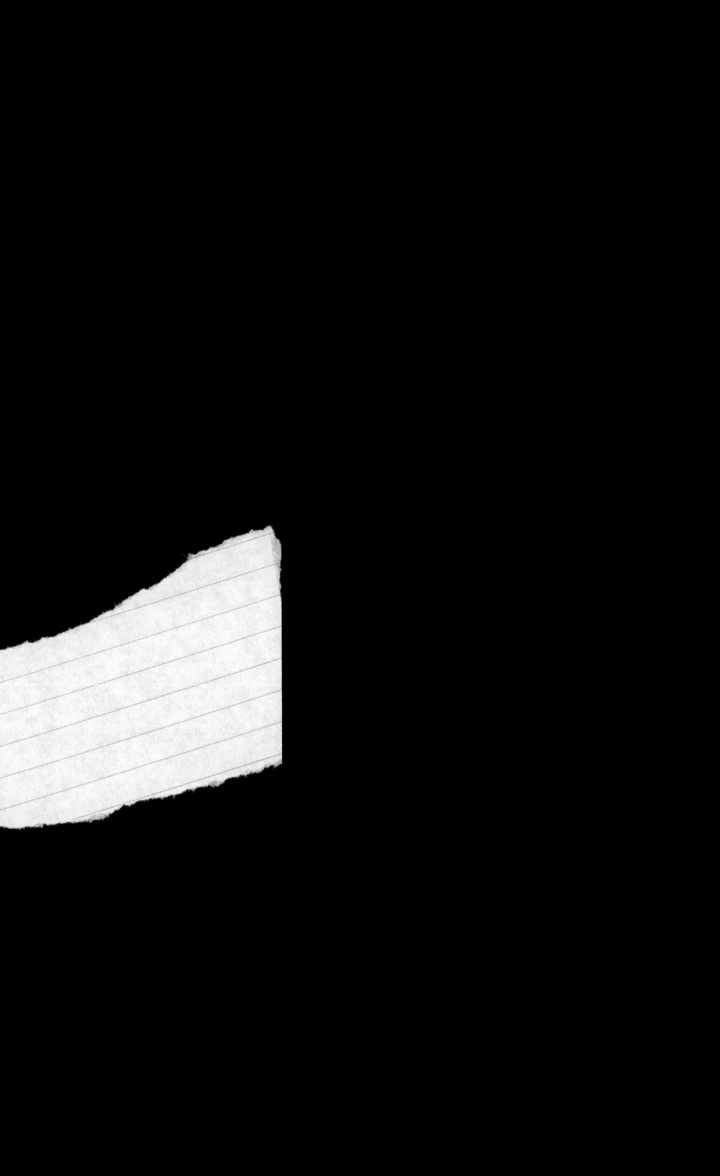

in the kingdom. The tracks used by pack-horse trains suffered from steep gradients while even the main roads were often deeply rutted by wagons and became muddy quagmires in the winter months. Once the ironworks began to increase production from the mid-eighteenth century onwards, there was considerable pressure from industrialists for improvements to be made. Turnpike trusts offered a solution and from about 1750 onwards they began to make an impact on improving communications. An act of 1752 led to the Shrewsbury-to-Wrexham road being made up and shortly afterwards a further section through Mold and on to Chester also came under the control of a turnpike trust. This set in motion a minor road mania in the northern Marches and during the next decade it spread to other parts, especially Montgomeryshire where the woollen industry was flourishing and needed better contacts with the English markets.

Apart from the needs of industry there was another influence which led to road improvements in the area. After the Act of Union in 1800, it was imperative that routes to Ireland should be firmly established if the new link was to succeed. Although the argument as to the best route through north Wales and the choice of a packet station was to continue for many years, the improvement of the Holyhead road, the present A5, became a priority and was soon to engage the attention of the foremost road engineer, Thomas Telford. The route from Shrewsbury through Llangollen and thence across the Denbighshire Moors had been brought into use for a mail coach service following the opening of the Capel Curig road in 1808. The latter was a private venture by Lord Penrhyn, one of many by rich landowners and industrialists who lamented the lack of a national road policy. The main difficulty lay in the numerous different trusts who controlled sections of a through-route and adopted varying standards of maintenance. The Holyhead route, for example, was in the hands of six different turnpike trusts who thought only of their own needs. Telford was aware of their general incompetence and so in 1819 he persuaded Parliament to take away their powers and set up an entirely new trust with a grant of £15,000 for road improvement. Telford, as engineer, at once set about improving the gradients for stage-coach travel. The Dee gorge at Chirk was a considerable obstacle and to overcome this Telford carefully graded his approach roads down each side of the valley. Similarly, beyond Corwen, where the road climbs out of the Dee valley in a twisting gorge section, he carefully rebuilt the approach to his own standards. These included a stipulation that gradients should not exceed 1 in 20 so that coaches could maintain a speed of ten miles an hour throughout their journey. In many places the original route of the old turnpike was abandoned in favour of a new road with better foundations and adequate

179

drainage. As it was still a turnpike road, new toll houses were built and some still survive, as in the section between Llangollen and Corwen. Distance milestones were placed at regular intervals and again many are still in place, each with a distinctive ridge top.

When Thomas Telford was called upon to improve the Holyhead road, it was not his first contact with the northern Marches. At the turn of the century he had been in the area supervising perhaps two of his best known engineering works, the canal aqueduct across the Ceiriog river at Chirk and the famous Froncysyllte aqueduct across the gorge of the River Dee. Although the canal era had begun as far back as 1758 with the building of the Duke of Bridgwater's canal by James Brindly, it was not until the last decade

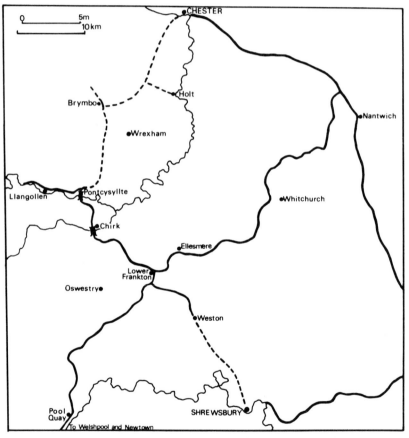

17. *Canal network of the northern Marches with the ill-fated scheme for connecting the Mersey and Servern.*

180

of the century that activity reached its peak in the so-called era of 'canal mania'. Such was the interest shown at the time that shares in the canal-building companies were often over-subscribed many times. With capital readily available it is clear that many over-ambitious schemes were floated without real feasibility studies being made of their likely trade. Many canals were so hastily conceived that they inevitably ran into constructional difficulties and turned out much more costly than the original estimates.

The northern Marches was served by the Ellesmere Canal which began life after a bill was presented to Parliament in 1793. Altogether 110 miles of waterway were proposed as part of a grand design to connect the Mersey with the Severn and thereby establish an inland route between the major west-coast ports of Liverpool and Bristol. This major objective was never achieved, at least not under the proposed plan of 1793. Money was not a difficulty at the outset for the capital was subscribed in less than eight hours after dealings began, such was the euphoria which surrounded the scheme. Among the many industrialists on the committee was the ironmaster John Wilkinson whose nearby works at Bersham would benefit considerably from a canal nearby. It was Wilkinson who persuaded his fellow committee members to appoint Thomas Telford, perhaps because he knew of the engineer's interest in building with iron wherever possible. In this case he was not disappointed. Telford's salary was to be £500 a year, out of which he had to employ a foreman as well as pay his own travelling expenses!

As a road-builder, Telford had learnt that it was necessary to go over the ground in detail in order to map out the best route and he adopted the same principle before beginning work on the Ellesmere Canal. There were two major physical obstacles to be overcome, namely the gorges of the Dee and Ceiriog valleys. Long flights of locks, perhaps sixteen in all, would be needed to descend to the valley floor and then climb back on to the original level, so slowing up traffic and therefore adding to the transport costs. Telford therefore decided on his famous iron trough aqueducts to cross the gorges. Great pillars of stone were to raise the aqueduct 127 feet above the Dee gorge at Froncysyllte. The foundation stones of the first pillars were laid in the summer of 1795 but it took another eight years to complete the aqueduct. In order to reduce the actual length of the structure to a minimum, Telford built a huge embankment out into the Dee gorge on its southern side and this left only about 1,000 feet for the iron aqueduct. Once the stone pillars were finished, the iron trough was placed in position. Although it was not the first time this type of construction had been used – Telford himself had earlier experimented with a short, sixty-yard length on the Shrewsbury Canal – no comparable major piece of engineering had ever been attempted. It inevitably attracted attention as one of the new wonders of Wales and the tourist guide books were soon instructing their readers not to miss the great structure on their travels through this part of the borderland country. Praise came from unexpected quarters. Sir Walter Scott described the aqueduct as 'the most impressive work of art he had even seen'.

30. *Telford's iron trough aqueduct which he used to carry his canal across the gorge of the Dee.*

   The Dee and Ceiriog aqueducts had proved costly in money and time and it is not surprising that it was November 1805 before the canal was officially opened. By then the heady days of the 1790s had given way to the much more sober, economic judgements of the new century. The shares of the canal company, which had earlier attracted a 20 per cent premium, were now to be had at a 50 per cent discount. The reason for the rapid change of fortune was that the original scheme of a Severn–Mersey connection had been abandoned. Constructional difficulties and the lack of further financial support meant that the section from Wrexham to Chester was never started while in

182

the south the Ellesmere Canal got no farther than Weston, still a long way from its intended connection with the River Severn. It was only the middle section of the original network that was built and it therefore had to link up with other systems which severely limited its effectiveness as a trade route. In the context of the original Severn–Mersey connection it was a white elephant of gigantic proportions. Wharves and basins built at places like Pontcysyllte in the expectation of heavy traffic were now far too large. Only in recent years, in a leisure-conscious age, have they really proved their worth with the increasing popularity of 'long boat' holidays. Curiously enough the Llangollen Canal, which was originally designed as a feeder to bring water to fill the canal system, is now one of the most popular sections, with its attractive scenery along the northern banks of the Dee valley.

Fortunately a major branch along the upper Severn valley was built as far as Newtown so that together with the northern limb around Chirk, the canal became a major north–south artery serving this part of the border country. This southern extension, known as the Montgomeryshire Canal, had its beginning in 1793 when permission was given for a link to be built to the limestone quarries around Porth-y-Waen (2623) from Newtown. Interested parties who became shareholders included landowners, industrialists and quarry owners like the Earl of Powis and his son, Lord Clive. The canal would carry lime to improve the newly enclosed lands of central Wales while in the reverse direction it would provide access to the English markets for the woollen industry centred on Newtown. This was made possible with the link-up forged with the Ellesmere Canal which was already constructing a branch from Lower Frankton (3631) to Llanymynech (2620). The more distant limestone quarries were given access to the canal by short tramway connections. Progress southwards was painfully slow and it was not until 1819 that Newtown was finally reached. The other major town of the valley, Welshpool, was brought into the canal system much earlier and to the benefit of its industry; warehouses were built and a distinct canal quarter of the town developed which is still recognisable today. The canal has recently been cleaned and is now used by pleasure boats. Its most distinctive feature is the picturesque lift bridges which straddle the waterway in places. The section near Newtown, however, has been infilled in recent years while farther north there is no longer any link with the former Ellesmere Canal.

The benefits which would follow the construction of a canal link with an inland town were often stressed in the prospectus which accompanied the floating of a new company. As a means of importing bulky materials like coal and lime, the canal had no rival and it is not surprising therefore that towns like Hereford, Leominster, Brecon and Abergavenny in the southern

Marches were anxious to take part in the intense activity of canal building which occurred in the 1790s. The Leominster Canal, for example, was completed in 1795 and ran from the Forest of Wyre coalfield at Mamble (SO 7273). Immediately there was a sharp reduction in the price of coal in both Leominster and Tenbury. The opening of a canal was a great event for the surrounding countryside and an excuse for great jollification. The ringing of church bells, the playing of brass bands, perhaps even a military display with the firing of cannon, a gaily decked procession of boats led by the principal shareholders, were the usual accompaniments of the opening ceremony. The initial euphoria was often to subside quite quickly if the commercial traffic did not come up to expectation. For the Leominster Canal receipts were reasonable but not sufficient to proceed with the original plan of a connection with the River Severn at Stourport, a town whose very being depended on the canal building era. As in so many cases it was the railway which brought about the downfall of the Leominster Canal and the whole system was drained in 1859. Now only the observant can trace its former course across the rural acres of north-east Herefordshire.

The city of Hereford, with its much larger population, would appear to have been a much greater prize for the canal builder. It is true that the River Wye did offer some means of natural water transport but its variable levels often made navigation difficult. It was because of this that an act was obtained in April 1791 for a canal to the River Severn at Gloucester. Work began almost immediately and in 1798 the section from Gloucester to Ledbury was opened for traffic. Money was now short and the time not ripe for further extension. For over forty years the original scheme lay dormant and then suddenly, between 1840 and 1845, the remaining section was completed by tunnelling under Aylestone Hill to reach the outskirts of the city of Hereford. In many ways the decision to complete the canal was an act of financial lunacy, coming as it did when the railway boom of the mid-nineteenth century was spreading even into rural areas like the Welsh borderland. The Hereford-to-Gloucester waterway was the last of the main-line canals to be built in England and clearly came far too late to stand much chance of success. Inevitably it was soon for sale and after prolonged negotiations it was a railway company that took over part of its route in 1882. Substantial remains of the canal still exist in the rolling landscape of east Herefordshire around Ashperton (6442) but elsewhere there is only the occasional hint of this ill-conceived and ill-fated project.

The Brecon Canal has fared much better and when renewed interest was shown in it about twenty years ago for pleasure boats it was sufficiently well preserved to be quickly restored. The canal, like so many others, can trace its origin to the Act it obtained in 1793 when the economic benefits of transporting heavy commodities like coal and iron attracted support from a public only too willing to buy its shares. The northern section was started straight away and by 1800 it had reached Brecon. Coal which had previously sold at 1s 2d a hundredweight now cost only 9d. The connecting link at the other end, to give access to the Monmouthshire Canal, was not completed until 1812 when it was possible to travel by water all the way to Newport. Running as it did around the margin of the coalfield, its only practicable route, the Brecon Canal was fortunate in being able to tap the coal and limestone trade in its path. As elsewhere in the borderland, nearby collieries and quarries were connected to the canal by short tramways. Lime kilns were built at intervals

31. *The Brecon Canal, now restored as a leisure amenity of the National Park.*

and some have survived by the canal bank at Llangattwg Park (2017). For large sections of its course the canal runs along the southern side of the Usk valley and this gives fine views of the Beacons to the south and the Black Mountains to the north. Not surprisingly it is an asset to the tourist industry for it lies almost wholly within the Brecon Beacons National Park. The industry on which it formerly depended has retreated more and more to the valleys of the south so that today the canal has a distinctive rural charm.

The topographic controls exerted on canal routes meant that many areas of mineral working were out of reach and, as has been noted above, the solution was to build a supporting system of short tramways. The Ellesmere Canal built its own tramway to the collieries around Ruabon while in Montgomery-shire the limestone quarries in the hills to the west of the Severn could only be reached by a specially constructed mineral line. In extreme cases, where physical obstacles prevented canal construction, the tramway took over completely. The best known of these was the Hay Tramway which ran from a point in the Usk valley below Brecon, then across the fairly low watershed into the Dulas valley, a tributary of the Wye. Once in this main valley the easy gradients allowed rapid progress to the town of Hay and beyond. The line was scheduled to end at Eardisley (SO 3149) where the river would take over. When work began on the tramway in 1812, the line offered a con-nection between Brecon and the rich agricultural lands of Herefordshire. More importantly, by using both the tramway and the Brecon Canal, coal could be brought from south Wales to Hereford. Brecon also benefited, for although it had a population of 5,000 it could not in itself generate enough traffic. Now it became a transit point rather than a terminus and it quickly led to goods being carried both to the east and north, the rate charged being 3d per ton/mile. The wagons of the Hay Tramway also carried passengers for a charge of 6d for six miles. It must have been a leisurely journey on the horse-drawn trains as they climbed ponderously out of the Usk valley and then over the watershed towards Glasbury and Hay. The gauge of the iron track was 3 feet 6 inches, which was normal for existing tramways then in use in the south Wales coalfield.

When the tramway was nearing completion at its northern end at Eardisley in 1818, interest was aroused in another part of the county. The townspeople of Kington were anxious to have the benefits which a tramway might bring, both for trade and easier contact with the outside world. An Act was presented 'to make and maintain a railway or tramroad for the passage of waggons and other carriages from the Hay Railway to or near the Town of Kington and from there to or near certain lime works at or near the village of Burlingjob for the conveyance of lime, corn and other commodities towards and into the county of Brecon greatly relieving the turnpikes and other roads which are at present in a very ruinous state'. This preamble adequately sums up the difficulties, thoughts and feelings of promoters of the early tramways which were increasingly favoured for those areas where the lie of the land prevented canal construction. The scheme also had commercial attractions for the Hay Tramway in that it would allow it to tap the rich grain-producing area of north Herefordshire and enter into the south Wales market. In theory, at least, the coal-carrying wagons coming north could return with corn and to a lesser extent with lime to be distributed *en route*. One of the main supporters was James Watt, the engineer, who owned land at Burlingjob and perhaps was looking ahead to the time when steam traction could take over from horses.

The route chosen for the Kington Tramway was necessarily a circuitous one in order to keep the gradients at less than 1 in 60 for the horse-drawn trains. Brilley Ridge, which stood in its way, had to be circumvented and this meant adding over two miles to the more direct route. William Hazeldine, the engineer in charge, was a friend of Telford and well versed in the art of following the contours from his canal-building experience. In many ways the early tramroads inherited the ideas and principles of the canal age which was now coming to a close. The Kington section was opened in 1820 and for over thirty years proved its worth. In 1857, however, a direct railway link was forged with Leominster, a town better situated than Hereford to serve the needs of this part of the borderland. In consequence the Hay–Kington tramway lost traffic and might have been closed completely but for the fact that a railway company took it over and replaced its track with a normal standard gauge. The tramway running westward from Kington to Burlingjob limestone quarries remained in use for some years but it, too, in 1875 was replaced by a railway. This continued as far as New Radnor (2160) which became the limit of railway penetration in this part of the borderland. Now even the railways have all closed and little remains save the outline of the track, the occasional bridge, embankment or cutting as a reminder of a past age. Stations like Talgarth (SO 1533), once the pride of the Hereford-to-Brecon line, have now become private houses but many have simply been abandoned, the platforms neglected and the former goods yards overgrown with weeds. All this has happened since the early 1960s when the so-called Beeching axe brought about the closure of many of these border railways in face of increasing competition with road transport. It is becoming increasingly difficult, even in the short space of time that has elapsed since closure, to recall the image and influence of these rural lines when perhaps an old steam locomotive pulled one or two carriages at a comfortable speed between the small market towns they served. Old photographs and the timetables of the line when in full operation perhaps can conjure up an era when the railway was the life-blood of the rural community. For the ever-ambitious Victorian traveller, perhaps with a Murray's Guide in his pocket, it was a means of exploring remote areas which had previously been out of reach.

The railways, like the canals of an earlier age, had a period of glory from about 1840 onwards when they carried all before them. They caught the imagination of a public only too willing to finance the most revolutionary innovation in transport history since the invention of the wheel. It is now difficult to imagine the impact which trains rushing through the countryside

187

at speeds up to fifty miles an hour must have had on a population used only to the ten-mile-an-hour average of the stage coach. The main emphasis initially was on forging a link between the principal towns of the region. But even the officials and businessmen of small county towns, as well as some influential landowners, were anxious to see themselves part of the national railway network. Many schemes never advanced further than the drawing board but a few managed to clear the major hurdle of Parliamentary approval and become a reality.

In terms of railway history the Welsh Marches has some distinctive facets. At various times it became a battleground between some of the major companies, perhaps symbolising the borderland role which had characterised the region over the centuries. It was also a desired area for many companies who were anxious to provide a link between the industrial towns

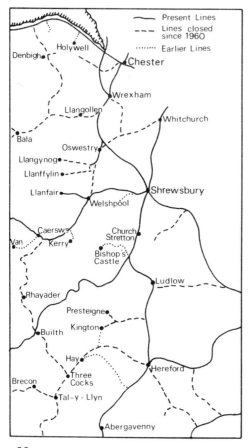

18. *The contracting rail network of the borderland. Many of the closures have resulted from policies operated since 1962.*

of England and south Wales and the coast of Cardigan Bay. Another distinctive feature of borderland railway history was the existence of many short, privately owned branch lines with limited resources. Many were forced to establish working arrangements or even sell out to the national companies. Even at the outset they were dependent on bigger concerns for the use of rolling stock and other operating equipment for which they paid a fixed proportion of their receipts. Finally the area had a multitude of mineral lines which reached out into the isolated corners of the region where worthwhile mineral deposits could be exploited.

Perhaps the most famous of the borderland companies was the Cambrian Railways, always given a plural designation because it resulted from an amalgamation of five separate entities in the 1860s. It was also a local railway in the sense that much of its track ran through the borderland countryside and it had its headquarters at Oswestry. Its network began at Whitchurch, well inside Shropshire, and had a main axial route running through Oswestry, Machynlleth and then to the coast at Aberystwyth, with a long circuitous route around Cardigan Bay to Pwllheli. Its interest in reaching the Welsh coast lay in the hope that perhaps it could win some of the lucrative Irish traffic from a specially developed packet station at Port Dinllaen on the north coast of the Lleyn Peninsula. This had been a planner's dream for half a century though by the 1850s the chances of fulfilment had virtually disappeared with the building of the Chester-to-Holyhead north-coast route. By buying out the Mid Wales Railway, the Cambrian acquired a long branch to the south as far as Tal-y-Llyn Junction (SO 1027) and this gave it access to Brecon and hence a through-route to south Wales. Although this long southern section never carried the traffic it had hoped, the route was scenically most attractive as it followed the narrow, twisting valley of the Dulas southwards from Llanidloes and then across the watershed into the upper Wye drainage system. Just before reaching Rhayader there was a difficult piece of engineering through the narrow gorge around the rocky precipices of Gamallt. From Rhayader the valley widened a little though the railway was forced to cross the river several times as it negotiated the succession of meander loops *en route* for Newbridge. At Builth Road (0253) it crossed under the Central Wales line and maintained its own station. To all intents it was a Wye valley railway for it continued to use the valley floor as far as Three Cocks Junction (1637) where it linked with the Hereford–Brecon line (owned by the Midland Railway). The latter had running rights over the Cambrian track as far as Tal-y-Llyn junction, a few miles east of Brecon. Thus the Cambrian covered a vast amount of territory in central Wales and linked some of the larger market towns. This gave it an important role as a passenger line but its commercial aspirations remained unfulfilled. It was also looked upon as a local line for, although it gave rise to a north-to-south through-route, it suffered badly from slow times because of the difficult country it ran through. Inevitably it suffered competition from the more direct borderland route which ran from Shrewsbury through Ludlow and Hereford to Newport which had opened in 1853. Much of the track bed of this now defunct Mid Wales railway can still be traced on the ground but it is quickly being swallowed up by the profusely growing vegetation. It is hard to believe that it only closed in 1962. A bottle gas company has now taken over the station buildings at Three Cocks Junction while at Newbridge the site has been used

32. Talgarth Station and the abandoned railway line which is being steadily submerged beneath the encroaching vegetation.

for a housing estate. Each year developments such as these claim a little more while the track itself is gradually submerged under scrub and weeds. What was once a dominant feature of the man-made landscape, often fought over by landowners who resisted its coming, the country railway is gradually sinking, leaving hardly a trace.

Although the Cambrian Railways liked to think of itself as the operator of through-routes like the above and the line which ran across to Cardigan Bay, it also controlled a number of short but interesting branch lines. None could ever hope to be a commercial success and it is surprising that they were ever built or managed to survive for so long. The Kerry branch line is clearly in this category. It ran from the Severn valley at Abermule (SO 1694) and climbed steeply up the Mule Gorge on to the plateau top of the Kerry Hills, a total length of only four miles. John Wilkes, a prosperous local farmer who founded the breed of Kerry Mountain sheep, was the main initiator of the railway scheme. Perhaps its early date (it opened in 1863), meant that sound commercial reasoning found no place in the decision to proceed. From the outset it carried very little goods traffic and insufficient passengers to the main line to ever cover the cost of maintaining the railway. For long stretches it had gradients in excess of 1 in 43 and this made it relatively costly to operate and keep the track in good order. Once it reached the plateau top it ended in a simple cottage-type terminus at Glanmule (1690), even though this was still a mile from Kerry village. In the depression of 1931 the railway was closed for

33. *The former terminal building of the Kerry Hill branch railway.*

passengers but it still lingered on for goods traffic right up to 1956. In its life span of almost a hundred years, the area of the Kerry Hills which it served hardly changed. Certainly the railway made no lasting impact on the land-scape, nor did it arrest the steady migration of people from the region. It is now difficult to make out the former track as it twists through the woodland of the Mule Gorge but the terminal station at Glanmule still survives as a private house, perhaps symbolic in its country setting of the gentleness and unobtrusiveness of this most rural of rural railways. As remarkable as the railway itself was a system of narrow-gauge tramways which spread out from the terminus at Glanmule to reach the outlying sheep farms and forestry plantations of the Kerry Hills. The tramways had a relatively short life and had been abandoned by 1922 when road transport was beginning to make an impact on these isolated areas.

The Kerry branch was one of a number of lines that formed feeders to the main Cambrian trunk. Perhaps the most purposeful and successful was the Llanfyllin Railway (SJ 1419) which followed the floor of the Cain valley. A practising solicitor in the town, John Pugh, was the most active of a band of local enthusiasts who wished to see their town restored to its former importance as a market centre. The railway company, however, was looking at the project through national eyes so that any line through Llanfyllin would be part of a route through to the west coast, perhaps to Port Dinllaen and a share of the Irish traffic. There were great physical difficulties, not least the barrier of the Berwyns range which would involve costly tunnelling. It was therefore decided at a meeting in Llanfyllin Town Hall in October 1860 to settle for a local branch line. John Pugh opened the subscription with £3,000 and this inspired confidence in local landowners and gentry to do the same. Three years later the nine-mile branch line was opened in a typically festive manner. A twenty-three-coach train was run from Llanfyllin to the seaside resort of Borth using the new branch to join the main Cambrian line at Llanymynech (2721). After this auspicious opening the line proved its worth for local trade. Passenger expansion was difficult, for the area was suffering depopulation and it was soon apparent that the line would lose money due to rising costs. The building of the nearby Vyrnwy reservoir in the 1880s by Liverpool Corporation brought a rapid increase in freight receipts, but this was only a temporary phase and once the work was completed the line reverted to its normal level of goods traffic, mainly farm produce. Nevertheless the Llanfyllin branch managed to survive until the mid 1960s when it was forced to close with the abandonment of the main Cambrian line between Welshpool and Oswestry.

A few miles to the north is the Tanat valley which heads back right into the Berwyn range at Llangynog (SJ 0526). When the nearby Llanfyllin branch was proposed in 1860, the Tanat valley was also considered as a possible route through to the west coast but again this project foundered because of tunnelling under the Berwyn range. With the great speed at which the Llandfyllin Railway came into being, there was no possibility of a similar line in the Tanat valley only a few miles away and the proposal was dropped for thirty years. After the passing of the Light Railways Act in 1896 the earlier scheme was revived for now it was possible to build more cheaply. An enquiry held in August 1897 decided that the proposed line should make straight for the Cambrian system at Llanymynech and not attempt to link with the Llanfyllin branch. Construction work on the fifteen-mile length of light railway began in 1901 but it was three years later before it was opened, largely because of delays caused by costly flood prevention works. The Cambrian was to operate the line on a promise of 60 per cent of the takings. One possible source of traffic and revenue, namely the lead workings around Llangynog, never materialised for by the turn of the century the richest veins had been worked out. The Tanat Valley Light Railway therefore became a farmers' line carrying local produce to market at Oswestry and serving a scattered rural population in the valley and surrounding hills. Although after the 1914–18 war mineral traffic became more important and brought in revenues twenty times that of passenger receipts, it was insufficient to keep the line solvent and by 1921 the railway was in the hands of a receiver. It was then taken over completely by the Cambrian and absorbed into the Great Western a year later. Although it struggled on until 1952, running three trains a day in each direction, increasing competition from road transport caused a gradual running down of the line. Local farmers found it more convenient to carry their livestock to market by lorry and a Mr Owen began a private bus service from Llanrhaeadr through Llanfyllin to Oswestry on market day. The scattered population of the outlying valley farms and hamlets was never really served by the line. Llanrhaeadr-ym-Mochnant (1226), the largest settlement, was more than a mile from its station. Even the Great Western Railway itself found it more convenient in the 1930s to run their own bus service to these side valley villages and thus was really in competition with itself.

The problem of providing transport for the scattered rural communities in the borderland was a pressing one throughout the latter half of the nineteenth century. With the main Cambrian Railways trunk line concentrating traffic in the Severn valley and thus enhancing the importance of places like Welshpool and Newtown, former small market towns like Llanfair Caereinion (1006) felt increasingly isolated. There was considerable local pressure for railway branch lines, the only practicable means of transport for both produce and people at the time. Without a rail link a once important market centre with a number of roads converging on it could find itself dying almost overnight. Whether a railway was built depended very much on local support and the emergence of a strong forceful personality who was determined to overcome the many difficulties which any scheme was likely to encounter. Unfortunately Llanfair Caereinion had no such enterprising local worthy to press its claims as at Llanfyllin, so that although schemes were put forward in 1862 and 1875 they came to nothing. As in the Tanat valley, it was the passing of the Light Railways Act of 1896 that led to renewed interest and in the following year a meeting held at Welshpool approved the building of a narrow-gauge railway. Work did not begin until 1901 and it was a further two years before the short line from the now decaying Llanfair Caereinion was opened. It followed the Banwy valley for the first two miles but then had to climb to cross the low watershed into the headwaters of the Sylfaen Brook close to Castel Caereinion (1605), the only other village the railway served *en route* to Welshpool. It was always intended that there should be a direct link with the main Cambrian system at Welshpool but with the Powis Estate blocking the southern approach the railway had to run through the streets of the northern outskirts of Welshpool to a point close to the Cambrian main line station. From the beginning the Welshpool and Llanfair Railway had to depend on the limited resources of an agricultural community for its traffic. Farmers in the upper part of the Banwy valley were enthusiastic and brought their livestock to the railhead at Llanfair Caereinion. The rail traffic generated undoubtedly benefited this small country town built on the sloping valley sides running down to the Banwy and for a time the streets were thronged with people, a situation that it had not known since the days of the drovers. The main hotel in the town, the Wynnstay Arms, advertised itself as a first class hotel for families and tourists. In spite of the attempt to attract both commerce and visitors the railway was not a financial success and by 1934 the Great Western Railway, which had taken control of the line, found it more profitable to run buses than operate a rail passenger service. It still continued to carry livestock until its enclosure in 1956. Its end was marked with as much ceremony as its opening some fifty years earlier. A special train carrying 150 enthusiasts left Welshpool on a still, late-autumn afternoon to the accompaniment of the local brass band and a similar reception awaited them on their return. The whole aura of sentiment which surrounded the occasion was seized upon by a small group of narrow-gauge railway followers and a few weeks later they formed a preservation society. Perhaps the time was just ripe to save one of the dwindling number of former branch lines from complete extinction. There was no particular virtue in this line compared with many others whose death had hardly attracted attention. It was simply a case of a group of people willing to make an effort to preserve the line. To this end they succeeded for the western part of the former railway was re-opened for passenger traffic in April 1963. In time it is hoped to re-open the other section into Welshpool though it is unlikely to ever operate in the streets of the town again. Its future seems assured if the increasing number of tourists in the border country continue to support it in the summer months when it is running.

For this single Llanfair–Welshpool railway which has survived there are up to a dozen former branch lines in the Welsh Marches which have disappeared with perhaps only the line of the track, the occasional building or odd item of operating stock remaining. It is easy to condemn the lack of foresight, economic common sense or business acumen of the promoters of these nineteenth-century railways. For anyone living in a rural community in the border country in the latter half of the nineteenth century, the chance of a much-improved line of communication with the outside world was not to be missed even though it now looks foolhardy. It is only in this light that the multitude of schemes and proposals, many of which came to fruition, must be seen. Sometimes, as in the case of the Glyn Valley Tramway which ran up the Ceiriog valley for nine miles from Chirk (SJ 2937), there were valuable slate deposits awaiting exploitation once adequate transport was available. A road built between 1860 and 1863 helped but there was continuous agitation for a tramway to transport the heavy slates to the main line at Chirk for dispersal to the ever-growing industrial towns of Lancashire and the Midlands. At the opening of the tramway in March 1874, horses were used to pull the laden wagons down the valley and even the passenger cars which were later added to the freight trains. The opening of the quarry at Hendre in 1875 to produce granite setts led to increased traffic and brought about the introduction of steam traction. By 1893 over 20,000 passengers a year were making the railway journey down the valley to Chirk where trains could be caught to Liverpool and Shrewsbury. Places which were talked about but never visited save on special occasions could now be reached in a few hours even from the remote hamlets at the head of the Ceiriog valley. Granite rather than slate became the main revenue earner, especially in the 1930s, when crushed stone rather than setts were produced at the Hendre Quarry. Soon lorries were taking an increased proportion of the total output of chippings which were being used for road making. In 1932 a motor bus link was established with Oswestry and this sounded the death knell for the Glyn Valley Tramway. After three years of substantial operating losses, the tramway finally closed. Only the line of the tracks which ran alongside the valley road for much of its length and the occasional bridge over the river have survived to the present day of what was once a prosperous mineral/passenger line.

Many of the branch lines did not have the mineral traffic to boost their revenues and yet miraculously survived as working entities for well over half a century. The attractive Golden Valley line running the length of one of the major dip-slope valleys of the Black Mountains, began life in 1881, mainly to serve the villages of the valley but also to provide a link between Pontrilas on the Hereford-to-Newport line with Hay-on-Wye on the Hereford-to-Brecon line. From the outset the railway had a struggle to survive and throughout its independent life it had to make do with a ramshackle engine and two second-hand coaches. The cost of building the line was well over £30,000 and yet it was finally sold to the Great Western in 1898 for a mere £10,000. Things improved under Great Western control and the line continued to carry passengers until 1946 and goods over certain stretches for another ten years.

The Golden Valley Railway began its history with a letter to the *Hereford Times* in August 1875 which set out, in effusive language, the sense of deprivation felt by the writer and his countryfolk friends through the absence of a railway in the valley. The letter began, 'In such a time of railway and telegraphic communication as the present is it not very strange that so lovely and fertile a part of Hereford as this should be declared unworthy to participate in the general advance of the time by being deprived of cheap and quick transit?'. Local landowners were asked to support the venture by providing traffic while the gentry were to put up the necessary capital and give the whole proposal an air of respectability. Although 10,000 passengers a year were carried, the receipts never quite matched even the modest expenses of running the line, less than £2,000 a year in 1882. The Golden Valley Railway of which so much had been hoped lurched from one crisis to the next, holding off lawsuits and continually seeking to borrow money. There was also the pipe dream of the line becoming part of a great north-to-south route across the borderland provided the southward extension from Pontrilas to Monmouth could be built. Parliamentary approval for this line was indeed given but nothing ever came of it. By 1901, when the Great Western took over the Golden Valley Railway, the idea was completely forgotten. For a short period at the beginning of the century the line did make a modest profit of about 10 per cent and brought tourists to places like Abbey Dore. As elsewhere the motor car and rural bus led to a continuous drop in passenger receipts and gradually parts of the line were closed, the last section from Abbey Dore to Pontrilas in June 1957. Perhaps the most remarkable fact about the railway was that it managed to survive for so long.

The same can be said of another borderland line, the Bishop's Castle Railway which began life in 1865 with a nine-mile link to Craven Arms. Initially it was never intended that it should simply remain a branch line but rather continue to Montgomery to join up with the Cambrian system. Repeated and long-drawn-out negotiations with other companies came to nought and its own insecure financial footing left it as a single branch line for seventy years. Typical of many border lines, it had to take a very circuitous route from Craven Arms (SO 4373) in order to pass through the Plowden

Gorge and thus avoid steep gradients. Once on the flat of the former glacial Lake Camlad, the route was much easier and more direct. At Lydham Heath (3490) a spur to the west was built, perhaps in the hope that an extension would ultimately be built to Montgomery. The decline in the fortunes of the former borough of Bishop's Castle this century and the general depopulation of this rural area of west Shropshire brought about the closure of the railway in 1935, much earlier than the valley branch lines of the borderland country farther north.

Perusal of any of the Ordnance Survey sheets covering the Welsh Marches will show the former widespread coverage of these now 'forgotten' railways. All the branch lines, save the mineral line to the Nantmawr Quarries (SJ 2524) from Oswestry, have now gone and even the former trunk system of the Cambrian is very much dismembered and shrunken. Apart from the main-line routes which run across the border country to reach the north and south coasts of Wales, the former Cambrian Railways route through to the west coast at Aberystwyth is still retained. As it serves the border towns of Welshpool and Newtown it remains a vital artery of communication, especially for an ageing population, even though its economic future looks bleak.

The other line under constant threat of closure is the Central Wales line running from Shrewsbury through to Craven Arms and then across the plateau of Radnorshire to Llandrindod Wells and the group of former small spa towns before reaching the south Wales coast at Llanelli and thence on to Swansea. Although providing the only through-route across the interior of Wales, it began life as the result of the amalgamation of four separate companies, each owning a particular section of the present through-route. Ultimately, under economic pressure, the four independent companies came together under the umbrella of the London and North Western Railway. The various sections were opened at different times between 1857 and 1868. The starting point was Craven Arms on the earlier built Shrewsbury-to-Ludlow and Hereford line. At that time Craven Arms was only an inn within the manor of the Earls of Craven. The opening of the Shrewsbury-to-Ludlow railway in 1851 and the later junction of the Central Wales line made Craven Arms a small railway town, perhaps not quite in the same class as Crewe or Swindon, but nevertheless unique as a border settlement. The Central Wales Railway, even today, has a character which sets it apart from other lines. It links a succession of small market towns like Knighton, Llandovery and the Victorian spas like Builth and Llandrindod before passing down the Towy valley *en route* for Llanelli. For long stretches it runs through empty country but nevertheless serves a useful social function for it is often, even now, the only link between isolated hamlets. Unstaffed halts pepper its route and they are still used, as any traveller on the line will know from the slow journey times.

The railway line likely to outlive the rest of the borderland lines was the first built. Although connecting the two English towns of Shrewsbury and Hereford, it forms the only real link between north-east and south-east Wales. The fifty-mile length of railway was sanctioned by Parliament in 1846 but owing to financial difficulties it was not started until 1850 under the guiding hand of Thomas Brassey. The Shrewsbury-to-Ludlow section was opened in 1852 and the remainder of the line to Hereford by December 1853. As a southern extension to Newport was already in existence, having been built some seven years earlier, a through-route running almost the entire length of the borderland was in being at a relatively early date. With its direct route and minimum gradients giving opportunities for reasonably fast journey times, the Shrewsbury to Newport line seems to fulfil the oft-used expression 'first to be built, last to be closed'. Perhaps the sound economic and geographical realities which surrounded the history of the earliest railways was soon abandoned amidst the euphoria of later years. The full impact of this became only too apparent in the post-war period when hundreds of miles of borderland railway disappeared almost overnight from the countryside scene.

8

Borderland Towns and Cities

Towns act as focusing points for greater or lesser areas of their enveloping countryside. The primary task of the town is that of a market centre, a task that has marked off urban communities at whatever time in history we start to examine the topography and geography of towns. The market-place forms a primary element in the plans of Roman towns just as, centuries later, the Norman architects of Ludlow made the focus of their new town in a huge market-place that filled the space between the castle and parish church on the flat top of a limestone ridge above the meandering Teme. Closely joined to the function of towns as markets is their role as centres of industry. The new towns of the Middle Ages, of which there are scores in the Marchland countryside, encouraged the occupation of their burgage plots by craftsmen – weavers, gold and silversmiths, leather workers and all those occupations that provided the luxuries and industrial equipment of the medieval world. In the past these tight, articulate settlements provided shelter and security within their walls and within the compass of their castles. As a long drowsy peace settled over the Marches after the Tudor Act of Union, towns began to lose their defensive role. In the process many places were to lose all meaning as urban centres, surviving as expanded villages dominated by the huge green mounds and crumbling walls of a medieval castle. Other towns, favoured by fortune and the harsh determinants of geography, were able to adapt themselves to the new demands of the long centuries of peace. In the eighteenth and nineteenth centuries Monmouth, Hereford and Ludlow, among several others, were to emerge as regional centres where the landed gentry could retire for the winter to comfortable Georgian town houses to enjoy an organised social round of balls and gambling, concerts, theatrical entertainments, literary societies and improving lectures. Slowly the successful towns among the many urban settlements of the Marches were to acquire their modern face and functions. The similar façades of the chain stores and supermarkets were to cast a film of uniformity over medieval market-places and shopping streets. Local newspapers, library services, the cinema in its heyday in the first half of the twentieth century were to create urban fields – zones over which each regional urban centre exercised a magnetic attraction in the surrounding countryside.

The towns and cities of the Welsh Marches not only express in their topography and functions a series of social and economic relationships with their surrounding region, they also display through their street patterns and names, their buildings and building materials a summary of their evolution through time. The topography of the Marchland town epitomises so much of the history of the region. The medieval walls of Chester, much restored since the eighteenth century when the ancient defences were converted into a promenade, follow for part of their course the line of the Roman wall. Again, at Shrewsbury the surviving black and white timbered houses, built by the Rowleys, Owens and Irelands – prosperous wool and cloth merchants – speak of the years at the turn of the sixteenth century when this regional capital of the middle Severn plain formed a focus of the wool and textile trade from the huge hinterland of the Welsh hills. The buildings of present-day Shrewsbury also reflect the connections of this regional capital with the formative years of the industrial revolution in the country of the Severn gorge below Ironbridge. In the northern suburb of the town we find a former flax spinning mill of revolutionary design, erected about 1800, with a complete framework of cast-iron columns and beams and window-frames of iron. This was the prototype of so many mills that sprang up in the industrial areas of early nineteenth-century England. Perhaps an even more striking memorial to the technological changes of the years about 1800 in the townscape of Shrewsbury was the building of St Chad's Church in 1792 on a hill overlooking the great southward bend of the meandering Severn. Thomas Telford, who has left his mark widely on the landscape of the Marches apart from the building of the great coach road to Holyhead, had forecast in 1788 that the tower of Old St Chad's, an Anglo-Saxon foundation, was in danger of collapse. Three days after his alarming pronouncement the church was destroyed. The new St Chad's, designed by George Steuart, the architect of Attingham Park, employed the techniques and materials of the new iron age in a plan composed of two intersecting circles. The smaller circle forms the entrance hall while the larger comprises a circular nave. The great circular gallery is supported by cast-iron pillars and the winding staircase that curls round the walls of the entrance hall displays the prolific use of iron that was to characterise the Industrial Revolution.

The topography of the Marchland towns reflects the cycles of prosperity and poverty that make up their individual histories. Chester, on the northernmost fringe of the Marchland, entered a phase of expansion in the late nineteenth and early twentieth centuries that is not matched elsewhere in the borderland. Already by 1850, it stood at the junction of four important railway lines and its communications controlled the greater part of the traffic with North Wales, a role that was equalled by none of Chester's counterparts in the middle or southern Marches. Chester's period of Victorian prosperity is abundantly revealed in the buildings of the city. The many timbered, black and white buildings that lend a 'picturesque' quality to the townscape of the medieval core are all the product of an extensive phase of redevelopment in the closing years of the last century. As Nikolaus Pevsner has written in his monumental survey of the buildings of England, 'Chester became one of the most thorough-going Victorian and Edwardian towns in the country, though the layman does not realise it'. To the hundreds of thousands of tourists who every summer explore the streets of the inner city this is the perfect exemplar of a long lost 'olde' England. The detailed and accurately imitated motifs of the black and white buildings in St Werburgh Street and Eastgate Street reveal few clues to their Victorian origin. Ninety-five per cent of Chester's 'black and white' belongs to the late Victorian and Edwardian decades, an age in which nailed-on boards had replaced the timber-framed structures of medieval and Tudor craftsmen.

As we survey the towns of the Welsh Marches at the present time, it is evident that many different patterns of urban history are concealed in the buildings and streets laid out before our eyes. In the townscape of Chester we can still find visual evidence of its role as a military capital of Roman Britain, while its fine shops, busy streets and expanding suburban ring testify to its vitality in the twentieth century. On the other hand, at Caus Castle (SJ 3307) on the southern foothills of Long Mountain, the massive banks and mounds, thickly overgrown with summer-scented hawthorn, tell of a medieval borough that failed to evolve any stable elements of urban life. The tantalising question arises of why Caus lacked the quickening pulse of urban development while Chester succeeded down the centuries in adapting itself to the changing conditions of economy and society in the British Isles, displaying in the course of time many functions from garrison town and border fortress, county town and centre of administration in a medieval palatinate, a busy port engaged in trade with Ireland, to one of England's leading tourist resorts. The glib answers seem to lie in the realms of geography and topographical relationships. Caus, lost in a tangle of lanes among the Shropshire Hills, appears to lack any connection with the major topographical features that geographical textbooks have always associated with the growth of communications, the focusing of trade and the development of urban communities. Chester, by this argument, thrived down the centuries because of the natural gifts of its site on a sandstone bluff that controlled the lowest bridging point of the Dee and which coincided with the tidal head of the river and the limit of sea-going shipping. In addition Chester's access to North Wales seemed to predestine the city for an important role in trade and conflict with the principality. The explanations offered by geography for the successful growth of towns appear to be as incontrovertible as they are simple. But if the Corbet family, the founders of Caus, had played a more powerful role in Marcher politics and if they had succeeded in carving out an extensive lordship from the ancient territories of Powys, it is not impossible that Caus might have evolved into a successful borough – a small town of the size of Ludlow that might have overshadowed and perchance eradicated its much older near-neighbour of Westbury. Our latter-day geographers might then have explained the town of Caus by its site 'at the northern entrance of the Rea Brook–Camlad corridor, a primary route into the upper Severn basin whose importance was already foreshadowed centuries earlier by the Romans when they constructed a road along the length of Long Mountain and established their fort, close by the Severn, at Forden Gaer'.

The first towns in the Welsh Marches were founded by the Romans. Caerwent, Caerleon, Kenchester, Viroconium and Chester remind us of the elements of urban geography that the Romans sketched on the landscape of the Marchland. The contrasted patterns of growth and decline in these settlements over the subsequent centuries illustrate the complex factors in urban history. Viroconium provides the most striking example and propounds the most difficult problems. Here was one of the most important towns of Roman Britain, ranking with Silchester and St Albans as one of the great central capitals. The streets of Viroconium covered almost two hundred acres and even in the earliest stage of its complex history, towards the end of the first century, a recent estimate of its population has proposed a total of between 8,000 and 10,000 people. Apart from a few shattered remnants of the most massive Roman masonry, the quiet fields of Wroxeter today convey no obvious signs of the former extent and greatness of Viroconium; only the techniques of aerial photography and a long history of excavation have uncovered the true character of a lost Roman city. At some time after the fifth century, in the largely unrecorded history of Dark Age

Powys, Viroconium's role as the regional capital of the middle Severn plain was taken over by Shrewsbury. Wroxeter, a completely rural community, possessed the lands of the lost city. Only the name faintly recalls one of the greatest among the tribal capitals of Roman Britain. Chester's course of development has been utterly different from that of Viroconium. Since the closing decades of the tenth century an active urban community has occupied the site that was first demarcated by the defences of the Roman fort and settlement. Medieval merchants, monks and craftsmen have been succeeded down the centuries in the inner city by store managers, hoteliers, solicitors, estate agents and the officials of local and county government. The continuity of life at Chester for more than a thousand years is reflected in the variety of its building styles and the great wealth of the city's street names.

Lying between the contrasted evolutionary patterns of Chester and Viroconium we find the history of Caerleon (ST 3390). Among the towns and cities of Roman Britain the functions of Caerleon most closely resembled those of the fortress settlement on the Dee. Strategically placed on the navigable River Usk, Isca Augusta, was the legionary fortress through which the conquest and control of south Wales was secured. The original fortress, with four symmetrically placed gateways and a grid-iron pattern of streets, covered almost as much ground as the original military station at Chester. Later extensive suburbs developed between the fort and the river where archaeology has revealed the sites of temples, baths and an amphitheatre. More than two thousand coins have come to light at Caerleon, dating from the first century until the opening decade of the fifth century. All the evidence suggests that urban life in Roman times was just as firmly rooted at Caerleon as at Chester and Viroconium. But later centuries have witnessed the transference of urban functions to Newport. Today Caerleon is not even a market town, though some of the elements in its urban topography and the evidence of its Dark Age importance as the chief ecclesiastical centre of Wales and a place of learning hint at the possibility of its evolution into a regional capital of the magnitude of Chester, an evolution that was not to take place.

Caerwent (ST 4690), lying inland from the Severn estuary between the mouths of Wye and Usk, presents an even more striking example of the fickleness of fortune in the history of towns. The site of a Roman town, covering an area almost as great as Caerleon or Roman Chester, is occupied by a handful of farms and cottages. Lanes and hedgerows follow the lines of former Roman streets and in places the extensive foundations of buildings are exposed to the light of day. Caerwent, named by the Romans *Venta Silurum* or the market of the Silures, has long lost all urban functions and even the outward aspect of a town. The ramparts of the Roman town now shelter a village and, as at Viroconium, some tantalising questions arise concerning the time and nature of its demise. Not that Caerwent failed to attract the great town-makers of the Middle Ages, for we find the mound of a Norman castle placed within the south-western corner of the Roman site. The great age of urban growth that occupies the two and a half centuries after the Norman Conquest saw the creation of active urban communities around castles on the navigable estuaries of the Usk and the Wye at Newport and Chepstow. Caerwent was to remain one among scores of medieval castle sites in the Marches that failed to generate an active and lasting urban life.

The Romans sketched out the first network of towns in the borderland between the mouths of Severn and Dee, but, as we have already hinted, the connection between the Roman ground-plan and the subsequent development of towns after the Norman Conquest is extremely obscure. The second important period of urban development and one that has determined the present map of towns in the Marchland occupies the high Middle Ages, the three centuries after the Norman Conquest. In this period of expanding population and growing trade, conditions in England and all over western Europe favoured the founding of new towns with rights to hold markets and fairs. The Welsh Marches were as favoured as almost any part of Britain in the making of the new towns or the raising of rural communities to a new status and a different way of life through the granting of market rights and borough charters. The abundance of urban experiments in this region is largely explained by the complex political geography of the Marcher lordships. Close on 150 territorial units in the Marchland led to a proliferation of nascent boroughs. Castles gave protection to the clusters of merchants and craftsmen who settled in the new towns. A list of major castles provides an almost complete gazetteer of the towns of the Marchland, that does not agree with the urban map of the twentieth century largely because the medieval process of town-making went too far and outran the economic capacities of the borderland to support urban communities.

By the time of the Act of Union in 1536, many of the sites that had received borough and market charters in the twelfth and thirteenth centuries had failed to live up to the ambitions of their founders. At New Radnor (SO 2160) it is still possible to trace in the hedges of adjacent fields the lines of streets that were planned but never finished in the new town, a town established about the year 1250 to take over the functions of Old Radnor. At Stapleton (SO 3265), close by Presteigne, the landscape today provides few suggestions of the efforts to plant an urban community there in the twelfth century. There is only a green space and a cross-road where markets were once held.

34. *New Radnor — in the latter half of the thirteenth century a new town was founded to replace Old Radnor. In this air view we can see the huge motte at the head of the broad main street, the enclosing Town Wall (marked by the dark line of trees on the left margin) and the incomplete grid-iron of streets that are now indicated by hedge-lines.*

One of the greatest attractions of the Welsh Marches for the traveller of today is the number of places that have at some time in the past eight hundred years borne the proud title of borough. At Caus, Cefnllys (SO 0861) and White Castle (SO 3716) it is hard to believe that an urban community was ever successfully settled; only the documents of the medieval centuries with their references to markets and burgesses make it plain that some kind of a settlement with urban functions of trade and industry once existed there. At many other places – Clun and Wigmore, Richard's Castle and Grosmont to mention only a few – the landscape still shows many traces of a livelier urban past in castle ruins, empty spaces where markets were once held, and rows of

205

cottages whose continuous façades recall the earliest years of the establishment of these urban settlements with the marking out of their burgage plots.

The founding of scores of new towns in the centuries after the Norman Conquest provided the Marchland with more than sufficient sites for its urban requirements down to the present time. The region has been left unscathed by Britain's latest phases of urban growth, in the nineteenth century with the vast expansion of industry and population and in our own times with the founding of new towns to solve problems of overcrowding and dereliction in the big cities. The coalfields of north-east Wales and Shropshire experienced a rash of urban development in this period. In the twentieth century the only new settlement, planned from the outset like so many of the medieval boroughs with all the legal accoutrements of an urban community, is Telford.

The three great regional capitals of the Welsh borderland, Chester, Shrewsbury and Hereford, were all in existence before the Norman Conquest, although much obscurity surrounds the history of all three settlements in the pre-Norman centuries. What is evident is that each settlement had very different beginnings. The foundations of medieval Chester were planted on four centuries of successful urban life as a Roman town and fort. One of the greatest problems that faces the local historian of Cheshire's county town is the question of a continuance of life there in the dark centuries between the abandonment of Deva by the Twentieth Legion and the late Saxon centuries when there is once more clear evidence of a flourishing community at Chester. Shrewsbury's early development is perhaps even more puzzling. Roman finds there have been so scanty as to discount any idea of a permanent settlement in this strategically valuable loop of the Severn between the first and fourth centuries. Yet in the timeless mist of the three centuries between the withdrawal of Roman power and the advance of the frontier of Saxon Mercia into the Marchland, Shrewsbury seems to have emerged as one of the major centres of government in the late Celtic kingdom of Powys, for it has a strong claim among several other places to be the site of Pengwern, the mysterious seat of the princes of Powys. Hereford offers an even more intriguing variation on the same theme. Just as Shrewsbury seems to be the logical successor to Viroconium as the organising centre of the middle Severn plain, so Hereford would appear to succeed Kenchester as the chief urban centre of the rich lowland of the middle Wye.

There are still many obstacles in the way of understanding the shaping of the urban pattern of Hereford and its surroundings. Kenchester was not another Viroconium, a splendid regional capital in the fullest meaning of the phrase. Recent research has suggested that it was little more than a large Romano-British village. The absence of a Roman settlement at Hereford is still more inexplicable when one remembers its proximity to a crossing of Roman roads in this part of the plain of the Wye. In the past decade archaeological research on the line of an ancient and now largely vanished earthwork at Hereford has revealed the shape of a substantial late-Saxon settlement on the north bank of the Wye, a settlement that in later centuries was to be occupied by the cathedral and the core of the medieval town. Shrewsbury probably began as the Dark Age successor to Viroconium. There the heart of the medieval town may well lie within the bounds of a long-vanished rampart of an Iron Age camp of which the only surviving evidence today is the 'bury' element in Shrewsbury's place-name. Hereford, unlike Shrewsbury and Chester, seems to be the first town worthy of the name within its surrounding region. It looks like the Saxon successor to the cluster of Iron Age camps, large British settlements of the Roman and Dark Age centuries, that crown several of the wooded hills rising from the Wye plain within sight of the county town.

In the first long centuries of urban development before the Norman Conquest, Chester presents the richest evidence and the most baffling problems. Here, where the River Dee swings close to a sandstone bluff, the Romans had established a fort by A.D. 79. Chester became a legionary centre, the base for thousands of Roman soldiers, and on the eastern flank of the military settlement a civil community of shopkeepers and craftsmen came into being. Even though Chester's history as an urban settlement appears to begin with the coming of the Romans and their need to secure a firm base for the conquest of North Wales after A.D. 60, it is far from certain that this was virgin ground for the Romans. The name *Deva* is of Celtic origin and the discovery, in 1966, of plough-marks beneath the site of the Roman parade ground suggests that there was some kind of settlement at Chester before the establishment of the fortress town.

The visual evidence of Chester's first three centuries as a Roman town is far from abundant. A considerable section of the medieval wall bounding the northern and eastern parts of the ancient urban core follows the line of the perimeter of the Roman fort, but the only substantial piece of Roman masonry today lies just to the east of North Gate. Here the Roman facing-stones reach to a height of sixteen feet and some old tombstones built into the wall suggest that it was part of a reconstruction at some time early in the fourth century. Elsewhere one can see a fragment of an angle turret that stood at the south-eastern corner of the Roman fort, and in the cellars of several

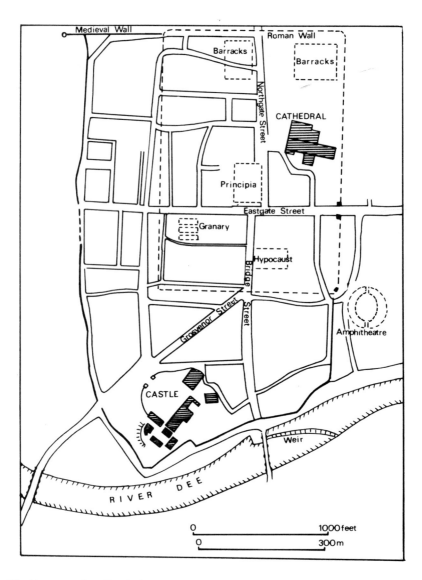

Medieval Wall
Roman Wall
Barracks
Barracks
Northgate Street
CATHEDRAL
Principia
Eastgate Street
Granary
Hypocaust
Bridge Street
Grosvenor Street
Amphitheatre
CASTLE
Weir
RIVER DEE

| 0 | | 1000 feet |
| 0 | | 300 m |

19. *The Roman and medieval elements of present-day Chester.*

shops and offices in the heart of the city fragments of Chester's Roman underpinnings are visible. For instance, part of the guard-room of the eastern gate of the Roman fort is preserved in the cellar of the Leeds Permanent Building Society in Eastgate Street. The extensive clearance and redevelopment of properties in the heart of Chester since the Second World War has uncovered details of many buildings of the Roman settlement. A legionary bath-house and a barracks building were revealed in the making of a shopping precinct, and the digging of underground car parks in the central redevelopment area between Princess Street and Hamilton Place brought to light the remains of workshops, the praetorium or commandant's residence and the sacellum, a central shrine where the standards were kept. The making of the inner ring road also uncovered the western defences of the Roman fort for the first time. Recent discoveries have added detail to the picture of a flourishing Roman settlement through evidence gathered outside the city walls. On the edge of the Roodee, the site of Chester's racecourse once occupied by the channel of the Dee, a short section of the quay wall of the Roman harbour has been revealed. Again, near to St John the Baptist's Church, a Saxon foundation within the limits of the Roman civil settlement, the site of a Roman amphitheatre has recently been located.

After the withdrawal of the Roman legionaries, perhaps before A.D. 400, the history of Chester is wrapped in obscurity. Archaeology can produce no firm proof of a continuing occupation of the site after the beginning of the fifth century. The documentary record is equally scanty and uncertain until the opening years of the tenth century when it is evident that Chester was once again a flourishing settlement. For instance, the Anglo-Saxon Chronicle, under the year 907, records that Chester had been rebuilt and it is evident that by 910, the time of the settlement of part of the Wirral by Scandinavian soldier-farmers under Ingimund, Chester had re-established its importance as a military centre. But the intervening centuries from Roman to late Saxon times present an enigma. As Graham Webster, the eminent Midlands archaeologist, has written, 'so far no single piece of recognisable pottery of the Dark Ages has been noted from any of the extensive excavations in the city'. Even so, the Chester that is discerned through the documentary evidence of the late Saxon period was a mature urban settlement. It seems to have performed an important role in the revival of Saxon political power against the Danelaw. The building of a castle, close by the Dee on the site of the later Norman castle, probably led to the inclusion of Chester among the Saxon *burhs* of the north-west established by Aethelflaed. An even more striking clue to the size and permanence of a pre-Norman settlement at Chester appears in the number and location of

Saxon churches of which there are six. Their location suggests that the focus of the late Saxon town lay on the southern edge of the long-abandoned Roman fort, perhaps along the bank of the Dee between the Saxon castle and the church of St John the Baptist that was to become a cathedral church for a short time in the closing years of the eleventh century. Another strand of Chester's pre-Norman history survives in the numerous names of streets and persons in the medieval record of Scandinavian origin. The 'gate' element in three of the city's main streets – Northgate, Eastgate and Watergate – represents the Scandinavian term, *gata*, meaning a street. Scandinavian personal names are included among the moniers of Chester and the presence of a mint in the pre-Norman town is strong evidence of its importance. Again, Chester of the late Saxon period was governed by twelve *iudices civitatis* or law men, a form of local government and also a mode of reckoning, by units of a dozen, that belonged to the territories of the Danelaw in eastern England. Not only was Chester a thriving town, at least from the beginning of the tenth century, but it also appears to have had a strong Scandinavian element in its population. Was there perhaps a distinct Scandinavian community living there in the lower part of Bridge Street close to the Old Dee Bridge and the harbour? A faint hint of their presence may still survive in the dedication of the little medieval chapel there to St Olav, the patron saint of Norway whose dedications in other English towns have left a clue to the presence of merchants here from Scandinavian lands almost a thousand years ago.

The state of Chester in the great gap between the fifth and the tenth centuries still remains open to debate and speculation. As Graham Webster has written in his article on 'Chester in the Dark Ages', 'that the site of Chester remained derelict throughout the succeeding five centuries', after a slow disintegration of the Roman pattern of urban life into the fifth century, 'cannot be proved'. Archaeology has nothing of proof positive to offer and the reference to the Roman fort in Bede's brief account of the Battle of Chester in A.D. 614 has been used as evidence for the total desertion of the Roman site by that time. However, it is not impossible that outside the walls of the Roman fortress a British community survived close to the banks of the Dee and within the ambit of the former Roman civil settlement.

Despite the long blank of the centuries between the demise of Roman Chester and the founding of a late Saxon settlement over the ruins of Deva, there is no doubt that the city embarked on a long period of growth in the tenth century. An era of town-planning, perhaps as important as any in Chester's history, belongs to the high Middle Ages. During this time the limits of the city were redefined so that they no longer coincided exactly with the line of the Roman defences. To the west the course of a medieval wall was laid out well beyond the Roman works. Southwards the new limits of the city were defined by a wall that closely followed the bank of the Dee. The date when the area of Chester was more than doubled remains obscure. Did it happen before the Norman Conquest or was the line of the medieval wall determined in the twelfth century, an important period of population growth and urban expansion in many parts of England? One important clue to the reshaping of the city in the Middle Ages lies in the sites of several early churches. Three parish churches – Holy Trinity, St Bridget and St Michael – are built over the foundations of the Roman wall. Two others that have since been pulled down, St Chad and St Martin, lay within a few yards of the outside of the Roman defences. All these churches first appear in the documentary record in the twelfth or early thirteenth centuries. Holy Trinity is first recorded in 1188. St Michael and St Bridget, picturesquely facing each other across the site of the Roman fort's south gate, first enter the records in 1178 and 1224. It is evident that the Roman defences had been destroyed by the latter half of the twelfth century and that they provide valuable building sites in a growing town. But other scraps of evidence suggest that the medieval reorganisation of Chester, and particularly the realignment of the wall, was under way before the Norman Conquest. One of the gateways in the medieval extension of the wall beyond the Roman perimeter has been known as Newgate since its rebuilding in 1553. In a thirteenth-century document, the same gate appears as *porta de Wlfild*, a medieval rationalisation of the Old Norse personal name, Ulfaldi. There seems little doubt that Ulfaldi was one of the Scandinavian settlers in Chester living in the quarter around St Olav's Chapel. He must have been an eminent member of Chester's Norse community if his name became attached to one of the gateways in the newly extended wall of the town. Does Ulfaldi's personal name in this long obsolete medieval name of the Newgate provide an important clue to the building of the successor to the Roman wall at Chester? The Scandinavian community there was at its strongest in the tenth and eleventh centuries. It is likely that the wall was extended southwards from the line of the Roman defences to the bank of the Dee to include the Scandinavian settlement before the Norman Conquest at some time in the tenth century.

Shrewsbury and Hereford, the two other major urban centres of the Welsh Marches, were already well-established towns by the time of the Norman Conquest. Through the bare notes of Domesday Book we are able to discern some of the early topographical elements of Shrewsbury. The great Norman survey shows the presence of a flourishing town on the sandstone bluff within the meander loop of the Severn. It had 252 burgages, the properties of merchants and craftsmen who were the wealthier members of the urban community. Shrewsbury's undoubted status as a town at the time when it was viewed by the Domesday surveyors in the year 1086 is revealed in the record of a mint there and the presence of five churches. The churches, whose tall spires rising from the ridge above the Severn make one of the most attractive of English townscapes, also mark out the site of the late Saxon town. St Mary's red sandstone tower and spire that ranks among the highest in England dominates the heart of Shrewsbury. Here there is evidence of the Saxon structure that preceded the present medieval church in the form of a grave slab in the vestry and the evidence that the older building occupied only one-third of the length of the rebuilt church of the thirteenth century. T. Auden, in his history of Shrewsbury written at the beginning of this century, believed that the site of St Mary's as a place of worship dates back to the period before the making of the Saxon town, to the time when Pengwern, the capital of the Dark Age kingdom of Powys, occupied the sandstone ridge that is strategically placed within the natural moat of the meandering Severn.

Two other churches, St Alkmund and St Julian, lie within a stone's throw

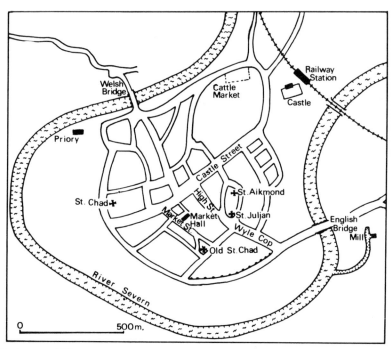

20. *The layout of Shrewsbury as it existed in the mid-nineteenth century prior to recent developments which have modified the early town plan set within a meander loop of the River Severn.*

of each other in this central quarter of Shrewsbury that expresses as strong a feeling of the medieval as almost any place in England, with its timber-framed houses, small and irregularly shaped spaces and narrow lanes with strange forgotten names. The dedication to St Alkmund takes the mind back to the centuries before the Norman Conquest. Alkmund was a Saxon prince of Northumbria and a church commemorating his name was founded on this site in Shrewsbury before the beginning of the tenth century. In its references to the time of Edward the Confessor, Domesday Book makes it plain that St Alkmund's was the owner of several manors in Shropshire. This town church was rich and well endowed before the Normans came. St Julian's was completely rebuilt in the mid-eighteenth century, but like the other restored and rebuilt churches at the centre of Shrewsbury it occupies a much older Saxon site, a site of importance in relation to the vanished topography of the original primitive pre-Norman town on the hilltop. St Julian's stood close against the line of the earliest medieval wall that followed the High Street. By the middle of the thirteenth century the town wall was rebuilt on a new line, incorporating land to the south and west of the older structure, on the lower slopes of the ridge that fall towards the flood plain of the Severn. The question remains; what was the age of the original wall of Shrewsbury that tightly enclosed the hilltop and the oldest core of the town? As an object of the present landscape this ancient feature has all but vanished. Only a sudden steepening of the slope by St Julian's remains to betray the presence of a former major topographical feature of the town. Was this an earthwork, like the one so recently investigated at Hereford, dating from the Saxon beginnings of the town? Or have we here in Shrewsbury the last faint marks of an Iron Age camp, a hint that is kept alive in the final element of the modern place-name?

The creation of a successful urban community at Shrewsbury in late Saxon times, itself perhaps a successor to Pengwern and some still earlier British settlement that occupied the earthworks of an Iron Age camp, is matched by the growth of Hereford in the two centuries before the Norman Conquest. Domesday Book's account of Hereford is even more fragmentary and obscure than the entries describing the other regional capitals of the borderland. For instance, the Norman survey makes no mention of churches at Hereford, a piece of evidence that goes a long way towards establishing the importance of Shrewsbury as a town. But elsewhere, in the records of the manors of rural Herefordshire, churches within the city are mentioned as holders of land. For instance, St Guthlac, a lost church the outlines of whose foundations can still be discerned on Castle Green in spells of dry weather, was the holder of ten manors in the surrounding countryside. Hereford too is listed in Domesday Book as a borough, the only place apart from the three new Norman castle towns, Clifford, Ewias Harold and Wigmore, then recognised as a town. The latter were all new foundations, part of the great expansion of urban life that was set off by the Norman invader. It is evident that Hereford, despite the incomplete record of the Domesday Survey, was the equal of Shrewsbury and Chester among the towns of eleventh-century England. Domesday Book mentions a mint and the presence of seven moneyers and there is an oblique reference too, under the manor of Eaton Bishop, of Hereford as a market centre.

But the most striking proof of a considerable settlement in the pre-Conquest centuries at Hereford has come to light as the result of archaeological excavations in the 1960s. The investigation of the earliest earthworks on the western side of the city have established beyond doubt the defences of a Saxon settlement. Archaeology has revealed the complex development of the earthwork over a considerable period of time. The earliest structure was an earth and gravel rampart fronted by a wall of timber made up of vertical posts and horizontal planks of half-round timbers. Later, the defences were reinforced with a wall of stone. Later still, most likely in the mid-eleventh century, the whole defensive structure was largely demolished to be buried under a great amount of clean gravel. The final works on the line of Hereford's western defences were made in the thirteenth century with the construction of the medieval town wall.

The detailed study of a piece of the western rampart and the discovery of its complex history has done little to solve the problems of the wall's date of origin, except to place it firmly within the Anglo-Saxon centuries. The earliest date for its construction probably belongs to the beginning of the eighth century when the westward advance of Mercia carried the frontiers of the kingdom into the plain of the middle Wye. The outline of the earliest rampart across a gravel terrace on the north bank of the river, now traceable through the directions of medieval lanes and property boundaries, seems to have enclosed a settlement of some fifty acres. Was Hereford then a newly planted town of the eighth century, designed to serve as a regional capital and bishopric of the sub-kingdom of Magonsaete within the greater state of Mercia? But the evidence, even with the latest findings of archaeology, is so slender and inconclusive that many conflicting speculations have been made about the ancient western earthwork, the oldest feature of Hereford's townscape. It has been proposed that Hereford was first fortified in the second half of the eighth century by King Offa. Another view suggests that the earliest clay bank with the timbered walling may not have been raised until the second decade of the tenth century when the Saxon struggle against the

Danes led to the foundation of a series of defended settlements, several of which, including Warwick and Stafford, were to evolve into important and successful towns. According to this thesis the elaboration of the western rampart by the addition of the pre-Norman stone wall probably took place about A.D. 930 when Aethelstan summoned the Welsh princes to Hereford. Still another consideration of the oldest defences at Hereford has assigned their building to the years immediately before the Norman Conquest when the army of Harold Godwinson is said to have thrown a defensive work around the town after a disastrous Welsh raid. A fresh shred of evidence in the form of radio-carbon dating of charcoal from the timbers of the rampart has done little to confirm any of the earlier speculations about the beginning of Hereford. It has given a date of A.D. 615 with a margin of error ranging between A.D. 550 and 680.

Whatever darkness surrounds the origins of the regional capitals in the Welsh Marches, there is little doubt that the century and a half before the Norman Conquest saw the evolution of urban communities that were to be adopted as centres of government by three of the most powerful among the Marcher lords. William Fitz Osbern, made Earl of Hereford in 1067, refortified the castle site that Leland, almost five hundred years later, was to describe as 'one of the fairest, largest, and strongest castles in England'. In the last quarter of the eleventh century, Roger de Montgomery, who had received the Earldom of Shrewsbury in 1071, affirmed the strategic importance of the Saxon town within the Severn's meander curve when he began building a huge castle in the northern quarter of Shrewsbury where the neck of land between the upstream and downstream channels of the Severn is less than three hundred yards across. At Chester too the Norman earls established themselves in a thriving town and port, a place that by the early thirteenth century had become the head of a palatine county, a remote part of the northern March that made its own laws, imposed its own taxes and until 1536, when the confused political geography of the Welsh borderland was simplified by the Tudor lawyers and civil servants, sent no members to the Westminster parliaments.

The closing years of the eleventh century ushered into the Welsh borderland three hundred years of urban development and experiments in town planning, many of which were to end in failure. In part, this activity in the making of new towns, unparalleled since the Roman period in Britain, reflected what was going on at the same time in the rest of England and indeed in many parts of Western Europe. But in the Marchland the movement towards the creation of new towns and market centres was perhaps more feverish than elsewhere. The fragmented political condition of the Welsh border country – a jigsaw of almost 150 different baronies, lordships and earldoms – provided a ground fertile for the establishment of new towns. Each unit of the new political order needed central places where trade and government could be carried on, and the logical focal point where these functions could be safely encouraged lay in the shadow of the walls of scores of new castles founded between the Norman Conquest and the beginning of the fourteenth century. It is one of the anomalies of the political geography of the Welsh borderland in the Middle Ages that an area whose regional history is filled with warfare, raids and arson should develop urban forms of society that demand security for their successful continuation.

The making of the towns of the Welsh Marches is closely related to the westward extension of the territories of the Marcher lords. The first great thrust of Norman power against the independent princedoms of Wales occupies the closing years of the eleventh century, in the reign of William II. From a base in the upper Severn valley that had already been established by the time of the Domesday Survey, the Earl of Shrewsbury's troops reached the shores of Cardigan Bay, overrunning the ancient Welsh princedom of *Ceredigion*. At the same time the valley of the Wye above Hereford was to provide a passage for the forces of Bernard de Newmarch in his conquest of Brycheiniog, an ancient kingdom of Wales whose continuous history in the basin of the upper Usk can be traced back to the closing decades of the Roman period. In the northern Marchland, the Earls of Chester had made a temporary inroad far into the heartland of north Wales by the 1080s. With a shrewd sense of strategic geography, Hugh of Chester anticipated Edward I's conquest of Wales by two centuries when he planted Norman castles on the Menai Strait at Caernarvon, Bangor and Aberlleiniog – the last a romantic, crumbling ruin deep in the wet woods and pastures of Anglesey.

The building of castles and the founding of the first towns quickly followed the expansion of Norman political power. Nowhere is this process of urban development better illustrated than in the history of Oswestry. The Lordship of Oswestry was created before the end of the eleventh century as part of the Norman plan for the conquest of Wales. Here, where the Welsh hills present a bold, clear front to the north Shropshire plain, was a district that had remained impervious to Mercian influences and settlement from the east. Medieval surveys of the Normal lordship of Oswestry reveal the pre-dominantly Welsh character of its society. Personal names suggest that it was entirely Welsh, Welsh customs persisted and the rentals recognised the ancient tribal structure of the region because they were made out by *gwelyau* – the basic social unit of Wales until the Act of Union began the transformation of the structure of Celtic society. In the elements that compose the present landscape of Oswestry and its surroundings one can read the main stages in the transformation of a Celtic pattern of organisation into that of medieval England.

Oswestry (SJ 2929) was always close to the focus of power in this part of Shropshire. Just beyond the northern outskirts of this little red-brick town that has served as a Norman frontier post, the 'Crewe' of the Cambrian railway system and a camp for twentieth-century armies, the complex ramparts of one of the greatest Iron Age camps of the Marches, Old Oswestry (SJ 2931), crown the summit of a low hill. Wat's Dyke, an early eighth-century earthwork and forerunner of Offa's frontier line, points northward from the flanks of Old Oswestry. By late Saxon times the focus of interest had shifted southward from Old Oswestry to Maesbury (SJ 3025), a large manor that formed the core of English settlement in this part of the west Shropshire plain. Maesbury stood at the head of the Saxon hundred of *Maersaete*, and it was here in the first years after the Norman Conquest that a castle, already mentioned in the Domesday Survey, was raised. The very name of Oswestry's castle in the Domesday record, *Luvre* or 'the work', speaks of the earliest years of the Norman occupation when the conquerors knew only an alien tongue.

If, as Domesday Book makes plain, a castle had been built at Oswestry by 1086, the foundation of a town there is much more obscure. The earliest surviving charter dates to the last decade of the twelfth century. In this document William fitz William fitz Alan refers to his burgesses at Oswestry as those 'who received messuages from my bailiff for the improvement of my market'. The phrase suggests an expansion of the settlement about the year 1190 with the attraction of fresh town-dwellers, burgesses, with the aim of improving trade and commerce at Oswestry. The pattern of streets at Oswestry is also different from the orderly grid-iron plan focused on a central market-place that is characteristic of the newly founded towns after the Norman Conquest. Here there is a cluster of streets, irregular in pattern, and a gently curving main street that today forms the sole reminder of the site of the castle, the proud *Luvre* that stood at the heart of the Lordship of Oswestry. Such hints, provided by an imperfect documentary record and the topographical evidence of the street layout, suggest that an older, pre-Norman village settlement at Maesbury evolved through the twelfth century into the borough of Oswestry. Another strange feature of the early history of this place is the lost name of *Blancminster*, a name that was once given to the town. It has been argued that this name was derived from the church, built perhaps of a pale limestone from the local hills at Llanymynech, and erected at about the same time as the castle. An examination of St Oswald's – the mother church of Oswestry – is of little help to us today because the present building is a reconstruction, dating from the seventeenth century. But the dedication of this church to St Oswald, a seventh-century king of Northumbria who was killed in battle at Maserfelth, close to the site of Oswestry, in A.D. 642, suggests again an important association of the place with a pre-Norman past. Was there, in fact, a Saxon minster at Oswestry when the Normans came there to set about the building of the castle? The evidence that tells against such an explanation of the early evolution of Oswestry is the Domesday statement that the manor Maesbury lay 'waste' in 1086. But the laconic phrase 'wasta est' that proclaimed a place as a barren source of tax revenue may not in every case be a record of absolute desolation. One shred of evidence points towards the presence of an active community at Maesbury in the latter part of the eleventh century, for a charter of Earl Roger mentions that the first Norman sheriff of the Marcher lordship of Oswestry had given to the monks of Shrewsbury Abbey the church of St Oswald and the tithes.

Among the several towns of the Welsh borderland that came into existence in the years of the late eleventh and early twelfth centuries Brecon (SO 0428) illustrates, perhaps more clearly than most, the relations between the westward advance of the Norman frontier and the planting of towns. By 1100 the army of Bernard de Newmarch had overrun the whole of the Dark Age Welsh princedom of Brycheiniog. In their wake three towns, Brecon, Builth and Hay, came into being. Brecon was planted at the junction of the River Usk with a tributary, the Honddu, draining from the north. The Honddu enters the wider valley floor of the Usk by a narrow gorge, and it was on the steep western bluff overlooking the two rivers that the first element of the new Norman settlement appeared with the building of a motte-and-bailey castle in 1092. Outside the north wall of the castle the foundations of the church of St John were laid, a church that later became a priory and today is the cathedral of Brecon. On the east bank of the Honddu, facing the site of the castle and the quiet respectable suburb around the cathedral, we find the new town of Brecon that seems to have been sketched out at about the same period as the building of the castle. Although documentary proof is lacking, there is a tradition that the town was brought into existence by the conqueror of Brycheiniog, Bernard de Newmarch. The great Norman lords whose decisions have played no small part in the making of the English landscape are shadowy figures. Bernard de Newmarch came from Neufmarché in Normandy, a name whose literal meaning is *new market*. Was he some kind of medieval property developer, a soldier more interested in the fortunes of commerce than the spoils of war? Whatever the beginnings of Brecon and the name of its founder, we can still see the elements of the new Norman town imprinted on the present landscape. The centre piece, as in every planned town of the twelfth century, is the great market-place, even though later building has encroached upon the original open triangle. The oval-shaped defences of the walled borough, once crowned by ten equally spaced towers, can still be traced through features of the urban topography – minor changes of level that betray the former presence of a ditch and a curving street pattern that follows the inner line of the wall. In the narrow courtyards of the back streets of Brecon one may still trace out the shapes of the original burgage plots, slim rectangles of land that were granted to the traders and craftsmen settling the new borough.

Like so many of the medieval towns of the Welsh borderland, Brecon has escaped the urban explosion of the nineteenth and twentieth centuries. As we explore its streets there is a strong feeling of continuity with the settlement that had emerged by the beginning of the thirteenth century, although much of the visual townscape has changed. The castle, alas, no longer dominates the scene. All that remains is transformed almost beyond recognition; it is now an hotel. Only two crumbling towers tell of the fortress town that eight centuries ago formed an English island surrounded on every hand by hills and mountains that were to remain Welsh in character. Since the seventeenth century, buildings in stone and brick have swept away the timber houses of the medieval town. But not all the elements of medieval Brecon have been lost. The compactness of an urban community, the original and primary purposes of the settlement – trade and defence – are still evident. Above all there is the sharp contrast of town and country. In whatever direction one walks from the market-place, and none better than towards the steep bluff where the line of the town wall overhangs the Usk, a wide view of the encompassing hills – the ancient limits of Brycheiniog – opens up before one. This perhaps is one of the most satisfying features of the small towns of the Marches. At Ludlow, Clun, Bishop's Castle, Ruthin and several others there is always the feeling of contrast between town and country – an aspect of medieval topography that has been lost to most of the towns of England through the spread of a suburban no-man's-land.

The southern Marchland, where the Usk and Wye flow through deep wooded valleys towards the Severn, was the setting of several successful urban plantations in the first years of the Norman Conquest. Chepstow and Monmouth were among the earliest of the new towns to mark the westward-advancing frontier of the Normans. Castles had already been founded at these places on the River Wye before the death of William the Conqueror in

1087. Chepstow's castle (ST 5394) occupies one of the most dramatic sites in the whole of Britain, its shaggy keep and massive curtain wall poised on the lip of a limestone cliff above a muddy arc of the tidal Wye. It is a pity that the town did not perpetuate the original name of its sheltering fortress, *Stroguil*, a name whose shape and sound hark back to a darker aspect of medieval England than that commemorated in Chepstow, simply meaning a market-place. That Chepstow came to replace the original name of this port and fortress town at the mouth of the Wye by the early fourteenth century reminds one of the commercial functions that later dominated the life of this successful urban foundation. A record of 308 burgages there at the beginning of the fourteenth century shows that Chepstow belongs to the largest and most prosperous of the Norman boroughs in the Marches. Domesday Book's entries on Chepstow also make it clear that the town came into being at the same time or shortly after the building of the castle. By 1086 there is little doubt that a flourishing trading community was in existence. We are told that Earl William made the castle and that 'in his time it returned forty shillings, and that from ships going up to the wood'. Here we find a hint that already this stronghold, dominating the estuary of the Wye from its cliff-top site, was already collecting tolls from the inland river traffic. Domesday Book goes on to record that by the time of Earl Roger, the son of the founding Earl of Hereford, William FitzOsbern, 'the town returned £16'. Chepstow was among the forfeited properties of Earl Roger in 1075; it is evident that a prosperous urban community had been established by that time.

The development of Chepstow has not lived up to the striking qualities of its site. The town, with its many shabby buildings and streets perpetually choked with traffic, lacks the spaciousness of Ludlow and the sense of a harmonious development of a medieval town plan that one feels in the Shropshire borough. Even the focus of Chepstow's trade, the market – known as Beaufort Square since the middle of the nineteenth century – has lost much of the spaciousness and visual importance that this great steeply sloping arena within the Town Gate must have provided at one time. Terracing and extensive infilling by several blocks of buildings have deprived it of most of the visual aspects of a central market-place.

Monmouth (SO 5012) must have come into existence at almost the same time as Chepstow. Its castle was founded by the same William FitzOsbern in the year 1070 in a tiny plain, encircled by wooded hills, where the Monnow flows into the Wye. Monmouth poses a problem that attaches to the histories of several of England's Norman towns. Was there already some kind of settlement at this place when the Norman castle-builders took over the site, a Saxon settlement that was to be reshaped as a medieval town? Or are we considering a fresh beginning, the planting of an urban community associated with the foundation of a castle in virgin territory? One or two clues in medieval records and some elements of the present topography of Monmouth suggest that a settlement was already in existence there before the Norman castle and its dependent town.

The site of the Roman predecessor of Monmouth, *Blestium*, lies on the west bank of the River Monnow close to the medieval bridge. Today we find here the suburb of Over Monnow occupying the space between the river and an ancient earthwork, the Black Dyke. Certain memories from the long history of the parish church of Over Monnow, St Thomas, suggest that here on the west bank of the river the primary settlement of Monmouth may once have stood. St Thomas stands close by the bridge over the Monnow. The original building, though considerably changed in two nineteenth-century restorations, dates back to the Norman period, and there is some evidence that the chancel arch is of Saxon origin. John Leland's account of the topography of Monmouth, written in Henry VIII's reign, contributes to the view that Over Monnow and its church were formerly of greater importance. In the mind's eye one traverses the bridge crossing the river beneath the Monnow Gate in the company of the great Tudor topographer. 'Beyond this gate is a suburb in the diocese of Llandaff, where once stood the parish church of St Thomas, but now only a little chapel dedicated to the saint. There is only one parish church in the town and it lies close to the priory of the Benedictine monks.' Leland's account makes it clear that at some time before the sixteenth century St Thomas had lost its status as a parish church, taking over a more humble role as a chapel of ease to St Mary, formerly the church of the priory at the heart of the Norman town. It looks as if the eleventh-century urban foundation at Monmouth, a new town, was laid out on empty land between the Monnow and the Wye, facing an older settlement that occupied the ground on the farther bank between the Black Dyke and the river. With the growth of the new town the older core whose original name is lost to us was transformed into the suburb of Over Monnow, gathered around the chapel at the bridgehead.

The earliest towns of the southern Marchland are closely associated with the chief rivers. The castles and castle towns of the Wye between Clifford and Chepstow mark out a temporary frontier of Norman power drawn by the Earls of Hereford in the last quarter of the eleventh century. The corridor of the Usk exhibits a similar design of isolated strongpoints where colonies of townsmen were brought into existence by the setting-up of markets and fairs and the granting of burgage plots. Brecon, we have already noticed, was already in the making by the turn of the eleventh century. Lower down the

36. *Monmouth, a medieval new town at the junction of the Monnow (above) and Wye (below), with the castle-site and priory church (centre right) and the older settlement of Over Monnow across the gated bridge (top left).*

223

Usk another Norman overlord, Hamelin de Ballon, was the founder of Abergavenny (SO 2914). The same principles of town-planning are apparent in the layout of Abergavenny that have been observed in the other markets and boroughs of this period. A Norman castle-site occupied a prominent bluff above the flood plain of the Usk. As at Monmouth, Chepstow and Brecon, land was set aside for the foundation of a priory. Some miles below Abergavenny the town of Usk similarly conforms to the features of the planned Norman town. Its foundation may follow a little later in time after Chepstow, Monmouth and Abergavenny for no document survives to tell of the date of its beginning or the name of the founder. The first mention of Usk (SO 3700) in the medieval records comes in 1131 when it is evident that an active urban community was already rooted there. The very name of the place arouses interest because it is of Celtic origin, after the river. Unlike the many Newmarkets and Newports that the aristocratic developers and speculators of the twelfth century have left scattered over the face of England, names that proclaim not only their newness but also their chief function as trade centres, the older names speak to a Celtic population that was completely alien to the ways and culture of the Normans. Were these new towns places in which a Welsh influence soon became dominant?

Usk became a large and prosperous place, if one is to judge from the records of the town in the thirteenth and fourteenth centuries. The borough rental of 1262 suggests that there were 141 burgages. In 1306 the number of burgage plots had grown to 294 and the records of that year show that Usk was still expanding with the addition of six new building plots granted to burgesses. An exploration of the streets of Usk stirs the imagination, but not for the merit of its present buildings that are devoid of any interest and visually without pleasure apart from the splendidly neglected ruin of its castle perched on a bluff at the north end of the town. The interest of Usk relates to its obscure origins and the waning of a busy medieval borough. Even the location of the centre of medieval trade there is beset with uncertainty. An open space between the parish church, a former priory, and the castle gate would seem to be the logical place for markets, but the presence of New and Old Market Street on the south-western fringe of the town provides a hint that commercial activity was focused near the river. Here too, alongside the River Usk, the remains of a Roman fort, *Burrium*, have been discovered. Is it not possible that Usk was a centre of activity in the Celtic centuries before the Norman Conquest and that the unknown founders of the new town in the years about 1100 merely added a castle and a planned urban settlement to an existing riverside community?

All along the Usk valley a striking connection exists between the planned towns of the early twelfth century and the sites of Roman forts. Both Usk and Abergavenny were planted on Roman sites, while there is a tradition that the medieval wall of Brecon used material quarried from the nearby Roman fort of Y Gaer. What one can never know in the search for an explanation of the similarity between the distribution of Roman forts and the castle towns of the southern Marchland is whether the strategic pattern was determined in the two periods of history by the unchanging dictates of topography or whether the founders of the new Norman towns deliberately chose the sites that had been developed by the Romans. Were such places of value to the masons and town planners of the early twelfth century as quarries or were they perhaps chosen because of their activity as centres of trade and social organisation in a pre-Norman society? The history of Newport, at the mouth of the Usk, suggests that the patterns of social organisation and the nodes of commercial life in Welsh society may have played some part in determining the new centres of Norman control in the Marcher lordships. Newport, bearing one of the most characteristic names of the medieval new towns, was a late foundation compared with several of its neighbours in the southern March-land. Giraldus Cambrensis, in his description of Wales towards the close of the twelfth century, records the presence of a new castle and the *novus burgus* at the crossing of the Usk in the year 1188. All the evidence points to the making of a new settlement there in the 1180s, a century later than the foundation of Cardiff and other boroughs of the southern March.

The late foundation of a Norman town at the mouth of the Usk gives rise to a fascinating line of speculation that in the present state of the evidence must remain unproven. On the outskirts of Newport, through some half-dozen swinging meander curves of the Usk, stands Caerleon – a place that still bears the name by which Chester was known to the Welsh in the centuries before the Norman Conquest, 'the fortress of the legion'. In the Roman geography of the southern Marchland, Caerleon is the equivalent of Chester. In the medieval evolution of the ports on the estuaries of Dee and Usk two different urban patterns emerged. Medieval Chester was focused exactly on the Roman site so that the cores of the medieval and Roman settlements were overlaid. On the Usk, and only after some decades of hesitation, the medieval borough was planted down-river from the older settlement. We can trace a succession of Norman castles along the tidal estuary of the Usk. The first was established by 1085 within the south-eastern angle of the rampart enclosing the Roman fort and settlement at Caerleon. About the same time, at the turn of the eleventh century, a Norman motte was thrown up at Gwynllwg, a Welsh *maesdref* or 'royal village' lying down the river from Caerleon and close to the site of the still later planned town of Newport that came into existence

225

after some decades, in the 1180s, beside the new castle that guarded the river crossing.

Castle towns arose out of periods of conflict when the Marcher lords were engaged in westward territorial expansion at the expense of the Welsh princedoms. Another critical phase of urban growth appears towards the end of the thirteenth century when Edward I successfully set about the conquest of the strongest of the Welsh kingdoms, Gwynedd, whose political and economic independence was founded on the inaccessible mountain retreat of Snowdonia and the cornfields of Anglesey. The submission of Gwynedd is marked by the founding of Edward's castle towns at Rhuddlan, Conwy, Beaumaris and Caernarfon. But it is along the valley of the upper Severn, above Welshpool, that one follows the intricate connections between national politics and the fate of towns. In the latter part of the thirteenth century two incipient boroughs competed with each other. Dolforwyn (SO 1595), a forgotten place today, occupies a romantic hilltop site steeply poised some four hundred feet above the Severn's floodplain near Abermule. (Newtown was to emerge as a successful settlement astride the same river.) The brief history of Dolforwyn shows that by the thirteenth century Welsh princes had learned much from neighbouring Marcher lords about the value of towns in stimulating trade and strengthening the political security of a region. Dolforwyn, whose site emphasises the strategic qualities of the location, came into existence in 1273 after two decades of increasing Welsh influence in the Marchland. In 1255 the prospects of the northern Welsh kingdom had brightened when Llywelyn ap Gruffydd became its ruler. Within three years a council of Welsh rulers had acclaimed him Prince of Wales and in 1267, by the Treaty of Montgomery, Henry III recognised Llywelyn's title as Prince of Wales and conceded to him the cantref of Cedewain. Cedewain included much of the hill country of what was to become the county of Montgomeryshire in the sixteenth century. On its southern margin the cantref of Cedewain reached to the corridor of the Severn above Welshpool. Llywelyn determined to strengthen his position in these newly acquired territories by the building of a castle on the hilltop at Dolforwyn in 1273, a place that grandly surveyed the hostile Marchland to the east. Today, from its silent grass-grown earthworks, you look across to the long northern face of the Kerry Hills and Clun Forest, scoured with deep wooded combes. Westward the Severn draws the eye towards the wilder hills of central Wales. Dolforwyn was an excellent place from which to make a last stand for Welsh political independence as it brooded over the castle and town that had been founded at Montgomery only half a century earlier.

Beside the building of the castle, Llywelyn announced the foundation of a market town at Dolforwyn. It was this last act that aroused the hostility of the English Crown. On 23 June 1273 the Council of Regents discussed the matter and the Prior of Wenlock was instructed to deliver personally a letter of protest to Llywelyn that said 'we forbid you to erect *de novo* a borough or town or market'. Less than a month later Llywelyn ap Gruffydd, Prince of Wales, replied asserting his right to build a castle and establish a market on his own land near *Abermiwl*. It could be argued from this contemporary reference that Llywelyn was intending to found a market-town at a more logical site in the Severn floodplain below the castle-hill of Dolforwyn – a development, if it had been successful, that would have resembled the relationship between Castel Dinas Bran and Llangollen in the Dee valley.

But the events that determined the fate of Dolforwyn were enacted on a much larger stage than that of the Severn corridor. In 1277 Edward I invaded Wales with three armies in a campaign to reduce the last stronghold of Gwynedd. As part of this strategy, troops under the Earl of Lincoln and Roger de Mortimer advanced on the upper Severn to lay siege to the new Welsh castle at Dolforwyn. The siege lasted scarcely more than a week. A Welsh chronicler of the events says that the garrison was forced to surrender from want of water, but reports from the English side suggest that a formidable military force was arrayed against the castle. Roger de Mortimer recorded that 'three good siege engines' inflicted severe damage, and after its capitulation the Sheriff of Hereford, Egidius de Berkely, claimed twenty-four shillings for the carriage of a catapult from Wigmore to *Dolvereyn* on Mortimer's instructions. The chance of the growth of a new town at Dolforwyn had vanished. In 1278 the castle and all the lands of *Ceri* and *Cydewain* were given to Roger de Mortimer. Now the possessions of the Mortimer family stretched across the trough of the Severn far into the dissected hill country north of the river. A year later, in 1279, Roger de Mortimer took the decisive step that was to change the settlement patterns of the upper Severn; he obtained a charter for him 'and his heirs forever that they may hold a market in his manor of Llanveyr, in Kedway'.

The emergence of a new market centre at Llanfair Cedewain, a place soon to be known as Newtown (SO 1091), can be traced through the half-century after the granting of the first charter to Roger de Mortimer. In 1279 there must have been a hamlet, called Llanfair Cedewain, in the great loop of the Severn where Newtown now stands. One element of Newtown's urban topography survives from this period in a ruined medieval church on the south bank of the river. At the time of the granting of the medieval charter this was a chapel within the mother parish of Llanllwchaiarn (SO 1292), located a mile below Newtown facing across the river to the enormous forty-foot-high motte of Gro Tump. Gro Tump is a relic of an earlier effort to plant Norman power in the upper Severn's plain. Soon after the granting of the market charter, perhaps even coincident with it, Llanfair Cedewain was raised to the status of an independent parish. No documentary proof survives of the exact date of this first stage in the evolution of Newtown apart from a reference of 1291 that describes Llanfair as an independent rectory. At some time between 1279 and 1291 the growing importance of the new settlement by the Severn had made it necessary to form a separate parish there. By 1321 the old name of Llanfair Cedewain is beginning to drop out of use because a document of that year refers to 'the new town in Kedewan'.

In the intervening years since the grant of a market charter and the first reference to a new town one can be sure that the outlines of an urban community had come into being at Llanfair Cedewain. Although no documents and little archaeological evidence remain to trace the process, we can still obtain some deep insights into the making of Roger de Mortimer's market town from a study of its topography. The main axis, Broad Street, is focused on the bridge across the Severn. For the rest it is still easy to trace the formal grid-iron plan that is characteristic of the new urban settlements of the Middle Ages. At the western end of the market town, in the grounds of Newtown Hall, stood the castle – a topographical feature that has given rise to much debate. Half of the motte survives as a weathered D-shaped mound, while the bailey was contained in what is now the north-eastern angle of Newtown Hall's park. In his excellent survey of the castles of Montgomery-shire, C. J. Spurgeon believes that the earthworks at Newtown were con-temporary with the grant of the market charter. The remnant of the motte suggests that it was a low, broad-topped earthwork with a diameter of almost 150 feet standing some sixteen feet above its ditch. Gro Tump, on the other hand, lying only a mile down the Severn valley from Newtown Hall, has a high-standing mound that towers some forty feet above its encircling ditch. It resembles so many primitive Norman castle works of the late eleventh century. The change of style at Newtown Hall suggests a later period of castle-building that could well belong to the end of the thirteenth century, about the time of the founding of the new town.

Whatever the exact date of the foundation of the castle at Newtown, there is little doubt about the success of Roger de Mortimer's urban experiment in the Severn valley. By the middle of the fourteenth century the records provide proof of a flourishing urban community paying annual rents of £6 6s 8d and whose markets and fairs yielded an annual toll of £24. Alas, the documentary history of Newtown is far from complete and one of the most important steps in its progress as a settlement, the acquisition of a borough charter, remains totally obscure. Some local historians have argued that the first grant of municipal privileges dates back to 1321, the year when the name Newtown began to supplant the older Welsh name of the settlement, Llanfair Cedewain. The first borough charter has long been lost, but oral evidence from the seventeenth century suggests that it was granted in the middle years of the fifteenth century. Certainly Leland, on his long journeys in Henry VIII's reign in search of the antiquities of these islands, was able to describe Newtown as 'well buylded after the Welsh fashion'. By that time its rectangular network of streets and lanes focused on Broad Street, the place where the markets and fairs were held, and Newtown contained a population of about five hundred. It was only in the years about 1800 with the expansion of the flannel industry and the opening of the Montgomeryshire Canal that the population began to grow rapidly, reaching almost a thousand by the first census of 1801.

Newtown was not the only town to come into existence in the upper Severn valley at the time of Edward I's conquest of Wales. At Llanidloes (SN 9584), a Welsh landowner, Owain de la Pole or Owain of Arwystli, obtained from the English king the grant of a weekly market and two fairs a year by a charter drawn up in the year 1280. Llanidloes seems to have prospered in the changed political geography of the upper Severn valley during the closing years of the thirteenth century. By 1309 a survey of the estates of Gruffydd, son of the founder of Llanidloes, shows that the town had sixty-six burgesses. As in the history of Newtown, no borough charter survives, nor is there any direct evidence of the date when it was granted. The presence of sixty-six burgesses in 1309 shows that Llanidloes had become a borough before that date, and it seems most likely that Owain's market was raised to the status of a town at some time in the last decade of the thirteenth century.

Just as Llanidloes came into being at the same time as Newtown, so the topographical evolution of the borough closely resembles that of its urban neighbour down the Severn. An ancient church close beside a traditional crossing of the Severn is the only feature of the topography of Llanidloes that survives from the centuries before the making of the town. As at Newtown, the parish church plays no focal role in the regular grid-iron of streets. Instead the market hall, at the crossing of the main axes, provided the chief concentration of interest in Owain de la Pole's new borough. Llanidloes, too, only became a parish in its own right after the founding of the town; previously it had looked down the Severn to a mother church at Llandinam.

Llanidloes Castle also presents problems similar to the castle at Newtown. The site of the motte, at the south end of the long axis of China Street and Long Bridge Street, is covered by the Mount Inn and other buildings. In

229

fact, the name of the inn, which is rare indeed among the names of Welsh inns, provides one of the few obvious clues to the site of Llanidloes medieval castle. The castle bailey, lying to the east of the motte and stretching as far as New Street, has left scarcely any visual evidence of its former presence. B. H. St J. O'Neil in his study of Llanidloes believed that the castle was thrown up at least a century before the founding of the market town, probably about 1160, when the territories of the upper Severn were once more in the hands of Welsh rulers after the failure of the Norman thrust to the west. If Llanidloes Castle was in being before the end of the twelfth century, it is not unlikely

37. *The Market Hall, Llanidloes, at the crossroads of the main axes of Owain de la Pole's new town in the upper Severn valley.*

that the shelter of the bailey was used for trade and commerce. It certainly stood close to an important ford across the Severn where an ancient trackway from the west that followed the long ridge between the Clywedog and the Severn came down to meet an eastern trail from the Kerry Hills. If this is the correct history of Llanidloes Castle, the granting of a market charter to Owain de la Pole and the subsequent founding of the borough represents the recognition, in the changed political atmosphere of the late thirteenth century, of an already established trading centre. Perhaps the narrow confines of the castle bailey were found to be too restrictive and the formal street plan of a new town was laid out in the 1290s – a town whose centre of interest became focused at the Market Hall at the junction of the main axes of Long Bridge Street and Great Oak Street. Both castle and church lay on the edge of the new Llanidloes and ceased to exercise a dominant role in the fortunes of the town.

Not all the urban experiments of the Middle Ages led to the successful creation of new towns. The abortive history of Dolforwyn reveals how the changing fortunes of politics in the last quarter of the thirteenth century could adversely alter the fortunes of settlements. Today the landscape of the Marches is littered with places that were once granted market charters and the rights of boroughs, places that have since failed completely. A rectangular-shaped field where cattle graze beneath tall trees may be the sole visual evidence of a former market-place. Narrow, high-hedged fields mark the plots that attracted burgesses to a newly founded borough eight centuries ago. Deep lanes and footpaths indicate the lines of former streets; and the castle of a forgotten founding Marcher lord is no more than a misshapen green mound, perilously steep to climb and defended now with an almost impenetrable thicket of hawthorn.

In Monmouthshire, among the broken hill country between the main corridors of the Wye and Usk, we find the traces of a number of failed urban experiments. One wonders whether the supposed hard laws of geography were at work in their demise. Was a location upon the banks of a main river with its prospect of trade essential to the success of an urban community? A comparison of the sites and histories of Chepstow and White Castle (SO 3716) would give credence to this argument. The building of White Castle began in the years 1184–5 on the summit of a high westward-facing hill in the parish of Llantilio Crossenny. Medieval records make reference to burgages there, but for centuries there has been no trace of an urban settlement apart from some vague unexplored earthworks in the fields around the castle that may yet be shown to conceal the house-plots of its former burgesses. Today White Castle is an utterly lonely place, its water-filled moat grey and menacing when clouds are piled above the mountains to the west. At Skenfrith (SO 4520), a small town seems to have come into existence about the year 1200. Its castle is first mentioned in a Pipe Roll of 1190. The borough of Skenfrith scarcely added to the primary elements of church and castle in the centuries after its foundation. Skenfrith probably failed to take off as a market town because of the overshadowing rivalry of its neighbours on the Monnow, Monmouth and Grosmont.

Scarcely three miles above Skenfrith, the ruined keep of Grosmont (SO

4024) stands perched above a precipitous river cliff. Castle-building had started at Grosmont in Henry II's reign, about the same time as the foundation of the other strongpoints of the triangle of defence in the Monmouthshire hills – White Castle and Skenfrith. As the head of a Marcher lordship, Grosmont had acquired the right to hold markets and fairs; its status as a borough lapsed only in 1860. Here we can still recognise all the basic elements of a medieval townscape and little has been added since. Between the castle and the church lies a long-deserted market-place where an early nineteenth-century market hall remains. The parish church bears witness to the declining population and prosperity of Grosmont over the centuries. Most of the building dates from between 1200 and 1400. Its elaborate cruciform plan and fine octagonal tower suggest a busy and prosperous urban settlement. For a long time St Nicholas has been too big for the dwindling population of Grosmont, which since the fifteenth century has found sufficient accommodation in the chancel and used the abandoned nave as a graveyard. Around the market-place the cottages stand on narrow rectangular strips of ground, the burgage plots that were sketched out early in the thirteenth century when Hubert de Burgh established his new town. Some of them have lost their buildings and are now used entirely as allotments, another visual proof of the shrinking population of the former medieval borough of Grosmont that now totals only five hundred.

Towns that have lost their role as boroughs await the discerning traveller from one end of the Marchland to the other. In the north, at the time of Edward I's conquest of Wales, successful new boroughs came into existence at Denbigh, Ruthin and Rhuddlan. At the latter the grid-iron of streets that was laid out in 1278 represents the third attempt to establish a successful urban community at the mouth of the Clwyd. Caerwys (SJ 1272), whose secluded site lies in the wooded hills above the Wheeler gorge, was granted a charter in 1290 – a charter that bestowed upon the new settlement all the privileges of the royal town of Conwy and those of the new borough of Ruthin, a town that Reginald de Grey had founded early in the 1280s. Although Caerwys belongs to the numerous towns whose course of development faltered, this large village in a very rural part of Flintshire still conveys the feeling of a planned town. Its rigidly rectilinear plan, so characteristic of the age, the small central market-place, and a large south-western quadrant occupied by the church recall the mind to the original purpose of its foundation as a market town.
market town.

Two other urban foundations in the northern March, Holt and Overton, date from the years of the Edwardian conquest of Gwynedd. They occupy

38. Grosmont, a medieval new town whose borough status lapsed only in the nineteenth century. In the foreground is the market-place with a disused Victorian market hall; the cottages occupy the burgage plots of the medieval borough and in the background is the raison d'être for this little town that was the head of a Marcher lordship, the castle.

233

dramatic sites on the Dee where the river meanders across the plain towards Chester after leaving the gorge above Llangollen. Holt (SJ 4154) seems to have been laid out as a town in the last years of the thirteenth century at the same time as the building of the castle by the Earl of Surrey. A survey of 1315, made about a quarter of a century after its foundation, shows that a healthy settlement had come into being, for it mentions more than two hundred tenants 'paying a shilling an acre' and 159 burgesses. Overton's site (SJ 3741) closely resembles that of Holt. Here too the valley takes on the shape of a shallow gorge where the meandering river has become entrenched in a harder band of sandstone. The castle site and the medieval borough are perched on the brink of a wooded sandstone cliff. Unlike Holt, Overton seems not to have been carved out of virgin country at the time of the granting of its borough charter. Indeed, there was a castle at Overton early in the twelfth century, but history is silent about the nature of the settlement before Edward I's charter created a new town in 1292. The record of the granting of market rights to Overton a dozen years before the acquisition of a borough charter suggests that a rural settlement was slowly transformed into a town towards the end of the thirteenth century.

The last great phase of the making of new towns came to an end in the Welsh borderland by the beginning of the fourteenth century. One late competitor for borough status seems to be Hope, grandly situated astride Wat's Dyke where the River Alyn enters a winding wooded gorge. Its borough charter was granted in 1351, a model of the rights and privileges that had been given to Rhuddlan and Hereford. Hope presents a familiar problem to the historian of our medieval towns. Was there perhaps already a settlement that was raised to urban status by the granting of a charter? At least one sinister fact has been preserved about the beginning of Hope. It was the first borough in North Wales whose charter specifically excluded the settlement of Welshmen there. Hope suffered the fate of so many of the marchland castle towns. By the sixteenth century and the political revolution that was worked through the Act of Union, many of the little urban settlements were now superfluous, bereft of all meaning in the larger political structure of counties that took the place of the Marcher lordships. The centuries of peace that descended on the borderland deprived them of their primary military functions. A favoured group of towns, most of them already prosperous by the sixteenth century, succeeded in changing with the times. They acquired new functions and industries as old activities faded. The regional capitals grew in importance. Coal-mining, iron-making, brick-burning created an ugly, formless conurbation at the northern end of Offa's frontier in the latter years of the nineteenth century.

By and large the great upsurge of population and industrial activity in nineteenth-century Britain left the borderland untouched. Oscar Wilde made of Shropshire an outlier of the rural home counties when it was named as the retreat of the fictitious Bunbury. A. E. Housman's *Shropshire Lad* and settings of some of the poems by Butterworth and Vaughan Williams have served to enhance the idea of the Welsh Marches as a place where the elements of a long-lost, pre-industrial England had been preserved. In the years between the two wars the novels of a now almost forgotten Shropshire writer, Mary Webb, wove a dark, primitive fantasy out of the landscape of the Middle March. Even the place-names, still sounding from the forgotten Celtic world before the Saxons, were taken over as the surnames of some of the characters in those books.

Now, as the twentieth century moves into its last quarter, we can still sense some of the features of the lost and ancient landscapes and their society. The long road may no longer lie white in the moonlight, but at least there are few miles of motorway in the Marchland. Only two new towns have been planned for the border country. Telford burgeons into existence on the eastern edge of the region, sprawling across the derelict land of the Shropshire coalfield. In truth it represents a northward extension of Birmingham and the Black Country. But in the hilly heartland of the March, in the valley of the Severn above Newtown, a new urban settlement has been talked about that would stretch over fourteen miles with its focus on Caersws (SO 0391). A government report, published in 1966, proposed a population of some 70,000 for this new city in mid-Wales. The arguments that developed around the scheme have shown that this region is still a Marchland, a border zone between two cultures. It was feared that a large new urban plantation of such a kind, 'combining manufacturing, recreational and resort functions' as the report expressed it, would only worsen the problems of mid-Wales in the twentieth century. Depopulation of the surrounding hills would be accelerated and the town itself, its links with the West Midlands strengthened through improved communications, would become little more than an adjunct and overspill for the conurbations of Birmingham and the Black Country. Faintly through this debate one can perceive the age-old social differences of the Celtic West and the English Plain. Fortunately, and largely with the object of preserving, if that is still possible, the older patterns of life, the plan for a fourteen-mile-long city beneath the western scarp of the Kerry Hills has been abandoned. Instead there is a plan to double the population of a number of small and active towns in the borderland. Newtown will be raised from 5,000 to 11,000; over a span of twenty-one years Brecon will increase to 12,000, and it is aimed to inject new life into Welshpool,

39. Cefnllys. In the middle years of the thirteenth century the Mortimers built a castle and founded a borough on a site that had been settled in the Iron Age. It belongs to the completely desolate town sites such as Dolforwyn and Caus.

236

Rhayader and Llandrindod Wells. Something like this, small-scale local improvements, must have happened many times to sustain the economies of the small borderland towns. At several other places – Caus and Cefnllys, Painscastle and Trellech to mention only a few – the impetus to change has been wanting and an urban way of life has failed at some time in the eight centuries that have passed since their foundation.

Select Bibliography

Chapter 1

BROWN, E. H., *The Relief and Drainage of Wales* (1960).

DAVIES, M. (ed), *The Brecon Beacons National Park* (1967).

DREGHORN, W., *Geology explained in the Forest of Dean and the Wye Valley* (1968).

EARP, J. R., 'The higher Silurian rocks of the Kerry District, Montgomeryshire', *Quarterly Journal of the Geological Society*, 94 (1938), pp. 125–60.

EARP, J. R., 'The geology of the south-western part of Clun Forest', *Quarterly Journal of the Geological Society*, 96 (1940), pp. 1–11.

EDLIN, H. L. (ed.), *Dean Forest and Wye Valley*, Forestry Commission Guide (1972).

GREIG, D. C., 'Geology of the country around Church Stretton, Craven Arms, Wenlock Edge and Brown Clee', *Memoirs of the Geological Survey* (1968).

HAINS, B. A., *The Geology of the Craven Arms Area* (1968).

HAINS, B. A., *The Geology of the Wenlock Edge Area* (1970).

HOLLAND, C. H., 'The Ludlovian and Downtonian rocks of the Knighton District, Radnorshire', *Quarterly Journal of the Geological Society*, 114 (1959), pp. 449–82.

LOCKE, S., 'The post-glacial deposits of the Caldicot Level, Monmouthshire', *Antiquity*, 3 (1970), pp. 1–15.

MILLER, A. A., 'The entrenched meanders of the Herefordshire Wye', *Geographical Journal*, 85 (1937), pp. 160–78.

NORTH, F. J., 'The geological history of Brecknock', *Brycheiniog*, 1 (1955), pp. 9–77.

RAILTON, C. L., *The Ogof Ffynnon Ddu System*, Cave Research Group Publication, 6 (1953).

SPARROW, G. W., 'Some environmental factors in the formation of slopes', *Geographical Journal*, 132 (1966), pp. 390–5.

THOMAS, T. M., 'The geomorphology of Brecknock', *Brycheiniog*, 5 (1959), pp. 55–156.

238

TROTTER, F. M., 'Geology of the Forest of Dean Coalfield and Ironstone Field', *Memoirs of the Geological Survey* (1942).

WATERS, I., 'High tides and flood', *Severn and Wye Review* (1972), pp. 57–60.

WATTS, W. W., 'On the igneous and associated rocks of the Breidden Hills', *Quarterly Journal of the Geological Society*, 41 (1885), pp. 532–46.

WATTS, W. W., 'Geology of South Shropshire', *Proceedings of the Geologists Association*, 36 (1925), pp. 321–63.

WELCH, F. B. A. and TROTTER, F. M., 'Geology of the country round Chepstow and Monmouth', *Memoirs of the Geological Survey* (1961).

WILLS, L. J., 'The geology of the Llangollen district', *Proceedings of the Geologists Association*, 31 (1920), pp. 1–15.

WHITAKER, J. D. McD., 'Geology of the country round Leintwardine', *Quarterly Journal of the Geological Society*, 118 (1962), pp. 319–51.

WRIGHT, J. E., *Geology of the Church Stretton Area* (1968).

Chapter 2

BOULTON, G. S. and WORSLEY, P., 'Late Weichselian glaciation in the Cheshire–Shropshire Basin', *Nature*, 207 (1965), pp. 704–6.

CROMPTON, E. and OSMOND, D., 'The soils of the Wem District of Shropshire', *Memoirs of the Soil Survey of Great Britain* (1954).

CROSS, P., 'Aspects of the glacial geomorphology of the Wigmore and Presteigne District', *Transactions of the Woolhope Club*, 39 (1969), pp. 198–220.

DERBYSHIRE, E., 'Late glacial drainage in part of north-east Wales, an alternative hypothesis', *Proceedings of the Geologists Association*, 73 (1962), pp. 327–64.

DWERRYHOUSE, A. R. and MILLER, A. A., 'The glaciation of Clun Forest, Radnor Forest and some adjoining districts', *Quarterly Journal of the Geological Society*, 86 (1930), pp. 96–129.

EARP, J. R. and HAINS, B. A., *The Welsh Borderland* (1971).

EMBLETON, C., 'Late glacial drainage in part of north-east Wales', *Proceedings of the Geologists Association*, 67 (1956), pp. 393–404.

EMBLETON, C., 'Sub-glacial drainage and supposed ice-dammed lakes in north-east Wales', *Proceedings of the Geologists Association*, 75 (1964), pp. 31–8.

EMBLETON, C., 'North-east Wales', Chapter 3 of C. A. Lewis (ed.), *The Glaciations of Wales* (1973), pp. 59–82.

GRINDLEY, H. E., 'The superficial deposits of the basin of the Middle Wye', *Transactions of the Woolhope Club* (1918), pp. 2–7.

GRINDLEY, H. E., 'The Wye Glacier', in Centenary volume of the Woolhope Naturalists and Field Club (1951), pp. 36–47.

HODGSON, J. M., 'Soils of the Ludlow Region', *Memoirs of the Soil Survey of Great Britain* (1972).

HODGSON, J. M. and CROSS, P., 'New evidence for the glacial diversion of the River Teme near Ludlow, Salop', *Proceedings of the Geologists Association*, 86 (1975), pp. 313–32.

LEWIS, C. A., 'The glaciation of the Brecknock Beacons', *Brycheiniog*, 14 (1970), pp. 97–120.

LEWIS, C. A., *The Glaciations of Wales and Adjoining Regions* (1973).

LEWIS, C. A., 'The upper Wye and Usk Region', Chapter 7 in *The Glaciations of Wales and Adjoining Regions*, pp. 147–73.

LUCKMAN, B. B., 'The Hereford Basin', Chapter 8 in *Lewis, The Glaciations of Wales and Adjoining Regions*, pp. 175–95.

PEAKE, D. S., 'Glacial changes in the Alyn river system and their significance in the glaciology of the north Welsh border', *Quarterly Journal of the Geological Society*, 117 (1961), pp. 335–66.

POOLE, E. G. and WHITEMAN, A. J., 'The glacial drifts of the southern part of the Shropshire–Cheshire Basins', *Quarterly Journal of the Geological Society*, 117 (1961), pp. 91–130.

WILLS, L. J., 'Late glacial and post-glacial changes in the Lower Dee Valley', *Quarterly Journal of the Geological Society*, 69 (1912), pp. 180–98.

Chapter 3

BEVAN-EVANS, M. and HAYES, P., 'Excavations of a cairn on Cefn-Goleu, near Moel Fammau', *Flintshire Hist. Soc.* 13 (1952–3).

CONWAY LLOYD, J. and SAVORY, H. N., 'Excavations of an early Iron Age hill-fort and a Romano-British iron-smelting place at Gwernyfed Park, Aberllynfi, 1951', *Brycheiniog*, 4 (1958).

CROSSLEY, D. W., 'Excavations at Pen y Gaer Roman fort, Brecknock, 1966', *Archaeologia Cambrensis*, 117 (1968).

DUNN, C. J., 'Recent prehistoric discoveries from a ridge east of Radnor Forest and their significance', *Radnorshire Society Trans.*, 40 (1970).

FORDE-JOHNSTON, J., 'Fieldwork on the hill-forts of North Wales', *Flintshire Hist. Soc.*, 21 (1964).

FORDE-JOHNSTON, J., 'The hill-forts of the Clwyds', *Archaeologia Cambrensis*, 114 (1965).

FOSTER, I. Ll. and DANIEL, G., *Prehistoric and Early Wales* (1965).

FOX, C., *The Personality of Britain* (4th edition, Cardiff, 1959).

GRIMES, W. F., *The Prehistory of Wales* (2nd edition, Cardiff, 1951).

HALE, M., 'Roman Roads in Herefordshire', *Trans. Woolhope Nat. Field Club*, 39 (1969).

HOGG, A. H. A., 'The size-distribution of hill-forts in Wales and the Marches', in I. Lynch and C. Burgess, *Prehistoric Man in Wales and the West* (Bath, 1972).

JONES, G. D. B., 'Roman Montgomeryshire', *The Bulletin of the Board of Celtic Studies*, 19 (1962).

NASH-WILLIAM, V. E., *The Roman Frontier in Wales* (Cardiff, 1954).

SAVORY, H. N., 'Prehistoric Brecknock', *Brycheiniog*, 1 (1955).

SAVORY, H. N., 'The excavations at Dinorben hill-fort, Abergele, 1961–9', *Trans. Denbighshire Hist. Soc.*, 20 (1971).

SAVORY, H. N., 'Prehistoric Brecknock', *Brycheiniog*, 15 (1971).

SPURGEON, C. J., 'Enclosures of Iron-Age type in the Upper Severn Basin', in I. Lynch and C. Burgess, *Prehistoric Man in Wales and the West* (Bath, 1972).

STANFORD, S. C., 'Croft Ambrey Hill-fort – some interim conclusions', *Trans. Woolhope Nat. Field Club*, 39 (1969).

STANFORD, S. C., 'The Roman forts at Leintwardine and Buckton', *Trans. Woolhope Nat. Field Club*, 39 (1969).

STANFORD, S. C., 'Invention, Adoption and Imposition – the evidence of the hill-forts', in D. Hill and N. Jesson, *The Iron Age and its hill-forts* (1971).

SYLVESTER, D., *The Rural Landscape of the Welsh Borderland* (London, 1969).

THOMAS, C. (ed.), *The Iron Age in the Irish Sea Province* (1972).

WEBLEY, D. P., 'Aspects of Neolithic and Bronze Age agriculture in South Wales', *Bulletin of the Board of Celtic Studies*, 23 (1970).

WEBLEY, D. P., 'How the West was won: prehistoric land-use in the southern Marches', in G. C. Boon and J. M. Lewis, *Welsh Antiquity* (Cardiff, 1976).

WEBSTER, G., *The Cornovii* (London, 1975).

Chapter 4

ALCOCK. L., 'Pottery and settlement in Wales and the March, A.D. 400–700', in I. Ll. Foster and L. Alcock, *Culture and Environment* (1963).

ALCOCK, L., 'Wales in the Arthurian Age', in G. Ashe, *The Quest for Arthur's Britain* (1968).

BOWEN, E. G., *The Settlements of the Celtic Saints in Wales* (Cardiff, 1965).

BOWEN, E. G., *Saints, Seaways and Settlements in the Celtic Lands* (Cardiff, 1969).

CHADWICK, H. M., *Studies in Early British History* (Cambridge, 1954).

CHARLES, B. G., 'The Welsh, their language and place-names in Archenfield and Oswestry', in *Angles and Britons*, O'Donnell Lectures (Cardiff, 1963).

CHITTY, L. F., 'An introduction to Shropshire Archaeology', *The Archaeological Jnl*, 113 (1956).

CRAMPTON, C. B., 'Ancient settlement patterns in mid-Wales', *Archaeologia Cambrensis*, 116 (1967).

DOBLE, G. H., *St Dubricius* (Guildford, 1943).

ELLIS, A. J., 'On the delimitation of the English and Welsh languages', *Y Cymmrodor*, 5 (1882).

FENN, R. W. D., 'The character of early Christianity in Radnorshire', *Radnorshire Soc. Trans.*, 37 (1967).

FENN, R. W. D., 'Early Christianity in Herefordshire', *Trans. Woolhope Nat. Field Club*, 39 (1969).

FINBERG, H. P. R., *Lucerna – studies in some problems of the early history of England* (London, 1964).

FOSTER, I. Ll., and DANIEL, G., *Prehistoric and Early Wales* (London, 1965).

FOX, A., 'The Early Christian Period', in *A Hundred Years of Welsh Archaeology* (Cardiff, 1946).

FOX, C., *Offa's Dyke* (London, 1955).

JONES, G. P., 'Notes on the political history of early Powys', *Archaeologia Cambrensis*, 85 (1930).

JONES, G. R. J., 'The pattern of settlement on the Welsh Border', *Agricultural History Review*, 8 (1960).

JONES, G. R. J., 'Post Roman Wales', in H. P. R. Finberg (ed.), *The Agrarian History of England and Wales*, vol. I (ii), A.D. *43–1042* (Cambridge, 1972).

LAING, L., *The Archaeology of Late Celtic Britain and Ireland, 400–1200 A.D.* (London, 1975).

LORD RENNELL OF RODD, *Valley on the March* (Oxford, 1958).

SYLVESTER, D., 'Settlement patterns in rural Flintshire', *Flintshire Hist. Soc.*, 15 (1954–5).

SYLVESTER, D., *The rural landscape of the Welsh Borderland* (London, 1969).

TAYLOR, C. S., 'The origin of the Mercian shires', in H. P. R. Finberg, *Gloucestershire Studies* (Leicester, 1957).

WADE-EVANS, A. W., *Welsh Christian origins* (Oxford, 1934).

Chapter 5

ATKIN, C. W., 'Herefordshire', in H. C. Darby and I. B. Terrett, *The Domesday Geography of Midland England* (2nd edition, Cambridge, 1972).

ASHTON, O. S., 'Eighteenth-century Radnorshire – a population survey', *Radnorshire Society Trans.*, 40 (1970).

BROOKSBY, H., 'The houses of Radnorshire', *Radnorshire Society Trans*. 40 (1970).

CATHCART KING, D. J. and SPURGEON, C., 'The mottes in the vale of Montgomery', *Archaeologia Cambrensis*, 114 (1965).

CHARLES, B. J., 'An early charter of the abbey of Cwmhir', *Radnorshire Soc. Trans.*, 40 (1970).

CRAMPTON, C. B., 'Hafotai platforms on the north front of the Brecon Beacons', *Archaeologia Cambrensis*, 115 (1966).

DAVIES, A. S., 'The charcoal iron industry of Powysland', *Montgomeryshire Collections*, 46 (1940).

DAVIES, A. S., 'Excavations at Coed-y-Bwynydd, Bettws Newydd', *Monmouthshire Antiquary*, 2 (1968).

GARETH-THOMAS, J., 'The distribution of commons in part of Arwystli at the time of enclosure', *Montgomeryshire Collections*, 54 (1955–6).

GAYDON, A. T. (ed.), *A History of Shropshire*, Victoria Histories of the Counties of England, vol. VIII (1968).

GWYNDAF, R., 'Sir Richard Clough of Denbigh, 1530–70', *Trans. Denbigh Hist. Soc.*, 22 (1973).

HAGUE, D. B. and WARHURST, C., 'Excavations at Sycharth Castle', *Archaeologia Cambrensis*, 115 (1946).

LLOYD-KENYON, R., 'The Domesday manors of Ruyton, Wikey and Felton', *Trans. Shropshire Arch. and Nat. Hist. Soc.*, 2nd Ser., 12 (1900).

RALEIGH RADFORD, C. A., 'Tretower: the castle and the court', *Brycheiniog*, 6 (1960).

ROWLEY, R. T., 'The Clee Forest – a study in common rights', *Trans. Shropshire Arch. Soc.*, 58 (1965–8).

SAUNDERS, V. A., 'Shropshire', in H. C. Darby and I. B. Terrett, *The Domesday Geography of Midland England* (2nd edition, Cambridge, 1971).

SAYCE, R. U., 'The study of farm names', *Montgomeryshire Collections*, 54 (1955–6).

SAYCE, R. U., 'The old summer pastures', *Montgomeryshire Collections*, 54 (1955–6).

SMITH, P., 'Rural housing in Wales', in H. P. R. Finberg and J. Thirsk, *The Agrarian History of England and Wales, 1500–1640*, IV (Cambridge, 1967).

SMITH, P., *Houses of the Welsh Countryside* (H.M.S.O., 1975).

SMITH, P. and OWEN, C. E. V., 'Traditional and Renaissance elements in some late Stuart and early Georgian half-timbered houses in Arwystli', *Montgomeryshire Collections*, 55 (1957–8).

SYLVESTER, D., 'The rural landscape of eastern Montgomeryshire', *Montgomeryshire Collections*, 54 (1955–6).

SYLVESTER, D., *The Rural Landscape of the Welsh Borderland* (London, 1969).

STANFORD, S. C., 'A medieval settlement at Detton Hall, Shropshire', *Trans. Shropshire Arch. Soc.*, 58 (1965–8).

STANFORD, S. C., 'The deserted medieval village of Hampton Wafer, Herefordshire', *Trans. Woolhope Nat. Field Club*, 39 (1965).

VAUGHAN-OWEN, C. E., 'An Arwystli Notebook', *Montgomeryshire Collections*, 55 (1957–8).

WILLIAM, E., 'Farm buildings in the Vale of Clwyd, 1550–1880', *Folk Life*, 2 (1973).

WILLIAMS, D. H., 'Grace Dieu Abbey', *The Monmouthshire Antiquary*, 1 (1964).

WILLIAMS, D. H., 'Tintern Abbey; its economic history', *The Monmouthshire Antiquary*, 2 (1965).

WILLIAMS, D. H., 'Abbey Dore', *The Monmouthshire Antiquary*, 2 (1966).

243

Chapter 6

BEAZLEY, E. and BRETT, L., *North Wales – A Shell Guide* (1971).

DAVIES, A. S., 'The charcoal iron industry of Powysland', *Montgomeryshire Transactions*, 46 (1940), pp. 31–66.

DAVIES, A. S., 'The early iron industry of North Wales', *Transactions of the Newcomen Society*, 25 (1945), pp. 83–90.

DINES, H. G., 'The West Shropshire mining region', *Bulletin of the Geological Survey of Great Britain*, 14 (1958), pp. 1–43.

DODD, A. H., *The Industrial Revolution in North Wales* (1951).

DODD, A. H., *History of Wrexham* (1957).

EARP, J. R., 'Mineral veins in the Minera-Maeshofen district of North Wales', *Bulletin of the Geological Survey of Great Britain*, 14 (1958), pp. 44–69.

EDWARDS, I., 'Iron production in North Wales', *Denbighshire Hist. Soc. Trans.*, 14 (1965), pp. 140–85.

EVANS, M. B., 'Gadlys and Flintshire lead mining in the 18th century', *Journal Flintshire Hist. Soc.*, 18 (1960), pp. 75–130; 19 (1961), pp. 32–60; 20 (1962), pp. 58–89.

FOULKES, E. J., 'Cotton spinning factories in the Holywell Valley', *Journal Flintshire Hist. Soc.*, 21 (1965), pp. 91–7.

HARRIS, J. R., *The Copper King* (1964).

HOWELL, P. and BEAZLEY, E., *Companion Guide to South Wales* (1976).

JENKINS, J. G., 'Newtown and the woollen industry', *Journal of Industrial Archaeology*, 2 (1965), pp. 1–43.

JENKINS, J. G., *The Welsh Woollen Industry* (1969).

LETTY, G., 'The industries of Denbighshire from Tudor times to the present day', *Denbighshire Hist. Soc. Trans.*, 7 (1958), pp. 34–66.

LEWIS, W. J., *Lead mining in Wales* (1967).

LLOYD, H., 'The iron forges of the Vyrnwy Valley', *Montgomeryshire Collections*, 60 (1967–8), pp. 104–10.

MINCHINGTON, W. E., 'The place of Breconshire in the industrialisation of South Wales', *Brycheiniog*, 7 (1961), pp. 1–69.

NEAVERSON, E., 'Medieval quarrying in North Wales', *Denbighshire Hist. Soc. Trans.*, 14 (1953), pp. 1–21.

NORTH, F. J., *Mining for metals in Wales* (1962).

RAISTRICK, A., *Dynasty of Ironfounders* (1954).

RAISTRICK, A., *Quakers in science and industry* (1968).

REES, D. M., *Mines, Mills and Furnaces* (1967).

REES, D. M., *The Industrial Archaeology of Wales* (1975).

REES, W., *Industry before the Industrial Revolution* (1968).

RHODES, J. N., 'Early steam engines in Flintshire', *Transactions of the Newcomen Society*, 41 (1968), pp. 217–25.

RICHARDS, P. S., 'The siting of two Flintshire paper mills', *Journal of Industrial Archaeology*, 2 (1965), pp. 161–6.

RICHARDS, P. S., 'Viscose rayon manufacture on Deeside', *Journal Flintshire Hist. Soc.*, 23 (1968), pp. 75–81.

RICHARDS, P. S., 'The Darwen and Mostyn Iron Company', *Journal Flintshire Hist. Soc.*, 24 (1969), pp. 86–94.

THOMAS, T. M., 'The mineral wealth of Wales', *Proceedings of the Geologists Association*, 83 (1972), pp. 365–83.

TYLECOTE, R. F., 'The blast furnace at Coed Ithal, Llandogo, Monmouthshire', *Journal of the Iron and Steel Institute*, 204 (1966), pp. 314–19.

Chapter 7

APPLETON, J. H., *Disused Railways in the Countryside of England and Wales* (1970).

BAUGHAN, P. E., *The Chester and Holyhead Railway*, Vol. I (1972).

BOYD, J. I. C., *Narrow Gauge Railways of Mid Wales* (1970).

CARTWRIGHT, R. and RUSSELL, R. T., *The Welshpool and Llanfair Railway* (1972).

CHITTY, L. F., 'The Clun–Clee Ridgeway', in *Culture and Environment: essays in honour of Sir Cyril Fox* (1963), pp. 171–92.

CHRISTIANSEN, R. and MILLER, R. W., *The Cambrian Railways*, Vol. I (1971).

CHRISTIANSEN, R., *Forgotten Railways, North and Mid Wales* (1976).

CLINKER, C. R., 'The railways of West Herefordshire', *Transactions of the Woolhope Club*, 35 (1955), pp. 286–93.

CLINKER, C. R., *The Hay Railway* (1960).

COLEMAN, V. H., 'The Kington Railway', *Transactions of the Woolhope Club*, 38 (1964), pp. 16–26.

DAVIES, D. L., *The Glyn Valley Tramway* (1962).

HADFIELD, C., *The Canals of South Wales and the Border* (1967).

HADFIELD, C., *The Canals of the West Midlands* (1969).

HALE, M., 'Roman roads in Herefordshire', *Transactions of the Woolhope Club*, 39 (1968).

MCDERMOT, E. T. and CLINKER, C. R., *History of the Great Western Railway*, Vol. I (1964).

MOWAT, C. L., *The Golden Valley Railway* (1964).

MEYNELL, L., *Thomas Telford* (1957).

NOBLE, F., *Offa's Dyke Path* (1969).

SHOTTON, F. W. and CHITTY, L. F., 'A new centre of stone axe dispersal in the Welsh Borders', *Proceedings of the Prehistoric Society*, 17 (1951), pp. 159–67.

SMITH, D. J., *Shrewsbury to Swansea* (1971).

TONKS, E. S., *The Shropshire and Montgomery Railway* (1972).

WREN, W. J., *The Tanat Valley, its Railway and Industrial Archaeology* (1968).

Chapter 8

BERESFORD, M. W., *New Towns of the Middle Ages* (London, 1967).

BERESFORD, M. W. and FINBERG, H. P. R., *English Medieval Boroughs* (Newton Abbot, 1973).

DODD, A. H., *A History of Wrexham* (Wrexham, 1957).

DODGSON, J. MC. N., 'Place-names and street-names of Chester', *Jnl of the Chester Arch. Soc.*, 55 (1968).

GANT, R. L., 'The townscape and economy of Brecon', *Brycheiniog* 16 (1972).

HEYS, F. G. and NORWOOD, J. F. L., 'Excavations on the supposed line of King's Ditch, Hereford', *Trans. Woolhope Nat. Field Club*, 36 (1958–60).

HILLING, J. B., 'Mid-Wales: a plan for the region', *Jnl of the Town Planning Institute*, 54 (1968).

JONES, E. V., *History of Newtown* (Newtown, 1970).

KISSACK, K., *Monmouth – the making of a county town* (Chichester, 1975).

LOBEL, M. D., *Hereford*, Vol. I of M. D. Lobel (ed.), *Historic Towns* (London, 1969).

MILES, H., 'Excavations at Rhuddlan, 1969–71', *Flintshire Hist. Soc.*, 25 (1971–2).

MILLWARD, R. and ROBINSON, A. H. W., *The Welsh Marches*, Landscapes of Britain, Vol. IV (London, 1971).

NOBLE, F., 'Medieval boroughs of West Herefordshire', *Trans. Woolhope Nat. Field Club*, 38 (1964).

PEVSNER, N., *Shropshire (The Buildings of England)* (London, 1958).

PEVSNER, N., *Herefordshire (The Buildings of England)* (London, 1963).

PEVSNER, N., *Cheshire (The Buildings of England)* (London, 1973).

PLATT, C., *The English Medieval Town* (London, 1976).

PRATT, D., 'The medieval borough of Holt', *Denbighshire Hist. Soc.*, 14 (1965).

REES, W., *The Medieval Lordship of Brecon* (Brecon, 1968).

SHOESMITH, R., 'Hereford', *Current Archaeology*, 33 (1972).

SYLVESTER, D., *A History of Cheshire* (Henley-on-Thames, 1971).

THOMPSON, F. H., 'Excavations at Linenhall Street, Chester, 1961–2', *Jnl of the Chester Arch. Soc.*, 56 (1969).

WATERS, I., *The Town of Chepstow* (Chepstow, 1975).

WEBSTER, G., 'Chester in the Dark Ages', *Jnl of the Chester and North Wales Architectural, Archaeological and Hist. Soc.*, 38 (1951).

WEBSTER, G., *The Cornovii* (London, 1975).

WILLIAMS, R., 'Dolforwyn Castle', *Archaeologia Cambrensis*, I, Series 6 (1901).

Index